During the early morning hours of September 11, 1777, British General William Howe split his army in a daring maneuver. American General George Washington's troops united behind the Brandywine River preparing for the army of King George III. In a dense fog, Howe and General Charles Cornwallis led a portion of the British army on a 17-mile march, crossing the Brandywine at two fords, and surprising the American army near the Birmingham Meeting House. The second portion of the British army under Hessian General Wilhelm Knyphausen pushed the American new light infantry under General William Maxwell back to the Brandywine and then held Washington's forces in check until Howe completed his flanking march. An American patriot, Squire Thomas Cheyney, heroically alerted Washington to the danger of Howe's flanking movement.

The Battle of Brandywine was the largest land battle of the American Revolution and the major conflict of the Philadelphia campaign that ended with Washington's army spending a hard winter at Valley Forge. Brandywine was also the first battle for a young French volunteer, the Marquis de Lafayette. Lafayette suffered a leg wound during the conflict. British Captain Patrick Ferguson's new invention, a breech-loading rifle, was also used for the first time at Brandywine. Ferguson had a chance to alter history that day as he had Washington in the sights of his weapon but declined to fire upon the brave Washington.

Howe's victory allowed him to capture Philadelphia, but he failed to destroy Washington's army and failed to rally the residents, including a large Quaker community, to the British cause.

September 11, 1777

Washington's Defeat at Brandywine
Dooms Philadelphia

By
Bruce E. Mowday

WHITE MANE BOOKS
SHIPPENSBURG, PENNSYLVANIA

The painting on the front cover of this book is Howard Pyle's *The Nation Makers*. It is from the collection of the Brandywine River Museum, purchased through a grant from the Mabel Pew Myrin Trust.

Adrian Martinez's painting, *Battle of the Brandywine,* is printed courtesy of Sue and Tim Coldren.

The maps credited for this book were made by Diane Cirafesi of Cirafesi Designs of West Chester, Pennsylvania.

The photograph of author Bruce E. Mowday on the inside front cover was taken by Sarah S. Bones of Sarah S. Bones Photography, Paoli, Pennsylvania.

The photographs of Douglas E. Brinton are from the collection of the Chester County Historical Society, West Chester, Pa. Brinton, who worked for the Oxford Press, was a member of journalistic family that spanned three generations. He was born in 1859 and was one of the first photographers to do a detailed study of the Brandywine Battlefield. The photographs in this book were taken by Brinton in 1899.

The acid-free paper used in this book meets the guidelines for permanence and durability of the Committee on Production Guidelines for Book Longevity of the Council on Library Resources.

For a complete list of available publications
please write
White Mane Books
Division of White Mane Publishing Company, Inc.
P.O. Box 708
Shippensburg, PA 17257-0708 USA

Library of Congress Cataloging-in-Publication Data

Mowday, Bruce.
    September 11, 1777 : Washington's defeat at Brandywine dooms Philadelphia / by
Bruce E. Mowday.
        p. cm.
    Includes bibliographical references (p.) and index.
    ISBN 1-57249-328-3 (alk. paper). -- ISBN 1-57249-342-9 (pbk.)
    1. Brandywine, Battle of, 1777. I. Title.

E241.B8 M69 2002
973.3'33--dc21

                                                                2002027218

PRINTED IN THE UNITED STATES OF AMERICA

Contents

Illustrations and Maps

Foreword

By Congressman Joseph R. Pitts
16th District of Pennsylvania

Decades do to history what months and years do to memory. An event that seemed momentous at the time will dissipate to become merely a fond or troubled memory. Eventually, it may be forgotten. Our high school graduations bring weak knees and tears when they happen, but years later we can barely remember the names of many of our fellow graduates. Likewise, with history. Details are forgotten. There are merely a handful of dates we remember. December 7, 1941. July 4, 1776. 1492. 1066. But does anyone remember what the date was when 444 Americans were taken hostage in Tehran? How many Americans can remember what the date was when Nixon resigned?

The same is true of the day the Battle of Brandywine was fought. At the time, it was a momentous battle. Washington's 8,000 Continentals and 3,000 Pennsylvania militia were all that stood between General William Howe and the fall of Philadelphia. In 1777 Philadelphia was no mere city. It was the "Athens of America." It was the seat of the Continental Congress. It was the city where William Penn had established the principle of Freedom of Religion in 1701, an act that was memorialized by the commissioning of the Liberty Bell 50 years later. It was the city of the Declaration of Independence, and the heart of America — both literally and symbolically.

Philadelphia represented the American cause, and the Battle of Brandywine was fought to defend it.

But the same tactics that won New York for Howe also gave him a victory at Brandywine, and within days the Continental Congress was fleeing to Lancaster and York. Though they lost, the Americans fought valiantly and determinedly. Outmanned, outmaneuvered, and very nearly outflanked, Washington's men (under the immediate command of Lord Stirling, also known as William Alexander, and Nathanael Greene) fought long enough and hard enough to allow Philadelphia time to evacuate. Had they not, Congress might have been captured and the war lost.

And the date was September 11.

Because Brandywine was a loss for Washington, it is not celebrated like Trenton or Yorktown. Only a small state park, off the actual main battlefield, preserves its memory for tourists.

Dates are forgotten, September 11, 1777, among them. But the date of the Battle of Brandywine is unique among all great historic days in that it has been revived in our minds by another, bloodier, national tragedy. On September 11, 2001, four hijacked airplanes took some three thousand lives in New York, Virginia, and Pennsylvania.

Now, again, September 11 is a date loaded with meaning. This time, for this generation, the memory is different. Yet, in many ways, the meaning is the same. We were reminded in 2001 that this nation of liberty is vulnerable if not defended. We were reminded, as the national memorial to the Korean War says, that "freedom is not free." Once again, American patriots donned uniforms to fight on to final victory.

The story of Brandywine is one that is not told as often as it should be. Perhaps it is not as easy to tell as those of Lexington, Valley Forge, or Yorktown. Perhaps we are embarrassed by it because Washington was outmaneuvered and had to retreat. Or perhaps we've just forgotten why the battle was important.

Yes, we failed to stop Lord Howe at Brandywine. The cause continued, however, and was eventually won.

Brandywine and its lessons need to be remembered, and the author of this book, Bruce Mowday, is a leading proponent of restoring this important American battle to general awareness.

The actual site of the battle remains, thankfully, undeveloped despite a crush of commercial and residential development in the region. I have worked closely with Mr. Mowday to see that it is preserved for future generations. A $3 million federal appropriation, matched with funds from the Commonwealth of Pennsylvania and from Chester County, was one result of this effort. This history is another product of Mr. Mowday's efforts.

By preserving the site and telling its story, we hope that in years to come September 11 will remind Americans of more than the worst terrorist attack in history. If the story of Brandywine continues to be told as ably as Bruce Mowday has told it here, many more Americans will realize that the lessons of both events are very much the same.

Acknowledgments

The acknowledgment section of a book is usually the least exciting text to the reader because of the list of persons unknown to them cited, but the section is most important to the author, especially in a work of historical nonfiction. This book wouldn't have been written without the cooperation of many historians, researchers, librarians, friends and family. Their efforts are deeply appreciated and they deserve recognition.

After obtaining a first-hand account of the Battle of Brandywine from an auction and discovering no detailed book on this important Revolutionary War battle had ever been published, the need for such a work was evident. James H. Duff, Executive Director of the Brandywine Conservancy, in Chadds Ford, Pennsylvania, was one of the first to urge me to research and write a researched history of Brandywine. He also was key to obtaining permission from the Brandywine River Museum to use Howard Pyle's painting *The Nation Makers* on the cover. Pyle's work captures the spirit and patriotism of those Americans who fought at Brandywine on September 11, 1777. Pyle's masterpiece was completed about the time of the 125th anniversary of the battle. Downingtown artist Adrian Martinez, who is achieving national recognition for his work, painted another rendering of Brandywine displaying the passion of the American troops during the battle, and his painting is also contained in this book.

Delving into records that were written more than two centuries ago required time, energy, and organizational skills. Katherine Harlan, my wife, devoted many hours conducting Internet searches and looking through the files of libraries and historical organizations for sources of information on the battle. She also helped in deciphering some two-centuries-old, hard-to-read documents. Katherine's research abilities and patience with the author helped me to maximize valuable research time. My brother, Barry L. Mowday, was recruited to look for specific information on John Marshall, a participant at the Battle of Brandywine and United States Supreme Court Justice, at William and Mary College in Williamsburg, Virginia, where Barry did his graduate and undergraduate work and now teaches at a nearby college.

Without exception, everyone contacted for this project helped without question. Edward G. Lengel of the University of Virginia shared his work on the George Washington papers involving the Battle of Brandywine. A trip to London in August 2001 to view documents related to the British army resulted in help from the staff at the Public Record Office in Kew and the National Army Museum where Michael Ball assisted me in gaining access to many important documents in his research facility. Lt. Col. Graham Hazelwood of the British army, who has researched the battle and given lectures on Brandywine, was extremely helpful in getting this book project started.

Diane Cirafesi of Cirafesi Designs of West Chester used her extreme talent to create the maps in this book. Her cartography work also appeared in my postcard history book, *Along the Brandywine River*. Photographer Marc McCarron provided the image of Adrian Martinez's painting in this book.

A number of trips to historical organizations in the Brandywine area were necessary and staff directed me to specific documents or pulled them for my review. Those organizations included the Chester County Historical Society; Brandywine Battlefield Park; the Pennsylvania Historical and Museum Commission; The United States Army History

Institute in Carlisle, Pennsylvania; the David Library of the American Revolution at Washington's Crossing; Valley Forge National Park; the National Archives; the Library of Congress; and the Pennsylvania Historical Society.

Susan Hauser and Kathy Wandersee opened files at the Delaware County Planning Commission for my inspection and copied many pages for me. Carol Grigson identified the files containing information on the Battle of Brandywine at the Chester County Historical Society and made the search a lot easier. Diane Rofini and Pam Powell of the Chester County Historical Society helped me obtain illustrations from the society's collection. Diane Shaw and Michelle Webb at Lafayette College were extremely helpful on gathering information from the college's special collections section. Linnea Bass of the British Brigade of Guards in America sent notes on the Battle of Brandywine. Donna Williams of the Pennsylvania Historical Museum Commission directed me to those in her organization with vast knowledge of Commonwealth records. Lee Jennings, a Delaware historian, offered valuable help concerning Cooch's Bridge, Delaware's only Revolutionary War conflict. Diana Loreman, Research Librarian at the David Library of the American Revolution, helped me find my way around the library, a great treasure of documents related to the War for America's Independence. At Valley Forge, Lee Boyle pulled documents and gave me a tour of the records at the national park.

A number of good friends helped in a number of ways during the research and writing of this book. Susan Engle, a descendent of Lafayette, was always on the lookout for information on Brandywine, and Joe Lordi, librarian at the Bayard Taylor Library in Kennett Square, Pennsylvania, provided a copy of an article by Bayard Taylor on the battle. Another librarian and lifelong friend, Mike Geary of the Michael Margolies Library in Coatesville, Pennsylvania, aided with a search for material. Catherine Quillman, a fine writer of local history, shared research she had compiled.

Tom Spackman, whose family owns a portion of the Brandywine Battlefield, took a few hours on a spring morning in 2001 to lead a tour through some wild roses to view a location where a creek ran red with blood during the afternoon of September 11, 1777, after British troops pushed back Americans into the Sandy Hollow section of the battlefield. Richard Bowers, a Board member of the non-profit Brandywine Battlefield Park Associates, joined us as we traversed that still hilly terrain to the area where the Marquis de Lafayette received his wound in his first battle on American soil. This tour reminded me of one taken by teenager Bayard Taylor in 1840. Taylor became one of America's foremost writers and recorded his thoughts of his tour. That article is reprinted in this book.

Paul Rodebaugh, a Chester County historian, who has spent a lifetime researching, lecturing and collecting artifacts and papers relating to the county, opened his vast library of resources to me. The same goes for the wonderful people who run the Chris Sanderson Museum. Sanderson, himself, was responsible for keeping the spirit of Brandywine alive in the early 1900s.

A special thank you goes to the members of the Brandywine Battlefield Associates. I served as member of the Board and as President of the non-profit Board, and they all are dedicated to promoting Brandywine Battlefield Park and preserving the battlefield. Especially helpful were Sally Jane Denk, known as the Bard of the Brandywine because of her ballads, who got me involved with the Board, and Tom Stolfi, educational coordinator at the Park, who does a wonderful job bringing Brandywine to life to thousands of students each year. During one rainy winter's day Sally found a Brandywine document at the Chris Sanderson Museum and immediately gave me a call.

Congressman Joseph R. Pitts is a military veteran, student of history and an elected official who truly has the interest of those he serves at heart. Besides writing the foreword to this book, he has been active in preserving the battlefield. Much of the land is outside the state park in the private sector. Congressman Pitts and Harrisburg officials, such as Pennsylvania

Senator Bob Thompson and Representative Chris Ross, have helped gain money to buy development rights through the good work being done by the Brandywine Conservancy.

As mentioned earlier, the Brandywine has inspired many artists over the years, including Howard Pyle and Adrian Martinez. Leah Martinez, Adrian's wife, was extremely helpful in preparing the painting for reproduction. John Hall, an attorney who practices in the old village of Turk's Head, now called West Chester, offered help in obtaining illustrations. Jackie Van Grofski, a friend and member of the Board of the Chester County Historical Society, loaned me a book she read on Brandywine many years ago and kept, and generously offered the use of her family cabin in northern Pennsylvania as a quiet place to write and complete this book.

An obvious problem in identifying those assisting in the writing of this book is that I have left off someone who deserves recognition. I'm sure this is true, as everyone who took time to search for documents should be identified. I thank everyone.

Introduction

This book on the Battle of Brandywine is rooted in my childhood. When I was a child, my parents, Raymond and Ruth Mowday, took my brother Barry and sister Bonnie to the Brandywine Battlefield Park on Route 1 in Chadds Ford. We spent many hours running and having picnics on the 52 acres of Commonwealth parkland containing the reconstructed Ring House, headquarters of General George Washington during the battle, and the Gilpin House, the home that served as headquarters of the Marquis de Lafayette.

The family tradition continued as my daughters, Melissa and Megan, both spent time at the park, including watching the Revolutionary War reenactments sponsored by the Brandywine Battlefield Park Associates. In the 1990s I was asked to serve on the Board of the Associates and served two years as its president. The non-profit Associates, affiliated with the Pennsylvania Historical and Museum Commission, is dedicated to helping to promote the Battlefield Park and educating students and adults on the colonial history of the region.

During my more than twenty years in journalism I worked as a legal reporter, investigative reporter, columnist, and editor. After obtaining a first-hand account of the Battle of Brandywine from an unnamed participant under Count Casimir Pulaski's command, I decided to write a column on the battle. I went to a large local bookstore and asked for a work on Brandywine. I was told no such work was in print. I was surprised and appalled. Indeed, the amount written concerning the battle, the largest land battle of the war, is surprisingly sparse. Minimal accounts in books, magazine articles and pamphlets make up the bulk of material. Browsing through books written on the American Revolution reveals the details devoted to Brandywine amount to either no information, a couple of paragraphs or several pages. On a rare occasion a chapter is devoted to Brandywine. The index of one book on the decisive battles of the United States written in 1942 lists the battle as having taken place in New Jersey instead of Pennsylvania. The text of the book does give its correct location.

The Battle of Brandywine, the main contest between General George Washington's army and that of General William Howe in the Philadelphia campaign of 1777 that led to the awful winter at Valley Forge, does not receive the respect it deserves. When Washington took his defensive position behind the banks of the Brandywine River, only his army stood behind Howe and Philadelphia, the capital of the new American nation. A catastrophic loss for Washington, which was narrowly averted by brave patriots fighting and dying in the fields and roads leading from the Quaker Birmingham Meeting House to Dilworth during the late afternoon and early evening hours of September 11, 1777, would have led to the loss of the Rebel army, the Rebel government, and certainly would have dashed any hope of American independence.

The outcome of the battle is the reason for the lack of attention for Brandywine in the United States. Washington's soldiers, especially late in the day, stood and fought the best of the British army. Americans earned respect and a full measure of self-confidence on the fields of Chester County, Pennsylvania, that late summer afternoon. But the end result was that Brandywine was an American loss. Howe, as he had at Long Island the previous year, outflanked Washington, and Washington was badly outmaneuvered that day. Brandywine was not Washington's favorite battle and he did not mention Brandywine much after his defeat.

The British army near perfectly executed Howe's plan. The British soldiers were at their best at Brandywine. Hessian Lieutenant General Baron Wilhelm Knyphausen, who directed one half of the British troops, kept Washington guessing about the deployment of the British army. Knyphausen's work that day has not received the recognition it deserves. After driving back the just-formed American light infantry under General William Maxwell during the morning's portion of the battle and keeping Washington occupied as Howe and General Lord Charles Cornwallis executed their flanking maneuver in the early afternoon, Knyphausen drove across the Brandywine and dislodged a determined holding action by Brigadier General "Mad" Anthony Wayne, who was fighting in his home county.

The outcome of the war is the reason for the lack of recognition for Brandywine in Great Britain. During a research visit to London one of the library researchers was asked about documents on Brandywine. His response was: "I'm not aware of that battle." Brandywine was a major British military victory and should command more attention. Many units, including the American Rangers, distinguished themselves and won well-deserved reputations. Captain Patrick Ferguson's breech-loading rifle was effectively demonstrated and Ferguson himself demonstrated his sense of honor by not putting three rounds from his new rifle into the body of Washington when he had the opportunity that day. Ferguson saved Washington from being a casualty of war at Brandywine.

Brandywine offers many challenges to historians. After 225 years the paper trail of orders, letters, and diaries is fast disappearing. Indeed, there was a scarcity of written records from the date of the battle. Since none of the participants are living, no eyewitness accounts can be obtained. Source documents always provide the most reliable information and as far as possible those documents have been used in this book. It was reassuring to see the original documents, or copies of the documents, that have been quoted in many works.

The approach used in this book was the same I used as a journalist. No information was taken as true without investigation and verification. If a doubt exists concerning an issue, it is so noted. Common sense plays a big part in trying to piece together the past. If a piece of information doesn't make sense, it usually is incorrect, or leads to another aspect of the piece of the historic puzzle. As with most historic events, stories and legends are formed. Some are true and some are believed even when they are disproved, or at least when it is impossible to verify them. Descriptions of events written generations after the fact are suspect.

Brandywine is important, and interesting, for many varied reasons besides the participation of many leading generals of both armies — including Washington, John Sullivan, William Maxwell, Lafayette, Nathanael Greene and Wayne in the American army and Howe, Charles Cornwallis, and Knyphausen of the British army. Besides being the largest land battle of the war, it is also the first battle where the new American flag came under fire. Some believe the skirmish at Cooch's Bridge in Delaware has that honor, but there is no documentation of Maxwell's troops having the flag during that engagement. Signers of the Declaration of Independence were present at Brandywine. Brandywine was the first battle for Lafayette, who suffered a leg wound. Ferguson suffered a debilitating wound to his right elbow, and Ferguson had Washington in his gun sight but declined to fire on the gallant American officer bravely executing his duties.

This book is written so readers can understand what took place at Brandywine, the events that led to the battle and the effect it had on American history. One goal is to have readers becoming engaged in the study of American history and discover it isn't as stuffy as some teachers made it in school. Many articles written in the early 19th century state the details of the Battle of Brandywine need not be repeated because they are so well known. That is not true today. The conflict needs to be highlighted because Brandywine is not known.

Quotes are taken directly from documents, but this work won't dwell on misspelling or arcane wording that detracts from the readability of the book and offers no historic insights.

Brandywine is spelled different ways in documents, such as Brandy wine. The same goes for the name of the village where the battle took place, Chadds Ford. John Chads was the son of a shoemaker, Francis Chadsey. His historic home is known as John Chad's House. Chadds Ford has been called Chad's Ford and Chadd's Ford. Some people believe Brandywine is a creek and others call it a river. I've always called it a river. There is no "right" and "wrong" way to describe the Brandywine.

Sections of the Brandywine Battlefield have been saved from modern development through the efforts of many individuals, government entities and organizations, including the Brandywine Conservancy. After reading this book I hope you have a chance to visit the fields where brave American and British soldiers fought valiantly during a major battle of the American Revolution.

Battle of Brandywine Timeline

December 20, 1776   Lord Richard Howe tells Lord George Germain of intention of invading Pennsylvania.

December 25, 1776   George Washington is victorious at Trenton.

January 1777   Howe has second thoughts on invasion of Pennsylvania.

March 3, 1777   Germain approves Howe's attack on Pennsylvania.

May 18, 1777   Germain tells Howe to continue with his invasion of Pennsylvania.

June 17, 1777   General John Burgoyne begins New York operation.

July 3, 1777   Washington receives word from spies that Howe is preparing for a sea voyage.

July 23, 1777   Howe and British fleet set sail from New York.

July 30, 1777   British fleet arrives at the Cape of Delaware.

August 14, 1777   British spotted off Cape Charles, Virginia.

August 22, 1777   Congress told that Howe's fleet is in the Chesapeake Bay.

August 23, 1777   Betsy Ross flag flown by Washington.

August 24, 1777   Washington marches his troops through Philadelphia.

August 25, 1777	British arrive at Elk Point.
August 25, 1777	Washington makes his headquarters at Wilmington.
August 28, 1777	Washington appoints Maxwell to lead the American light infantry.
September 3, 1777	Skirmish at Cooch's Bridge.
September 9, 1777	Washington moves his army from Delaware to Chadds Ford.
September 10, 1777	British army forms at Kennett Square.
September 11, 1777	The Battle of Brandywine.
	(Approximate Times)
4:00 a.m.	Howe orders army to move.
5:00 a.m.	Baron Wilhelm Knyphausen begins his march.
7:00 a.m.	First shots fired near Welch's Tavern.
10:00 a.m.	Maxwell's light infantry retreats across the Brandywine.
11:00 a.m.	Howe crosses Trimbles' Ford.
Noon	Howe reaches Jefferies Ford.
1:15 p.m.	American troops skirmish with Howe's forces.
2:30 p.m.	British reach Osborne's Hill.
2:30 p.m.	Sullivan ordered to Birmingham.
4:00 p.m.	Howe launches attack on Birmingham.
4:00 p.m.	Knyphausen prepares to attack General Anthony Wayne.
4:30 p.m.	Washington departs Chadds Ford for Birmingham.
5:15 p.m.	Knyphausen launches his attack.
6:45 p.m.	Fighting near Dilworth concludes.
7:00 p.m.	Fighting concludes.
11:00 p.m.	Washington arrives in Chester.
Midnight	Washington reports to Congress.
September 16, 1777	Battle of the Clouds.
September 21, 1777	Battle of Paoli.
September 26, 1777	Howe takes Philadelphia.
October 2, 1777	Battle of Germantown.
December 19, 1777	Americans at Valley Forge.

A Visit to the Battle Ground of Brandywine

By Bayard Taylor

Having long desired to see this place, celebrated in the annals of our revolution, as having been the scene of a sanguinary conflict, I, in company with several others, determined to pay it a visit. Enlivened by the desire of beholding so distinguished a spot, we began our journey with alacrity. It was a lovely morning. The sun had just appeared above the horizon, the sky was clear and unclouded, and all nature wore the garb of beauty. After walking for a considerable time, we came in sight of the Brandywine, flowing in placid beauty beneath the shade of tall trees, which extended their long arms across, and, interlacing their boughs, seemed to form a protection. As the waved glittered in the sunbeams, I thought what a contrast it presented to the turbid and crimsoned stream, which flowed upon the day of that ever-memorable battle. Before reaching the bridge, we noticed on the left a small meadow, which, we were afterwards informed, is the burial place of a small body of Hessians, who were cut down by some American riflemen, stationed in the bushes, and behind the trees with which the adjoining hills were then covered. To the west of the bridge was a wooded knoll, part of which had been cut away to afford a passage for the road. This, we were told, was the station of Gen. Knyphausen's detachment, when the passage was disputed by the Americans, and when the bank was dug away, many cannon balls were found, indicative of the hot fire kept up between the contending armies. A few yards above the bridge (Chadds' Ford) is the site of the old fording place, there having been no bridge at the time of the battle. After viewing the landscape a short time, we were conducted to the hill, north of the tavern, which is the site of the American camp. It was, in many respects, similar to the one on which the Hessians were stationed, from which we may infer, that the advantages of situation were about equal on each side. Here we were shown the breastwork, thrown up by Gen. Proctor, on which the cannon were placed. It is now hardly distinguishable, but may be traced by means of semi-circular ridge extending along the brow of the hill. Bullets and grape shot are often found here, some of which were procured from the landlord, after an ineffectual search to find some ourselves. We were standing on the soil where our ancestors nobly defended the cause in that eventful conflict. Such thoughts caused our minds to wander back to the very day when this hill was occupied by the American army, and we almost imagined we heard the roar of discharging artillery, and saw the glitter of hostile bayonets.

An apple tree which stood at a short distance, is the only memorial left to mark the spot where a young and noble American officer was buried. A small and now very old house near by served at that time as the headquarters of Washington; and, on the flat meadow below the tavern, Gen. Wayne's troops were stationed. While at this place, Washington was not aware that the remaining portion of the British army had gone up the creek, to cross at some distance above; and this, in a great measure, decided the fate of the day. In the meadow near the Brandywine were deposited the bodies of many Hessians who perished by the unerring aim of some American riflemen, in the woods on the opposite side of the stream. After viewing the ground awhile, we entered a beautiful green meadow and proceeded up the creek to Mr. Brinton's mill, where, by means of a wire bridge, we crossed again and ascended a very high and steep hill, to a wood where we had been informed a tree was still standing into which seven cannon balls were fired, and still remain imbedded in the wood.

The view from the hill was beautiful. We could distinguish the course of the Brandywine for several miles, and all around, the hills crowned with wood, sloped gently away, until they faded in the distance. After searching a short time, we found the tree, which is a large and lofty poplar, and bids fair to resist, for many years, the ravages of time. The balls in the tree were fired from some American cannons, planted a few rods further up the hill. It is said that when the advanced lines of the British army forced the Americans to retreat across the stream, one brave young soldier being unable to find any cannon balls, filled the cannon with iron bolts, horse shoes, &c., and having fired, and opened a wide breach in the British lines, escaped across the stream. Recrossing again, we proceeded about a mile to the east, where we stopped at a farmer's house to obtain some information. The house was situated on the slope of a hill, to the east of which the principal struggle had taken place. Here we also obtained some musket balls which are still to be found on the fields. The farmer conducted us to the summit of the hill, and crossing one or two fields, we stood in the very center of the battlefield. It was the same, but how changed! In the fields where we were then standing, the ground was once crimsoned with the lifeblood of our ancestors — the fields now green with verdure, were once heaped with the bodies of the dead and dying, and where the hum of the bee and the song of the woodland bird are now heard, once echoed with the groans of the wounded, the clash of contending swords, and the shrill neigh of the fiery war horse.

Our guide was familiar with the history of the battle, and described to us the relative position of the two armies. During the retreat of the Americans many were killed in a wood to the north, which, being then small, was cut down to afford them a passage. On emerging from the wood, they were enabled to gain some distance on the enemy, and were then met by Washington, the cannon having been sent on before. From this wood to the brow of a hill to the south, (a distance of about half a mile), a constant retreating fire was kept up by the Americans, who would walk slowly a few stops, till they had loaded their muskets, and then, wheeling round, fire upon the British, being in this manner enabled to maintain their retreat in good order. The farmer stated that he had been told by an American officer, who was engaged in the battle, that for upwards of half a mile, the fight was as hot and spirited as any he had ever witnessed. At the eastern extremity of the wood, the greatest slaughter took place; the bodies being in some places literally heaped up. After the Americans had crossed the hill, on the south, the firing was discontinued, and the main body of the army took up its march to Chester. In the adjoining field the decayed stump of a walnut tree was pointed out to us, as being the spot where Lafayette was wounded, the first and only blood he shed in the American cause.

An officer who was engaged in the battle, informed the farmer that he was passing by the spot at the time when Lafayette was wounded; it is supposed by a cannon ball passing very near him, the concussion of the air produced a slight flesh wound. Many Americans were slain to the north of the woods, and it is a superstitious notion of some of the farmers, that, where the blood was shed in the greatest profusion, an abundant growth of thyme sprung up spontaneously! At the eastern extremity of the woods, some moldering cinders mark the spot where a blacksmith's shop formerly stood, of which there is an anecdote related, by the farmers around. It is said when the retreating Americans were pursued by the British, an officer belonging to the British army stopped there, and commanded the blacksmith to shoe his horse. This he (being a republican) refused to do so; but on being threatened by the officer, pretended to comply, and watching his opportunity, struck him dead with a hammer, and dragging his body to a well at a short distance, threw it in, and then turned the horse loose. This valley, known by the name of "Sandy Hollow," is reputed to be haunted, and many persons are said to have seen the courageous blacksmith performing his daring deed over again, in the dead silence of midnight! It is carefully avoided after dark by the ignorant and superstitious who are afraid of meeting with the ghost of the slaughtered Briton!

What was then a thicket of small trees, is now a fine lofty wood, being the same which the Americans cut down to afford a passage in their rapid retreat. To the north-west was a high hill, on the top of which the American cannon were planted by Gen. Greene, to check the British on their approach. On arriving at the summit, we were both astonished and delighted at the extended and beautiful prospect which burst upon our view. To the west it was unconfined for upwards of eight miles, presenting a fine landscape. It was here that Gen. Greene first made a stand, when he was aware of the approach of the British; but he was obliged, after a short resistance, to retreat, owing to the superior force of the enemy. After we had viewed the surrounding landscape for some time, we proceeded to Birmingham Meeting-House, a short distance to the north. Arriving there, we were conducted by Mr. Cook into the Meeting-House, which was used at that time as a hospital for the wounded. It has been somewhat enlarged since the battle, but is, in many respects, unchanged. At one end we observed stains upon the floor, said to have been caused by the blood of the wounded and dying, who were carried thither.

The burial ground adjoining the Meeting-House, was the stand of a small body of troops commanded by Gen. Sullivan, placed there to annoy the British and retard their progress. They took shelter behind the walls, but the main body of the British army coming suddenly upon them, they were surrounded, many being killed and the remainder compelled to fly. The grave-yard has been enlarged since but the spot where our unfortunate countrymen were buried is distinctly visible. We almost deemed it sacrilege to walk over and tread upon the graves of our country's brave defenders. Near the middle is the grave of Lord Percy, mentioned by Miss E.M. Chandler in her "Legend of the Brandywine." About one hundred yards from the burial ground, is the spot where he was struck by the ball which terminated his life. "His remains lie unmarked by a single memorial, to tell the passing traveler, where rest the remains of one of the proud race of Northumberland." Being shown a hill above a mile and a half to the north, where he beheld the landscape he is said to have seen in dreams, where in England, we resolved to ascend it, that we might have the satisfaction of viewing it. The hill was rather a conical shape, and commanded a view of a most lovely landscape. To the west, at some distance we saw the placid Brandywine, glittering in the sunbeams. To the north-east was West Chester, distinctly visible at a distance of three miles, and contrasted with the blue hills afar off, presented a most beautiful sight. Before us was the landscape. On the spot where we were standing, Miss Chandler in the "Legend," makes Percy to exclaim: "The scene of my childhood are not more familiar to me than this. It has appeared to me in my dreams, and when I have closed my eyes in the dim twilight." About a mile to the south, was a brick house, one of the bricks of which was shot away by a British cannon ball, on the supposition that the house contained spies.

The following is a brief account of the battle, as given us by some of the farmers who were conversant with its history.

The British army, upon finding that the Americans were determined to make resistance, divided into two bodies. The Hessians, commanded by Gen. Knyphausen, advanced to Chadds' Ford, where they were met by Washington, and Wayne, who kept them in check. The other and larger body, commanded by General Howe and Cornwallis, proceeded up the Brandywine above the forks, where they crossed and marched to "Osborn's Hill," as it now called. Washington, on learning this, immediately sent Lafayette and Greene to stop their progress, but before they could form, the British army appeared in sight, on the top of Osborn's Hill. Sullivan, with a small body, was stationed in the burial ground to retard the British, till Greene could plant the cannon; but being surrounded and forced to fly, the only alternative was to retreat.

Taking a "last lingering look" at the landscape before us, we slowly descended the hill, and wended our way homewards, highly gratified with our visit, which fully compensated for our fatigue. I conclude, by desiring every one who has never visited the far famed field of Brandywine, to do so, as they would find the gratification of beholding it a sufficient recompense for their time and trouble.

Unionville, April 5, 1840.

Bayard Taylor wrote about his tour of the Brandywine Battlefield as a teenager. This article, printed in the *West Chester Register*, was his first published work. Taylor was born in Kennett Square, where the British army began its march on September 11, 1777, and went on to become one of the best-known travel writers in the United States during the 19th century. He wrote for the *Saturday Evening Post* and *New York Tribune* and authored several books. "Views Afoot or Europe Seen with Knapsack and Staff" was written after hiking through England, Germany, Italy, France, and Switzerland. He also served in the Abraham Lincoln administration as secretary of legation in Russia and minister to Germany during the Rutherford B. Hayes administration.

Taylor's visit to Brandywine was made on "a lovely morning. The sun had just appeared above the horizon, the sky was clear and unclouded, and all nature wore the garb of beauty." General George Washington had little time to reflect on the area's beauty on the day of his encounter with General William Howe and the British army.

Battle of the Brandywine

Painting by Adrian Martinez,
courtesy of Sue and Tim Coldren

One

Fighting Blind

General George Washington was fighting blind. Somewhere to the west of his own Continental army in the rolling fields and wooded land of Chester County, Pennsylvania, was the bulk of a 12,500-man army under the command of British General Sir William Howe. Washington had placed his 11,000-man army in a defensive position behind the Brandywine River with Major General William Sullivan protecting the northern fords of the Brandywine from a crossing by Howe. Brigadier General John Armstrong with the Pennsylvania militia guarded the southern crossing at Pyle's Ford, even though the British were not expected to force a crossing in front of Armstrong because of the rugged terrain. The main portion of Washington's army was in the center, at Chadds Ford. Washington wanted, and hoped, Howe would attempt a frontal attack on his main force, assembled in defensive positions, across the Brandywine at the tiny crossing at Chadds Ford. Few scouts, however, had been dispatched by Washington to the west of the Brandywine to keep an eye on the movement of the British army. Early in the day Washington had lost contact with his enemy.

In the late morning hours of Thursday, September 11, 1777, Washington knew at least a portion of Howe's formidable army was stationed directly across from his main forces at Chadds Ford. Early in the morning — as a heavy fog shrouded the landscape — the newly formed American light infantry under the command of Brigadier General William Maxwell crossed the Brandywine and engaged enemy forces under the direction of Hessian Lieutenant General Baron Wilhelm Knyphausen. Maxwell's units challenged Knyphausen's forces in several skirmishes between Kennett Square and Chadds Ford, the main and most direct route from the British encampments at Kennett Square to Washington's army. Maxwell eventually retreated back across the Brandywine. Was Knyphausen leading the main body of the British army and preparing to assault Washington's forces at Chadds Ford? Knyphausen commanded a significant number of troops, but Washington was unsure if the whole army of his foe was entrenching across the Brandywine and preparing for a major battle.

Washington picked Brandywine as the best defensive spot to stop Howe's advance on Philadelphia and the attempt to capture the key Rebel city and possibly members of the Continental Congress. Washington would have liked nothing better than to have the British army conduct a frontal assault on his forces that had taken positions in the wooded hills behind the Brandywine. While the fighting between Maxwell and Knyphausen was brisk at times, it was not sustained. Was Howe attempting a flanking maneuver as he had successfully done against Washington the year before at Long Island? Had Howe somehow slipped around the inexperienced American forces and was his army on its way to capture Philadelphia, the nation's capital city? Washington had many troubling questions that needed immediate answers. If Washington reached wrong conclusions, the future of the American army and the fate of the young nation would be in jeopardy.

As the morning hours passed and the heavy fog that shrouded the beautiful landscape lifted, Washington still was not sure of where his main opponent was located. Hours earlier, Washington had directed Colonel Theodorick Bland's dragoons to scout out the British position and warn Washington of any British surprises. Washington's adjutant, Colonel Timothy Pickering, reported that as late as "11 a.m. or noon Washington was bitterly lamenting that Col. Bland had not sent him information and that accounts Washington received were of a very contradictory nature."[1] Those contradictory reports froze Washington. The commander kept his main forces at Chadds Ford on the eastern side of the Brandywine River. Sullivan's men protected the fords of the Brandywine immediately to the north of his position, but Sullivan did little probing outside of his assigned lines of defense. When Washington first heard reports that British, Hessian, and American troops loyal to King George were on the march above the right flank of his army, Washington sent Major John Jamison of Bland's dragoons to investigate.

At 9:30 a.m. Washington received his first information and it appeared to be good news for the American commander in chief. Sullivan reported, "Maj. Jamison came to me...at 9 o'clock (and said that he had) come from the right of the army, and I might depend there was no enemy there."[2] The British apparently were attempting a frontal attack on his forces. Washington was poised to inflict the first major defeat upon the British forces in the American Revolution. Washington was waiting for Howe to plunge across the Brandywine and into his fortified positions. Within an hour Washington received a second report from Sullivan. This one, delivered by Sullivan's aide, Major Lewis Morris, Jr., had the enemy definitely making a flanking movement. The information came from Colonel Moses Hazen at Jones Ford. Hazen commanded a unit of mostly Canadians, commonly known as the "Infernals," who joined the American cause in 1775.

Washington had received conflicting reports within an hour. Which one was accurate? Should Washington shift his troops north to blunt a flanking attack by Howe? Did he have enough time to charge across the Brandywine, attack and defeat Knyphausen, and then rush to meet and defeat Howe? Should he remain in his defensive positions behind the Brandywine to blunt the hoped-for frontal attack? He knew Knyphausen, with at least a large portion of the British army, was facing him across the Brandywine. Without reliable intelligence from Bland's dragoons, Washington was in a quandary.

An American general was fighting a major battle without information on the position of his enemy. This situation would be replicated 86 years later on another Pennsylvania battlefield during the American Civil War when Confederate General Robert E. Lee fought the first half of the Battle of Gettysburg without the aid of General J.E.B. Stuart and his cavalry. The lack of accurate intelligence on the positions of their enemies would play a large part in the defeats of Lee at Gettysburg and Washington at Brandywine. Robert E. Lee's father, Henry "Light-Horse Harry" Lee, fought at Brandywine and was assigned to Bland's Regiment of Virginia cavalry. Lee's performance during the Philadelphia campaign resulted in Captain Lee's being promoted. Later he commanded the highly regarded Lee's Legion.

While Washington was contemplating his options, an American patriot, Squire Thomas Cheyney, was riding hard to Washington's headquarters after personally seeing the main portion of Howe's army, under the leadership of Lieutenant General Charles Earl Cornwallis. Lord Cornwallis and the attacking column of the British army were in the process of flanking General Sullivan's troops by crossing two unguarded fords on the eastern and western branches of the Brandywine above Sullivan. Cheyney and Colonel John Hannum, a friend and fellow patriot, had been riding together that morning and turned out to be the most important scouts Washington had that day.

Over two centuries Squire Cheyney has emerged as a folk hero in the Brandywine Valley. Cheyney risked his life to warn the American army of the British movements on the morning of the battle. At first both Sullivan and Washington scoffed at Cheyney's accounts and neither one believed him. Indeed, Washington's staff believed Cheyney to be a British spy delivering deceptive information that would lead to Washington's splitting his army and being defeated. How could a civilian obtain information that the dragoons couldn't verify? No official army reports of Cheyney's actions exist and several versions of Cheyney's heroic actions have been recorded. An account of Cheyney's exploits entitled "Squire Thomas Cheyney: The Paul Revere of the Brandywine" was written by Duane Christman. The following is Christman's account of Squire Cheyney's ride to destiny:

> The evening before the battle, while Washington sat in the Ring House planning his tactics, Squire Thomas Cheyney's friends and neighbors rushed to his home in Thornbury and warned him to leave quickly — the British were about to leave Kennett Square and move east. Cheyney, a local farmer and landholder, was an outspoken Whig, and he made no secret of his sympathy for the Colonial cause. He had called early and openly for independence from the Mother County, a stand the British loyalists had long observed with angry frustration. For despite the clear target he made of himself, Cheyney somehow always managed to slip through British hands as they closed to seize him.
>
> Heeding his neighbor's warnings, Squire Cheyney left his home and spent the night of September 10 with his good friend and relation Colonel John Hannum at Centre House, in present day Marshallton. The next morning Cheyney and Hannum decided to visit the Colonist's camp at Chad's Ford. They set out early and rode down the hill along Northbrook Road in the direction of Trimble's Mill and Ford. But as they approached the ford they came upon a sight that brought a sudden halt to their morning ride and forced them to scurry for cover. Unseen, Cheyney and Hannum watched as endless lines of British soldiers flowed over and down the opposite hill and came splashing through the shallow waters of the ford. Cheyney leaned over and quietly conferred with Hannum. This was no patrol of British advance scouts; thousands of redcoats were pouring over the hill. Where was the American army? There was only one possible answer — General Washington must be unaware of this British movement. He must be warned, and quickly. The army was in danger![3]

In 1936 a relative of Cheyney, Edward P. Cheyney, delivered a speech to the Pennsylvania Historical Society[4] and he used family source material to conclude on the day of the battle Squire Cheyney was at his Thonbury home, some five miles from the scene of the fighting, and either heard the clash of Knyphausen's forces with Maxwell, or, in some other way was told of the battle. He rode to Washington's camp by way of Jefferies Ford, one mile above Sullivan's forces, and saw the British cross the Brandywine.

Squire Cheyney, a third-generation resident of Chester County, was born in 1731 and was a farmer. A year after the Battle of Brandywine he was made a justice of the peace. He also served as a sublieutenant for Chester County; a sublieutenant collected fines from those who did not perform military service. This fine was particularly troublesome for the peace-loving Quakers who lived in the Brandywine Valley. The Quakers vowed not to support either army, a stance that angered both Washington and Howe.

The accounts of both Christman and Edward P. Cheyney had the American generals not believing Squire Cheyney. Christman's account continues:

> Hannum and Cheyney backed quietly away and then leaping to their saddles, turned their horses up over the hills towards Chad's Ford. The Squire's fleet mare, Bess, despite the heavy load she carried, soon outdistanced Hannum's mount. Hannum eventually turned off to join his regiment, while Cheyney raced on towards Washington. At one point in his ride he crashed through the midst of a surprised body of British scouts. Bullets whizzed by his ears as, head down, he rode on.
>
> Continuing downstream Cheyney suddenly came upon General Sullivan and the units he was commanding some distance upstream. Flanked by his jeering staff, Sullivan listened with impatience to the Squire's story of imminent danger, making little effort to conceal his suspicion. This story was ridiculous, he told Cheyney. Had not he himself just heard from a corps of local militiamen

that no British troops were reported above the Brandywine? Indeed he had just now dispatched that very information to General Washington....Sullivan now leaned closer into the Squire's face. Persons supplying such false information, he said pointedly, could have only one purpose: to serve the British cause by confusing the American command. Shaking with fury at Sullivan's blunt dismissal, Cheyney remounted, demanded directions to Washington's Headquarters and galloped off cursing the ineptitude of subordinates.

He was still uttering dark oaths when finally he reached Chad's Ford. To his complete surprise and further indignation aides blocked his path to the General and, like Sullivan, treated his information with contempt and disbelief. The Squire's face, already flushed from his hard ride, grew redder with increasing fury. What was wrong with the American officers, he thought. Why wouldn't they listen to him? He began to bellow, insisting that he be taken immediately to General Washington.

Washington, who was sitting inside his quarters, could not help but hear the shouting. Going to the entrance he demanded an explanation for the uproar. Cheyney, sweaty and disheveled, poured out what he had seen at Trimble's Ford. The General listened quietly to his story, but it was obvious, with skepticism. When Cheyney finished the story, General Washington looked him in the eye and said sternly, "Sir, do you know the penalty for spying?"

Stunned by another rebuke and from the General himself! — the Squire exclaimed, "By Hell, it is so!" Jumping from his horse, he picked up a twig and scratched a quick map into the dirt, pointing to the spot where he had observed the British cross the Brandywine, and then to the area around Birmingham Meeting where he suspected the British had by now advanced.

Washington still did not look convinced. Cheyney tried again. "If you doubt my word, sir, put me under guard till you ask Anthony Wayne or Persie Frazer (Colonel Persifor Frazer of the local militia) if I am to be believed." The General's officers continued to sneer at him. He turned to them and yelled "I would have you to know that I have this day's work as much at heart as e'er a blood of you!"[5]

Just after Squire Cheyney delivered his eyewitness information and impassioned plea to Washington, Washington received the confirmation he was seeking from Sullivan. The dispatch said: "Colonel Bland has this moment sent me word that the enemy are in the rear of my right about two miles coming down. There are, he says, about two brigades of them. 2 of oclock PM he also says he saw a dust rise back in the country for above an hour."[6] There was no longer a doubt that Howe and Cornwallis had a major portion of the British army bearing down on Washington's exposed right flank. If Washington did not take quick action, Howe and his main army would force Washington to fight not only Howe to his east, but also Knyphausen, who still had a strong force facing the Colonials across the Brandywine at Chadds Ford. A repeat of the August 27, 1776, defeat at Long Island seemed imminent.

Washington was no longer blind, but he was in a serious bind. Howe and Cornwallis, with half of the British army, had outflanked him and were about to attack the undefended rear of his army. Knyphausen, with the remainder of the British army, held strong positions across the Brandywine and wouldn't be easily dislodged. Sandwiched in between Howe and Knyphausen were Washington's forces. The general was on the brink of having his whole army annihilated, the capital of Philadelphia captured, and the battle for colonial freedom lost.

* * * * *

At Osborne's Hill, Howe watched his magnificent British army prepare to deliver a crushing blow to the Rebel forces. His daring plan was being executed to perfection. The rudimentary elements of Howe's tactics called for his army to split into two sections, and while forces under Knyphausen held Washington in check in front of the Brandywine, Cornwallis' troops would outflank Washington. The simple plan contained many dangers. The mere act of dividing his forces would mean Washington's total force far outnumbered either wing of the British. Washington, with luck and reliable military intelligence, certainly could attack and defeat one wing of the British army and have enough time to do the same to the remaining isolated body of British troops.

The British army had just endured an excruciatingly long sea voyage where men, supplies, and horses were lost. Were the British troops physically recovered enough to execute Howe's plan? To outflank Washington's troops, Cornwallis' wing of the British army would have to march 17 miles, ford the Brandywine at two places, and then attack and defeat the American army. The terrain would both help and hurt Howe. Chester County was an agricultural community with fields and many wooded areas and rolling hills. The woods and hills would provide a screen for Cornwallis and hide him from the eyes of Washington's scouts and the civilian sympathizers of the rebel cause. The woods and hills would also make the march more difficult.

The weather on September 11, 1777, also was a blessing and a hindrance for Howe. A thick fog formed in the early morning of the late summer's day. Again, the fog would aid in hiding Cornwallis as he made his way north from his encampment at Kennett Square and toward the Brandywine. Would the Loyalists guiding the British army become lost in the fog? Did the guides actually know of fordable crossings of the Brandywine north of the position of Sullivan's troops? The Americans, on their home soil with local militia, apparently didn't know of their existence. The warm weather that aided in the creation of the fog also would sap the strength of the troops, in full gear, on their long march. The area had undergone a number of rainstorms in recent weeks. Did the rain muddy the roads enough to hinder the movement of troops, cavalry, and cannons? Had the rain swollen the Brandywine enough to make it impassable? On the day of the battle the river, at many places, was as high as a man's waist.

The success of Howe's plan depended on surprise and the ability of Knyphausen to make Washington believe that Knyphausen commanded the main force of the British army. The British, while relying on Loyalists in Chester County to aid them and the Quakers to stay neutral, knew many rebels lived in the area and would aid Washington with intelligence. Cornwallis would have to detain farmers and their families encountered along the march until the attack was made. The Quakers, a large and influential segment of the Chester County population of 30,000, could be counted upon by their religious creed to not take part in war on either side. The British would not receive any aid from the Quakers, but neither would Washington.

Knyphausen played a pivotal role in Howe's plans. The Hessian general had the responsibility of leading Hessian, British, and Loyalist troops against Washington's army. Knyphausen would have to clear out the rebels between Kennett Square and Chadds Ford and drive them to the eastern side of the Brandywine. While doing so, he would have to deliver the clear impression that he commanded the main British army. For Washington to discover that Knyphausen had only half of the British forces would be disastrous for not only Knyphausen, but also Howe and Cornwallis. Knyphausen would then have to deploy his troops on the hills and woods overlooking the western bank of the Brandywine in such a way as to defend against an attack from Washington and still be in a position to cross the Brandywine and sweep the remaining American troops from the field once Cornwallis began his assault in the American rear.

Even though Howe's strategy contained elements of danger for his army and he could not count on immediate help if he failed, Howe had every reason to believe he could defeat Washington. He had experienced, brave, and loyal troops at his command and the officers were professional. And, almost the same plan had worked before at Long Island.

Stationed at Staten Island, Howe conducted an operation that landed 15,000 troops and 40 cannons on Long Island. In this battle General James Grant played the role that Knyphausen handled at Brandywine. Grant had the duty of drawing away attention from Howe's main attacking force. Early in the morning Grant's 5,000 troops had drawn American reserves away from the spot where Howe was planning his assault. In all, more than 20,000 British troops were engaged against the American army of half its size. Howe's troops marched nine miles that day without his column being discovered by the Americans. Sullivan's troops were caught between British forces and at 9 a.m. Howe began his attack. British and Hessian forces would spend the next few hours chasing the outnumbered Americans from their defensive positions.

Long Island was a major British victory with the Americans losing more than 1,000 and the British less than 400. The defeat could have been far worse for the Americans as Howe failed to storm the depleted American defenses at Brooklyn. Late in the day at Brandywine Howe would have another opportunity to press Washington after a clear, but incomplete victory over the rebel army.

* * * * *

As lead elements of Cornwallis' forces began their attack on the American forces still taking up defensive positions on the hills west of the Birmingham Meeting House, Howe was seeing his daring plan executed to perfection. Knyphausen, indeed, had held Washington at Chadds Ford. The rebels had not detected Cornwallis' march until it was too late for Washington to shift troops and individually attack the separate British columns. The experienced British soldiers were about to engage an American army, while full of fight and valor, devoid of strategic military leadership.

The only mistake the British had made during this opening battle of the Philadelphia campaign was actually being at Brandywine.

In December 1776 Howe had Washington on the run throughout New York and New Jersey. Through battle fatalities and desertion Washington's army numbered about 3,000 men when Howe pushed Washington through Princeton and to Trenton. Washington and his forces barely escaped to Pennsylvania. Major General Charles Lee was one of the casualties of the American army as he was captured on December 13 at Basking Ridge by a patrol of the Sixteenth Light Dragoons, a unit he once commanded. Lee, a soldier of fortune who had served as an officer in the 44th Foot and later in the Polish army, was appointed second-in-command of the American army. While Washington was losing at Long Island, Lee was in charge of a victory at Charleston, South Carolina. Lee was sent to New York where he aided Washington's retreat from New York and warned against an impending disaster at Fort Washington. There, the rebel army lost 3,000 troops to the British. Lee's relationship with Washington was strained, evidenced by many of Lee's letters. During Lee's time as a prisoner of war with the British he authored a plan that would allow the British to "Rally the Tories, to 'unhinge and dissolve the whole system of defence,' and to end the war two months after its execution."[7] Lee was later exchanged even though some British officials wanted Lee executed for treason because of his prior service with the British army.

Even though there is no indication Lee's plan played a role in Howe's strategy for the Philadelphia campaign, Howe was counting on Loyalists to rally to his aid, as they did in New Jersey after Washington's army was forced from the state. A strike into the heartland of Pennsylvania offered Howe many opportunities. Mills and forges in the area provided food and materials for weapons of war for Washington's army. A disruption of supplies would be disastrous for Washington, as his army already suffered because of a lack of proper equipment, clothing, and rations. The American government was headquartered in Philadelphia. Capturing the capital city and members of the Continental Congress would do irreparable harm to the rebels, shake confidence in the fledgling rebel government, and maintain the loyalty of those colonists who were thinking about abandoning King George III for the rebel cause. Patriots who were not wholly committed to the American cause of freedom would have an opportunity to pledge their allegiance to King George without punishment. A victory in Pennsylvania in 1777 twinned with a successful campaign by General John Burgoyne attacking New York from Canada would sever the defiant New England colonies from the less militant Mid-Atlantic and Southern states.

Indeed, the 1777 Pennsylvania campaign offered Howe and the British government many rich opportunities.

At the end of November 1776 Howe wrote to Lord George Germain, British secretary of state for the American colonies, indicating that he wanted to isolate New England. That view, however, changed in another letter Howe penned to Germain on December 20, 1776. In that letter Howe said he proposed "to hold Rhode Island, New York, and the lower Hudson defensively only, employing ten thousand men for the invasion of Pennsylvania. He had, in fact, every intention of advancing on Philadelphia as soon as the Delaware should be frozen, and had returned with Cornwallis to New York to mature his plans, when his security was disturbed by a rude shock."[8]

The rude shock was about to be administered by Washington, as the American general was on the verge of reversing his fortunes and changing the course of the war. Indeed, with his army in critical condition, it was a desperate time. The troops were underfed, underclothed, and underpaid. Soldiers were deserting at a rate that threatened the integrity of the army, and the enlistments of many more units were due to expire by the end of December. Howe's troops were safely ensconced for the winter and by spring a good chance existed that a skeleton force representing the American army would be his foe. Hessians held the left of the British line, anchored at Bordenton and Trenton. At Trenton Colonel Johann Rall had about 1,300 men. Rall did not believe Washington was a threat to his men. He even ignored orders from Howe to construct a proper defense. "We want no trenches," Rall said. "We will go at them with the bayonet."[9]

Christmas night was cold and wet as Washington and 2,400 troops along with 18 cannons made their way across the Delaware from McKonkey's Ferry. Two supporting columns were to offer support to Washington but the weather prevented one group from crossing the Delaware and slowed down the other column so long that it arrived too late to become engaged. Rall and his troops celebrated on Christmas Day and Rall drank so much he had to be carried to his bed. Tories and American deserters had informed Rall of the impending American attack but Rall didn't believe the attack would be in force. Washington attacked at 8 a.m., hours later than he had planned. He didn't want to launch his assault in full daylight, but less than two hours later the Hessians surrendered. During the engagement Rall was shot and killed while directing his troops from his horse. The Hessians had more than 100 killed and almost 1,000 others taken prisoners. No Americans were killed during the battle.

Washington's surprise attack had shocked the British and altered their plans to subdue the rebellious Americans. Germain was being deluged with requests for additional troops for the British army by his generals in the colonies. And, Howe in a January letter had changed his mind and now thought better of the Pennsylvania operations. Germain's response on March 3, 1777, to Howe "approved an attack on Philadelphia; but simultaneously he reduced the promised reinforcement from eight thousand to three thousand men, and yet at the same time recommended a 'warm diversion' on the coasts of Massachusetts and New Hampshire."[10] Three weeks later Germain ordered Burgoyne to continue with his plans to strike at Albany and on June 17 Burgoyne began his thrust into New York. On May 18, 1777, Germain told Howe to continue with his plans to capture Philadelphia, but he hoped the operation would conclude in time for his army to join Burgoyne. "I trust that whatever you may meditate will be executed in time for you to cooperate with the army to proceed from Canada,"[11]

Germain wrote Howe. Germain seemed to have second thoughts concerning the Pennsylvania operation. An order was then drafted, but never sent, reversing Howe's objective and sending him to New York to aid Burgoyne. During May Howe received the March correspondence from Germain approving the Philadelphia campaign.

Indecision on the part of Germain and his attempt to run the war from London, along with the months of delays in sending communications back and forth across the Atlantic resulted in Howe's ill-advised Philadelphia expedition. The campaign was doomed to fall far short of its goals despite an overwhelming military victory at Brandywine. And, Burgoyne's offensive in New York would end in disaster for the British at Saratoga.

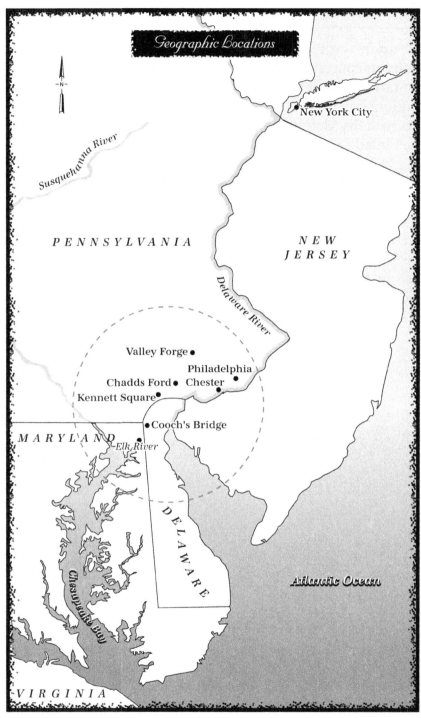

Diane Cirafesi of Cirafesi Designs
West Chester, Pennsylvania

Two

Howe's Frightful Sea Voyage

Colonel Carl Emil Curt von Donop arrived in America in August 1776 as one of the many German mercenaries, numbering about 30,000, hired to fight in the British army. More than 7,700 would die in the American Revolution and another 5,000 would desert the British. Von Donop was a veteran of the fight at Long Island where Howe soundly defeated Washington. Eleven days before Washington fought back and surprised Colonel Johann Rall's German command at Trenton, von Donop was relieved of command at Trenton and given overall responsibility of the chain of outposts along the Delaware River. Von Donop's brief time in the colonies didn't stop him from questioning the British strategy of invading Pennsylvania instead of concentrating forces in New England. He endured the protracted boat voyage from New York to Maryland along with his fellow Germans and his British comrades during the summer of 1777. Less than a month after arriving at Head of the Elk, the British would engage the American army at Brandywine. After disembarking in Maryland, von Donop made his thoughts on the campaign clear in a letter to the Prince of Prussia, who was the son of Augustus William, brother of Frederick II and soon to become King Frederick William II. The letter is dated Head of the Elk, September 2, 1777.

If I dared to tell you what I think of our present situation, I should say outright that our expedition into these parts of the south is not to my liking. For if, instead of coming here, we had set sail for New England and joined Burgoyne's army, we should without fail have forced that province and its capitol to return to their duty before the end of this month and, by so doing, have put an end to the war in that section of the north; our army would have been spared the excessive heat that it has been compelled to endure; and it would have operated in New England with eight battalions more, for it would have been joined by the eight battalions that are on Red Island (Rhode Island)....Our army could easily have repulsed that of Washington if he had tried to follow us and to cross the North (Hudson) River. More than that, we could have driven him back across the Delaware and before winter have chased him right into Virginia. For judging from all appearances, he would not have dared to risk a battle against an army that would have been 35,000 strong.

That way I think we should have had one of the most glorious campaigns, and perhaps peace before the end of it. For if all the provinces from Quebec to Virginia were cleared of rebels, the rest would be utterly lost unless they sought pardon and made peace. At present I cannot think of our army as anything but a flying corps that is doing a dangerous thing in entering a region where it will be entirely surrounded by the enemy, who need not worry about it much, knowing that it will very soon have to abandon its position. The outcome will show whether I am mistaken.

Washington has his force on the heights of Wilmington, but has at the same time two intermediate posts, one of 700 men on the iron mountains and another 4,000 who are supposed to be entrenched near Christianbruck (Christiana). His whole force is said to amount to 40,000 men. It may be that strong, for the rebel race has greatly increased of late. In the meantime, I hope that they will stay where they are, and that we (I mean the English) may be a bit more closely drawn together for the attack. For unless we are, I cannot yet reassure myself that infantry with its files four feet apart can capture entrenchments by escalade, or hold its ground against cavalry, of which the rebels have far more than we do, and judging by all appearances, it is not all bad, either. We have allowed the rebels too much time in which to become soldiers. They are drilled by French officers, and I am none too sure how our general is going to get himself out of this affair.

If Washington should decide to make a quick advance upon us, for two days now General Knyphausen has been detached with three brigades, and half of the Sixteenth Regiment of dragoons are on the left bank of the Elk river in the County of Delaware, it would be impossible for us to re-assemble this side of Christianbruck. Washington would find nothing to prevent him from falling either upon us or upon Knyphausen's corps; so I hope that we shall move as soon as possible and get possession of Christianbruck before the enemy gets his eyes open.

Above all, my genuine affection for the Howe brothers leads me to hope that our campaign will be successful...For they are, both of them, certainly persons of exceptional merit.

P.S. We have just at this moment received orders to march at four o'clock tomorrow morning. The enclosed proclamation will show that perhaps a bit too much humanity is being shown the rebels.[1]

Von Donop didn't receive any mercy from the rebels. On October 22, 1777, he was wounded in the attack on Fort Mercer in New Jersey and died three days later. Even though von Donop greatly overestimated the strength of Washington's army, his reasoning was sound. A united British army would certainly have averted the defeat at Saratoga and very well may have driven Washington's army from New England and the Middle Atlantic states into the far southern states. The South, with the North taken out of the war, would not have been inclined to fight alone.

Captain Friedrich von Muenchhausen, as early as April, believed Howe would not support Burgoyne's forces in New York. Von Muenchhausen was the wing adjutant to all German auxiliary forces. He wrote in his diary on April 17, 1777, "From all indications, I conclude that Gen. Howe is planning a secret expedition and I think that we will try to support the army of Carleton, since there has been no way of doing that. Everybody believes Gen. Howe will send a corps down into the Delaware River to land not far from Philadelphia. But personally I believe it would be better if we would send a corps up the Hudson River to Albany. But the Rebels have strong batteries and forts on the Hudson."[2]

Von Muenchhausen, unlike von Donop, would survive the war. He was born in Hanover, Germany, landed in America at Staten Island on August 12, 1776, and returned to Germany in 1778. He died on January 25, 1795.

* * * * *

Even though Howe joined von Donop, von Muenchhausen, and Lord Germain in having doubts about the wisdom of invading Pennsylvania and capturing Philadelphia, Howe was committed to the campaign. He had received orders from Germain to proceed with the operation, and as spring turned into summer Howe undertook the task of preparing his army for the campaign. Howe would not receive Germain's letter suggesting he help Burgoyne until he landed in Maryland in August. Burgoyne would have to succeed, or fail, on his own in New York. Howe was about to begin his assault on Pennsylvania by heading toward the Delaware Bay, and if the Americans had the Delaware too well defended, he would proceed to the Chesapeake. On July 23, 1777, after a delay of almost three weeks during which the troops were confined to the transport ships, Howe put to sea with about 17,000 troops and 266 ships with provisions for three months, according to the journal of Captain John Montresor, chief engineer of the British army. The British navy was under the command of Admiral Lord Richard Howe, brother of General Howe. While

William Howe's clear intention for the upcoming campaign was the capture of Philadelphia, only General Cornwallis and Brigadier General James Grant received details of his plan. The rest of his army was in the dark. When Howe set the armada in motion his troops were unsure whether they would sail north to aid Burgoyne, south to the Delaware River and on to Philadelphia, or, farther south to fight in the extreme southern colonies.

Washington was at a loss as to Howe's destination. During the early portion of the summer Washington and his troops, believed to have numbered only 6,000 at this point, kept Howe bottled up in New Jersey. Washington didn't risk a full battle in the open and also didn't allow Howe a direct route to capture Philadelphia by land or to march north to Burgoyne. As word reached Washington of Howe's force moving by sea, Washington had to be ready to advance to New York, defend Philadelphia, or watch as Howe sailed to Virginia or South Carolina. On July 1, 1777, Washington wrote, "there is the strongest reason to conclude that General Howe will push up the river immediately to co-operate with the army from Canada."[3]

On July 3, Washington's army was at Morristown, New Jersey. While at Morristown rebel spies reported that Howe was outfitting his ships for a long voyage, including the construction of stalls for horses. He asked the local militia to watch the movement of Howe's fleet. Washington wanted desperately to know if Howe was heading north or south. Washington moved his army north on false reports that Howe would aid Burgoyne. When word was received that Howe, indeed, was heading to sea and to the south, Washington asked Congress to have lookouts fixed along the capes of Delaware to detect Howe's movements. Philadelphia and the Continental Congress now seemed the likely target for Howe's 1777 campaign. Washington ordered his army to Philadelphia, his capital city. General Anthony Wayne, who lived in Chester County, was given the responsibility of rallying and organizing the Pennsylvania militia. Wayne, known as Mad Anthony, had little time to organize the volunteer soldiers before Brandywine. To bolster a crucial element of the defense of Philadelphia, Congress turned its attention to the defensive fortifications on the Delaware. Fort Mifflin, built before the war by British engineers, and soon-to-be-constructed Fort Mercer, the site favored by Washington for fortification, were partly responsible for Howe's deciding to forgo a direct assault on Philadelphia from the Delaware River.

By the end of July reports were reaching Washington, Congress, and Pennsylvania officials that Howe was near the Delaware Bay. On July 28, 1777, the Executive Council of the State of Pennsylvania issued two orders. The first one called for the driving off of "live stock on the frontiers of Chester County, whenever the enemy may approach." The second one called for the Prothonotary of Chester County to secure Chester County Court records. The order said, "Whereas it is highly necessary in this time of danger, the Enemy at present meditating an invasion of the state by the way of the Bay and River Delaware, on the bank of said River the Borough is situated, that said books, records, papers and seals should be removed to and secured at some place of greater safety."

Washington hastened his march to Philadelphia, urging his commanders to get their troops to the capital city. Washington had split his divisions and they were traveling by different routes to Philadelphia. Washington left his troops in the hands of General Nathanael Greene and hurried to Philadelphia to confer with members of Congress. During early August Washington again questioned Howe's ultimate destination. Was Howe drawing Washington's army toward Philadelphia and away from his ultimate destination in New York? To protect against that possibility Washington ordered a portion of his army, including General John Sullivan, to retrace its steps and head back toward New York. During this period Washington had the opportunity to meet his newest general, and youngest, Major General Lafayette of France. That is the Marquis de Lafayette, whose full name was Marie Joseph Paul Yves Roch Gilbert du Motier Lafayette.

On August 8, 1777, Lafayette had his first opportunity to review the American army. About 11,000 troops took part in the event. The troops did not have proper arms and equipment. The whereabouts of Howe was just one of the problems facing Washington in the summer of 1777. His soldiers were suffering from a lack of quality clothing, especially shoes. Also, Joseph Trumbull, member of a patriotic New England family and elected to the Continental Congress as an alternate from Connecticut, resigned as quartermaster general of the Continental army during this period because of lack of resources and support. Trumbull had held the position since July 1775, after serving for two years as commissary general of Connecticut forces. General Thomas Mifflin, a member of the Continental Congress, assumed control of the department, but failed to supply the troops with the materials they needed, which hindered Washington during the Philadelphia campaign and made the coming hard winter worse at Valley Forge. Washington was also concerned about protecting the stores he had established in the Philadelphia region. The Continental Congress had established storage locations at York, Lancaster, and Mill Town, the present-day Downingtown. When it became apparent Philadelphia would be a target of Howe's assault, Washington sent members of the Philadelphia militia to Mill Town, about 30 miles west of Philadelphia and 20 miles north of Chadds Ford, on August 23, 1777, to protect the supplies, including 900 barrels of flour, from the British.

During August Washington lost the use of one of his most dependable units as he ordered Morgan's Rifles north to help General Horatio Gates defend against Burgoyne. Daniel Morgan had organized a rifle company from Virginia in the beginning of the war and won praise for his leadership in the campaign for Quebec in 1775. Morgan and his riflemen played crucial roles in the victory at Saratoga. With Morgan fighting in the north, Washington needed a unit of light infantry, and on August 28, 1777, Washington tapped Brigadier General William Maxwell to head a new command of troops picked from various units of Washington's army. Each of the six brigades of the American army contributed nine officers and 109 enlisted men to form a light infantry corps. The unit would first fight at Cooch's Bridge on September 3, 1777, the only Revolutionary War battle in Delaware, and eight days later play an important role at Brandywine.

Besides not receiving proper supplies for his troops, discipline was becoming a problem for Washington. An officer in the 4th Continental Dragoons was charged with desertion and taking a horse. On August 19 he was found guilty and led round his regiment on horseback with his face toward the horse's tail and his coat turned wrong side outward. He was then discharged from the army. Also, 15 men were charged with mutiny and desertion and were sentenced to death, but mercy was shown and they were ordered barred from serving with the dragoons and sent to "foot service," the infantry. Other infractions resulted in 25 lashes on naked backs.[4] On August 7 Washington ordered each man should receive five ounces of soap per week as it was absolutely necessary to keep the soldiers decent and clean. Those selling their soap were to be severely punished.

By mid-August Washington was again befuddled about Howe's objectives and for a time was totally unaware of Howe's location. Had Howe wanted to attack Philadelphia by way of the Delaware or Chesapeake, Howe had plenty of time to find a landing place and begin his operations. American sympathizers on August 14 again sighted the British fleet at Cape Charles, Virginia. "I am now of opinion that Charles Town is the present object of General Howe's attention though for what sufficient reason, unless he expected to drag this army after him by appearing at different places and thereby leave the country open for General Clinton to march out and endeavor to form a junction with General Burgoyne, I am at a loss to determine."[5] A week after Howe was sighted in Virginia Washington sought out the opinions of his officers as to Howe's probable destination and the next move for the rebel army. The American military commanders concluded that Howe was on his way to South Carolina and they should march back to New York to take on Burgoyne. The consensus was wrong.

Washington's fretting over his foe's location was about to conclude. On August 22 Congress received word that Howe was in the Chesapeake Bay and about to make a landing. Washington's plan to proceed to New York was cancelled. He now had to contend with defending Philadelphia from an attack from the west. Washington ordered his units posted throughout New Jersey to rejoin the main force and head toward Chester, Pennsylvania. Congress also requested Delaware to contribute 1,000 militia members to support Washington's army. Caesar Rodney, signer of the Declaration of Independence, was placed in command, despite being ill. Maryland and Pennsylvania also received formal requests for militia. "The enemy is advancing rapidly towards the city, and unless every man exerts himself, they will, most undoubtedly, accomplish their design of stealing it," Congress declared.

Pennsylvania leaders also allowed for non-militia citizens to come to Washington's aid. On July 31, 1777, Chester County militia officers were issued the following proclamation from the Executive Council of the State of Pennsylvania: "Volunteers, animated by the love of liberty and their country who may step forward on this great and important occasion before it may be their turn to go into the field in the class to which they belong, and thereby render the most important service at this critical time, will be entitled to the highest esteem and respect and will most certainly meet with every countenance and encouragement which the Council can give. They will be entitled to same pay and rations with the militia."

Washington decided to perform a grand march through the streets of Philadelphia as he made his way to oppose Howe. A show of force should encourage residents of the city and Congress and give a message to the Tories that the American army was a formidable force. The army was made ready as clothes were washed and a green sprig was added to each man's hat as an emblem of hope. Washington issued orders to begin the march at 4 a.m. on Sunday, August 24, 1777, and proceed down Front Street to Chestnut Street and then turn to the area known as the Common, now occupied by Philadelphia's City Hall. The order of march was the divisions of Greene, Major General Adam Stephen, Major General Benjamin Lincoln and Lord Stirling with regiments of the Horse divided and assigned to the front and rear of the long column that took about two hours to pass any one location. To keep the appearance of a well-disciplined fighting force, Washington also ordered all women, including wives, laundresses, servants, and prostitutes, attached to the army to be kept away from the troops. The army kept marching until 8 p.m. They would need their rest as the British were reported as ready to land on the Elk River. Washington's troops were then ordered to proceed to Wilmington, Delaware.

The show of force impressed John Adams, who wrote to his wife, Abigail, in Braintree, Massachusetts: "We have now an army well appointed between us and Mr. Howe, and this army will be immediately joined by ten thousand militia, so that I feel as secure as if I were at Braintree...I find (the army) to be extremely well armed, pretty well clothed, and tolerably disciplined...Much remains to be done. Our soldiers have not yet quite the air of soldiers. They don't step exactly in time. They don't hold up their heads quite erect, nor turn out their toes so exactly as they ought. They don't all of them cock their hats; and such as do, don't wear them the same way."[6]

Washington's troops might have instilled a sense of security in Adams, a signer of the Declaration of Independence and future American president, but those same troops, who didn't exactly step in time and didn't properly cock their hats, were on course to meet the British army, whose experience, training, discipline, and supplies far exceeded those of the American army. Philadelphia would soon become a dangerous place for Adams and his fellow rebel leaders.

* * * * *

The British army and its German comrades found the voyage to Maryland full of hardships. Lieutenant Carl Philipp von

Feilitzsch wrote in his diary on August 6, 1777: "Dull weather and almost no wind. I will very briefly record my thoughts on this day concerning life at sea. Anyone who has a desire to experience misery and misfortune should go aboard ship. Everyone can believe me that when I am again in Europe, should the opportunity arise for another such trip, I would certainly not go. 1) There is no bread except zwieback, which is spoiled or full of worms. 2) Stinking water with all possible impurities mixed in, because on this trip, from the beginning until now, we have not had one good drop. 3) The meat is miserable and frightfully salted so that it can hardly be eaten, and then one nearly dies of thirst. 4) The entire ship is full of lice, and when it storms no one can think of anything else. Anyone who has never gone to sea cannot understand how miserable that can be. It is nearly impossible to take a step without risk of breaking your neck or a leg. Everything has to be securely fastened and still everything breaks and busts to pieces. If there is no wind the water is generally restless, which causes the ship to sway back and forth in one place in a dreadful manner. There is seldom a day when a person is satisfied, but how can I describe all of it as it is? God will surely help to return me to my fatherland. During the evening, at about six o'clock, there was a thunderstorm in the distance, accompanied by rain."[7]

Von Feilitzsch gave the following account of his time on board the ship *Martha* with Captain August von Wreden in command. Sickness, death, and a collision between his ship and another one of the British navy all contributed to a hazardous voyage:

- *July 26th:* The wind was contrary and very strong from early in the morning to the next morning. Once again I realized what an unfortunate life it is at sea.

- *July 28th:* Heavy fog and at ten o'clock thunderstorms and rain, and then a strong wind from the east. At six o'clock in the evening the thunder resumed and at seven o'clock we had a frightful weather. Here I will add something. Storms here in America are much stronger and last longer than in Europe.

- *July 29th:* The wind was from the northwest, very strong and good. However, I did not feel well and I considered my fate again and sincerely wished I were back in Germany. Who knows where we are bound? This day we passed Delaware. We changed our course toward Pennsylvania and believed we were going to Virginia. How much heat will we have to tolerate there?...At eight o'clock in the evening, Admiral Howe turned, unexpectedly, and we sailed directly for the Delaware.

- *July 30th:* At six o'clock the land was clearly visible and at seven o'clock we were in Delaware Bay....The sea was very restless, however, and during the evening we sailed into the ocean.

- *August 1st:* We still sailed southward toward Virginia. No one any longer knew where we were bound. Everyone said something different and everyone had to leave the decision to General Howe.... At seven o'clock in the evening we had a thunderstorm, which lasted two hours.

- *August 5th:* Although we are hardly thirty English miles from the Delaware, I still believe that we are going to Philadelphia and that this maneuvering is only a subterfuge in order to get the rebels away from the Delaware, and, upon news of that, we will at once enter. During the evening at eight o'clock there was frightful lightning, such as is never seen in Germany. It rained hard all during the night.

- *August 7th:* We saw land, which we considered to be Maryland, but we sailed on into the sea. During the evening there was frequent lightning but the weather remained pleasant.

- *August 8th:* The mate was very sick with a high putrid fever, very contagious and lying not far from my bed....On this day we saw a great many different fish.

- *August 9th:* We were below the 38th degree of latitude and hoped soon to reach land, which I wished from the bottom of my heart. Today we reached Cape Henry and we expect to enter tomorrow.

- *August 10th:* At about one-thirty in the afternoon the mate died. I must admit that I was glad, because he could not have recovered and was no longer able to resist death. At five o'clock in the afternoon he was buried at sea. This took place in the following manner — He was laid on a board to which twelve cannonballs had been tied. The second mate gave a short speech in English and finally asked some sailors if this death occurred naturally and not in a violent manner. They answered this with a yes and then the body was thrown overboard.

- *August 11th:* About six o'clock in the evening today became memorable to me. A year earlier this accident would have affected my mind. However, since my first sea voyage on the ocean, when everything seemed miserable and unusual, I have accepted that as long as I am in America, everything will be different and consider this as something to be expected. Therefore, for this reason, this incident did not affect me as much as otherwise.

  A large East Indiaman ship of about 800 tons, which had 1,000 English troops on board, and was three times larger than our ship, which had only 200 men on board, sailed directly at us with a strong wind and full sails. Everyone called for the ship's captain and mate, even while it was some distance from us. It did not turn and it appeared it would run us down. That ship, fortunately, only wiped out the after part of our ship. Two large sails with all their rigging and a small boat were smashed and broken into many pieces. The so-called bowspirit or nose of the other ship penetrated about two yards into our solid wall. On the other ship our anchor tore out a large piece of the cabin. Other than that, we know of nothing. All the jaegers and grenadiers reacted to the call and the terrible, frightful cracking on the deck. Everyone threw up his hands and shouted for help. Everyone can imagine how such an event seemed without my describing it further. The surgeon's mate from the Hessian Jaegers jumped from our ship onto the other ship. God, however, helped us out of this great danger. The ship's captain assured us that if it had hit at the middle of the ship, instead of the after part, we would all have lost. I was prepared for anything, even this, but God helped us once again.

- *August 14th:* It was excessively warm today. About six o'clock in the evening we saw land. It was the tip of Cape Charles. At this time we fired a heavy cannonade.

- *August 15th:* At one-thirty we again set sail and despite a heavy cannonade entered Chesapeake Bay. We also saw smoke and some ships. We assumed it to be frigates from our fleet engaged with the enemy but could not tell if the enemy were on water or on land.

- *August 16th:* By three o'clock we were completely within Chesapeake Bay. We saw Virginia to the right and left. During the night there was a thunderstorm such as has never been seen in Europe.

- *August 19th:* This was a rainy day with thunder. I also heard today that a few days ago, lightning struck an English ship, killing four dragoons and six horses.

- *August 22nd:* On this day we sailed quite close to the land on our right side. We saw many people. Today we had Baltimore behind us and sailed in another direction. We still did not know where we were bound.

- *August 23rd:* At five o'clock a frigate fired a cannon shot toward land and chased the people, who had ridden to the water's edge, away. At once we saw cannon fire, on land in the distance, against our ships, which then replied. The point of land where we lie is called Turkey Point, Kent Island. Today a jaeger from the Major's Company died and was immediately thrown in the water.

- *August 24th:* During the afternoon we received an order to disembark tomorrow morning at three o'clock, that is, the English Grenadiers and Light Infantry, and the Hessian Jaegers and us. These are the First Brigade and are to be the first ashore.

- *August 25th:* We entered the flatboats at two o'clock in the morning. The First Brigade formed and sailed eight miles into the Elk River. The entire fleet sailed behind us and at ten o'clock we arrived at Elk Point, where we landed. We occupied the heights at once, without seeing a single rebel. Later we marched three miles. The heat was terrible. A Hessian jaeger dropped dead and I was sick myself.[8]

The voyage was just as frustrating for Howe as it was to von Feilitzsch. The fleet battled bad weather as it attempted to stay out of sight of the rebels. On July 29 Howe was poised to enter the Delaware River and make a quick strike at Philadelphia. Admiral Howe positioned the fleet about eight miles south of Cape May as the British commanders awaited word from the frigate *Roebuck*, then exploring the Delaware Bay with Captain Sir Andrew Snape Hammond commanding. Hammond's report was not encouraging. General and Admiral Howe were told the enemy had both sides of the Delaware fortified and it would be dangerous for the fleet to attempt to approach Philadelphia. A decision was made not to land the army in Delaware even though a successful disembarking was possible in front of the American defenses at Philadelphia. Such a landing would have saved the British valuable time and provided Howe an opportunity to capture Philadelphia and also aid Burgoyne. When Admiral Howe led the fleet towards the Chesapeake, Burgoyne's fate was in his own hands. Howe would not be in a position to save Burgoyne when Burgoyne desperately needed his assistance. On July 31 the British fleet disappeared off the Delaware capes.

A series of storms battered the fleet during the first week of August, causing sickness, loss of life, and damage to several ships. The extreme heat of many of the days baked the soldiers on the ships. Fresh water was scarce, along with food for the sailors, soldiers, and horses. "The fleet and army much distressed for want of fresh water (the bay of course was brackish) having been for some time put on allowance, but not so much as the horse vessels which had been obliged to throw numbers of their horses overboard."[9] Crabs did offer a supply of food to the British army as the soldiers caught thousands of them.

Howe's element of surprise was also gone. As Admiral Howe skillfully led the fleet up the Chesapeake, the British fleet was spotted on August 12 and soon the Continental Congress knew of his imminent landing.

The long, painful voyage concluded on the morning of August 25 as the fleet anchored opposite Cecil Court House and Elk Ferry above Turkey Point. British officers reported 27 men and one woman died during the trip along with 170 horses. The woman died during one of the storms. Another 150 horses were rendered unfit for duty. In a letter dated August 30, 1777, from Head of the Elk River, George Osborn wrote to Germain that the Hessians lost 29 dead at sea and their sick list at landing amounted to 180.[10] The British lost even more horses after landing. "Upon reaching Head of Elk, the three hundred horses that survived were turned loose in a cornfield, where they so gorged themselves that half of them were felled by colic."[11]

The initial portion of the Philadelphia campaign did not unfold as Howe had planned.

Three

First Blood

Two pressing issues faced British General William Howe upon his landing at Head of the Elk. For almost two months many of his troops had been confined on board ships and the inactivity caused an erosion of their fitness for combat. They needed fresh water and food to restore their strength. His mounted troops also needed fresh horses. Too many of the horses died or were rendered unfit for service during the long sea voyage. The horses would have to be obtained from the local inhabitants and Howe was willing to offer a fair price for their purchase. The British army was in no condition to face a major assault from General George Washington's army. Luckily for Howe, the rebel forces were not in position to oppose his landing. The Americans were in the process of gathering near Wilmington, Delaware. Howe had the time he needed to refresh his troops.

The second problem facing Howe would be harder to solve. His troops needed provisions and plenty were available from the local farmers. Howe would not tolerate the plundering of local farmers. His troops had to act with restraint. Howe didn't want the citizens to have any reason to hate the British army and take up arms against him. Indeed, Howe wanted the citizens to rally to his army's side. If the residents remained loyal to King George III and offered assistance to his army, Washington and the American Revolution would be doomed. On August 27, 1777, a statement was issued from

British headquarters that offered protection for loyal British subjects and forgiveness to those who would defect from the rebel army and forgo any further armed resistance. Howe's pardon offer to the rebellious patriots, however, would be in effect only for a limited time.

The order, in part, said:

> Sir William Howe regretting the calamities to which many of his Majesty's faithful subjects are still exposed by the continuance of the Rebellion, and no less desirous of protecting the innocent, then determined to pursue with the rigors of war all those whom His Majesty's forces, in the course of their progress, may find in arms against the King, doth hereby appease the peaceable inhabitants of the Province of Pennsylvania, the lower counties on Delaware, and the counties of Maryland on the Eastern Shore of Chesapeake Bay; that in order to remove any groundless apprehensions which may have been raised of their suffering by depredations of the Army under this Command, he hath issued the strictest orders to the troops for the preservation of regularity and good discipline, and has signified, that the most exemplary punishment shall be inflicted upon those who shall dare to plunder the property or molest the persons of any of his Majesty's well-disposed subjects.
>
> Security and protection are likewise extended to all persons, inhabitants of the Province and Counties aforesaid, who, not guilty of having assumed legislative or judicial authority, may have acted illegally in subordinate stations, and conscious of their misconduct being induced to leave their dwellings, provided such persons do forthwith return, and remain peaceably at their usual places of abode.
>
> Considering moreover, that many officers and private men, now actually in Arms against His Majesty may be willing to relinquish the part they have taken in this Rebellion, and return to their due allegiance; Sir William

Howe doth therefore promise a free and general pardon to all such officers and private men as shall come and surrender themselves to a detachment of His Majesty's Forces, before the Day on which it shall be notified, that the said Indulgence is to be discontinued.[1]

Residents living near where the British landed didn't display any passion for either side. Local militia companies posted on the Chesapeake failed to fire a shot in opposition to the landing. "The most common political sentiment in all the districts...was impartial desire to be left alone by both political parties; and farmers were equally afraid of being plundered by the Hessians, and of being persecuted as Loyalists by the Republican committees after the Royal army had retired from their neighborhoods."[2] Howe's promise of harsh punishment for plundering and assaulting the local inhabitants didn't stop every British and German soldier from attempting to take advantage of the citizens. A Hessian officer, a member of the Regiment von Mirbach and a member of Lieutenant General Wilhelm Knyphausen's staff, wrote in a letter home, "In the first onrush the rigid orders against plundering were not strictly observed. General Howe sentenced some to be hanged on the spot and others to be flogged within an inch of their lives. On the other hand, the Hessian troops under Colonel von Donop and Lieutenant Colonel (Ludwig) von Wurmb were warmly thanked in the orders of the 28th for observing the necessary discipline in every way."[3] German soldiers were not as pure as the Hessian officer claimed. Ambrose Serle, civilian secretary to Lord Richard Howe, wrote in his journal on August 29, 1777, "Went on shore and mortified with the accounts of plunder, committed on the poor inhabitants by the army and navy.... Parties straggling for plunder, were surprised by the Rebels. The Hessians are as infamous and cruel as any."[4]

Serle wasn't happy about Chesapeake as a destination. In his diary on July 24, 1777, he wrote, "In the evening it was given out that we were bound to the Chesapeake, may GOD defend us from the fatality of the worst Climate in America at this worst Season of the Year to experience it!"[5] British soldiers reported that the constant rain made their camp a mud hole and Howe, two days after landing, wrote in his diary, "since the heavy rain continues, and the roads are bottomless, and since the horses are still sick and stiff, we had to...countermand the order of march."[6] Before dark on August 26, every soldier, field piece and wagon had been safely landed; and orders were issued to march at three the next morning, but that night "it turned to rain, and continued raining for six and thirty hours. The roads were reported to be impassable for such of the famished horses as had survived that dreadful voyage; and all the biscuits and cartridges served out to the troops were spoiled in the pouches. The Guards alone lost sixteen thousand rounds of ammunition."[7]

The loss of the ammunition and the horses might not constitute a problem for Howe, as he was unsure if Washington would stand and fight. In a letter to Germain on August 30, 1777, Howe wrote, "Fleet sailed July 23—arrived off the Capes of Delaware on the 30th following: when, from information, I judged it most advisable to proceed to Chesapeake Bay: but meeting with constant unfavorable winds, we did not enter the bay until the 16th inst.,...Enemy force of 15,000 men: I am of opinion it will be a difficult matter to bring them to a general action, even though it should be in defense of Philadelphia."[8] An American officer captured by the British on September 1 agreed with Howe by saying "Washington, in his present situation, cannot avoid battle. He is a fool, however, if he risques one."[9] Would Howe be able to capture Philadelphia unopposed? Would Howe's troops have been better utilized in New York with Burgoyne? The last correspondence Howe received from Burgoyne indicated that Burgoyne needed no help. The letter of Burgoyne to Howe dated camp before Ticonderoga on July 2, 1777, read: "The army is in the fullest powers of health, and spirit. I have a large body of Savages, and shall be joined by a larger (force) in a few days. Ticonderoga reduced, I shall leave behind me proper Engineers to put it in an impregnable state; and it will be garrisoned from Canada, where all the destined stores are safely arrived. My force therefore will be left complete for future operations."[10]

On August 28, 1777, the British army began its march from Head of the Elk at 4 a.m. Howe would either engage Washington or enter Philadelphia unmolested.

* * * * *

Washington was intent on stopping Howe before he reached Philadelphia. On August 25 he established his headquarters in Wilmington and made preparations for the upcoming campaign. One of the first concerns of Washington was the equipping of his own army and the removal of stores from the area of Head of the Elk so Howe wouldn't have use of the valuable materials.

General Nathanael Greene believed the stores were in jeopardy, especially the magazines located just a few miles from the British landing point, as indicated by a letter he wrote to Livi Hollingsworth, brother of Henry Hollingsworth, quartermaster for Maryland: "I arrived here last night and find this side of the country open to the enemy, and that they are daily driving off stock and removing publick stores from Elk Forge, 4 miles above the landing...unless a detachment of 1500 or 2000 men be speedily spent to support the removing the stores with wagons, they will fall into the hands of the enemy."[11]

Washington also ordered Brigadier General Caesar Rodney to cooperate with the militia from the Eastern Shore of Maryland in fighting against the British. On August 31, 1777, Washington wrote to Rodney from his Wilmington headquarters:

> ...taking every opportunity of harassing them, by alarming them frequently with light parties, beating up their Pickets, and intercepting as often as it can be done, whatever parties they may send out to procure Supplies of forage, horses, cattle, provisions and necessaries of every kind; which will equally serve to distress them and shelt(er) the Inhabitants from their Depredations, and ought therefore to be an object of your peculiar care. The more effectually to distress them in this respect, I would

have you to remove such grain, catt(le), horses, stock and other articles of subsistence, that lie so contiguous them, as to be in more immediate danger of falling into their hand(s) out of their reach, and to continue doing this as they continue the(ir) progress through the Country. You will also withdraw every kind of carriage which might serve to facilitate the Transportation of their Baggage and Stores to a distance from their Camp, than which you can do nothing that will be more injurious to them, as there is nothing they are more in need of.

One more precaution in this way I must recommend to you to use—which is, if there should be any Mills in their neighborhood, to take away the Runners and have them removed out of their reach. This will render the Mills useless to them and will be little or no detriment to the Inhabitants, more especially to the well affected, who it is probable will, for the most part, quit their homes where they appear, and to whom they can be restored at a proper time.

While you are attentive to annoying and distressing the enemy, you will not neglect any expedient necessary for your own Security—for this purpose, you will take posts the most advantageous and the least liable to surprise, you can find, and will station proper Guards at every pass by which you are accessible....As General Maxwell will want Persons well acquainted with the Country to remain with him, in the capacity of Guides, you will leave with him thirty or forty men fit for the business, out of the Battalions that are now advanced towards the Enemy. These should be select men, who have a thorough knowledge of the Country, intelligent and of known attachment and fidelity to the American Cause....We have no time to spare, and cannot be too soon prepar'd as we have reason every moment to expect the enemy will prosecute their march towards the object they have in view.[12]

Even though the letter to Rodney was issued on August 31 and Greene was worried about the stores being in danger,

Washington had written to Congress on August 27, "I am happy to inform you, that all the public stores, are removed except about seven thousand bushels of corn." The British, however, received significant supplies from the local citizens. A British officer reported in his journal on August 31 that the command of Knyphausen took "261 head horned cattle and 568 sheep and 100 horses."[13] Also, another British report said, "In the Elk River about 16 enemy boats were taken. The greater part of their cargoes, which consisted of tobacco, corn, coffee, sugar and flour was distributed among the army, but the flour and corn were delivered to the English commissariat."[14]

While protecting his supplies, Washington also wanted to protect the citizens and not alienate them. In that respect, Washington shared the same concern as Howe. Like Howe, Washington issued orders to his troops to properly treat their countrymen. And, Washington had as much trouble as Howe enforcing the edict. On September 4, 1777, from Wilmington, Washington wrote:

> Notwithstanding all the cautions, the earnest requests, and the positive orders of the Commander in Chief, to prevent our own army from plundering our own friends and fellow citizens, yet to his astonishment and grief, fresh complaints are made to him, that so wicked, infamous and cruel a practice is still continued, and that too in circumstances most distressing; where the wretched inhabitants, dreading the enemy's vengeance for their adherence to our cause, have left all, and fled to us for refuge. We complain of the cruelty and barbarity of our enemies; but does it equal ours? They sometimes spare the property of their friends: But some amongst us, beyond expression barbarous, rob even them! Why did we assemble in arms? Was it not, in one capital point, to protect the property of our countrymen? And shall we to our eternal reproach, be the first to pillage and destroy? Will no motives of humanity, of zeal, interest and of honor, restrain the violence of the soldiers, or induce officers to keep so strict a watch over the ill-disposed, as effectually to prevent the execution of

their evil designs, and the gratification of their savage inclinations? Or, it these powerful motives are too weak, will they pay no regard to their own safety? How many noble designs have miscarried, how many victories been lost, how many armies ruined, by an indulgence of soldiers in plundering?...For these reasons, the Commander in Chief requires, that these orders be distinctly read to all the troops; and that officers of every rank, take particular pains, to convince the men, of the baseness, and fatal tendency of the practices complained of, and that their own safety depends on a contrary conduct, and an exact observance of order and discipline; at the same time the Commander and Chief most solemnly assures all, that he will have no mercy on offenders against these orders; their lives shall pay the forfeit of their crimes. Pity, under such circumstances, would be the height of cruelty.[15]

One of the reasons for Washington's harshly worded pronouncement was rooted in an order issued the day before by the general. On September 3 Washington approved the sentences of men found guilty by a general court-martial that week. Besides disobeying orders to protect citizens, some soldiers committed other military crimes. Some of the findings include:

- Peter Linch a Matross in Capt. Gibbs Jones's company of artillery, charged with "Desertion," found guilty and sentenced to have the hair on the front part of his head shaved off without soap, and a quantity of tar and feathers fixed on the place as a substitute for hair, then to run the Gauntlet in the company to which he belongs, provided nevertheless, that the stripes which he shall receive while running the Gauntlet, shall not exceed one hundred; and then to be sent on board one of the Continental frigates to serve during the war.
- Daniel Fennel of Col. Proctor's regiment, charged with "Deserting from the said regiment," found guilty, and sentenced to receive one hundred lashes on his bare back, and to forfeit one month's pay for the use of the sick.

- Daniel Halley of the 11th Virginia Regiment charged with "Abetting the cause of a deserter from Col. Proctor's regiment of artillery, and with collaring Col. Proctor," found guilty, and sentenced to receive one hundred lashes on his bare back.
- James Martin of the 2nd Pennsylvania regiment charged with "Being drunk and asleep on his post while sentinel over prisoners," found guilty, and sentenced to receive one hundred lashes on his bare back, and to have the hair from the front part of his head shaved off without soap, and tar and feathers substituted in the room of the hair.
- Henry Hargood charged with "Desertion from the German regiment," found guilty, and sentenced to suffer death: But for the reasons mentioned by the court, they recommend him to the Commander in Chief's clemency and mercy. The Commander in Chief pardons the offender.
- Godrid Oxford of the 14th Virginia regiment charged with "Desertion, getting drunk and loosing his arms," found not guilty of getting drunk and losing his arms; and sentenced to receive one hundred lashes on his bare back, and to pay for his arms lost.[16]

For the most part, Washington's army was ready for a fight with Howe. Greene reported to his brother Jacob on August 31, "The army is in good health and high spirits but is not numerous as you very justly observe in your letter, yet I believe not inferior to Mr. Howes. The troops we have added by the militia will form a formidable force."[17] Captain Walter Stewart, in a letter to General Horatio Gates on September 2 concurred. He said, "Our army are in amazing high spirits and very healthy."[18]

Washington also strengthened his army by forming a division of Light Infantry to take the place of Morgan's Riflemen. His August 28, 1777, order read, "A corps of Light Infantry is to be formed; to consist of one Field Officer, two

Captains, six Subalterns, eight serjeants and 100 rank and file from each brigade." Washington wanted commanders of the seven brigades to pick only those who may be depended upon. Two days later Washington named Brigadier General William Maxwell of New Jersey, senior brigade commander, to take command of the light infantry corps.

The force, numbering less than 800 men, was designed to give Washington a weapon he hadn't possessed in previous engagements. The light infantry would be used to screen Washington's main army from the British, for scouting and for fighting. They carried the minimum amount of equipment needed to fulfill their duty, and thus were called the light infantry. Being selected for the light infantry was an honor and the command developed into an elite unit. Within two weeks of being formed, Maxwell's light infantry would play major roles in two engagements: a skirmish at Cooch's Bridge and the Battle of Brandywine.

During the last few days of August and the beginning of September a portion of Washington's forces flowed to the area where Howe landed. Washington, himself, took part in a scouting expedition on August 26 with Generals Greene, Lafayette, and Weedon and a small contingent of cavalry. They rode down the King's Highway to Newport and then on to Iron Hill, Delaware, close to the Maryland line. Washington and his staff learned little of use concerning the British army before beginning their return to Wilmington. Before completing the journey they were forced to stay the night with a farm family because of a heavy rainstorm. This is the same rain that hampered British movements and destroyed ammunition of both armies.

Lieutenant James McMichael of the Pennsylvania Line reported in his diary as marching at 3 a.m. on August 29, 1777, from the White Clay Creek and proceeding northeast for a few miles up the Lancaster Road before turning and marching to the heights of Newport on the Red Clay Creek where they made camp. "Our scouting party returned with 14 regulars, prisoners. They gave us to understand that their army was not advancing but that they intended shortly to attempt the conquest of Philadelphia. Our encampment here was exceedingly beautiful, and being chiefly surrounded by Whig inhabitants, very agreeable. (On September 2) an express arrived at 6 a.m. with news that the enemy was advancing. We struck tents and marched to an advantageous height at the intersection of the roads leading to Newport and Wilmington, and remained under arms to 3 p.m. when we learned that the enemy had advanced to the heights near Christiana Bridge and halted."[19] Greene reported to Congress on August 29 that between 30 and 40 prisoners and 12 deserters were captured but little intelligence was gained from them. The rebels found out the British troops were healthy but their horses suffered during the sea voyage.

Washington, ignoring advice from Greene to oppose Howe on the banks of the Christiana Creek, sent Maxwell's new corps of light infantry to meet and harass the British. "Maxwell positioned his light infantry around the wooden Cooch's Bridge, over Christiana Creek, extending his line to the nearby Iron Hill (elevation 325 feet). On September 2 he received notification from Washington to expect an enemy advance the next day. 'I beg you will be prepared to give them as much trouble as you possibly can,' entreated Washington. Maxwell should keep to the enemy's left flank, 'because in that case they cannot cut you off from our Main Body.'"[20]

* * * * *

The British army was slowly making its way to Cooch's Bridge. Captain John Montresor, chief engineer of the British army, reported that the severe rainstorm of August 27, 1777, delayed their marching orders and destroyed 16,000 cartridges. An order that day from Howe's headquarters said, "The March of the Troops this morning is countermanded on account of the badness of the Weather, and the Commander in Chief is pleased to order an extra day's Rum to be issued to the Army this forenoon." The British army at first encountered little resistance with only a few shots exchanged on their way to the town of Elk. Montresor reported finding "40 well built brick and stone houses" in the town. On August 29, Montresor said a "man came from Philadelphia, who had passed through the Rebel country who assured us that they are posted at Brandywine with a considerable body at White Clay Creek. The Welsh fusiliers fired a few shots at rebel cavalry and on August 31 a skirmish took place in the morning where a body of Americans fought the 23rd Foot. The rebels lost one killed, five wounded and two deserted."[21]

At daybreak on September 1, 1777, 200 British Rangers attacked the rebels, taking several officers prisoner and killing two and wounding one, according to Montresor's journal. The day turned hot and at night a gentle rain fell on the British army. Montresor also reported "two Rebel Light Horse deserted to us."[22] The next day another Light Horse and two other rebels deserted and Montresor reported that 500 of the British army were sick. Those ill soldiers would not be available for the first skirmish of the Philadelphia campaign, on September 3, 1777, at Cooch's Bridge in Delaware, that state's only Revolutionary War engagement. On the American side a future chief justice of the United States Supreme Court, John Marshall, took part in the skirmish. Marshall served as a captain in the 11th Virginia Regiment but was detached to Maxwell's light infantry and also would fight at Brandywine.

As Howe moved north to Pennsylvania, he split his troops into two divisions, one headed by Cornwallis and the other under Knyphausen. They marched toward Aiken's Tavern with Howe joining Cornwallis. Cornwallis arrived at Aiken's Tavern before Knyphausen and advanced toward Cooch's Bridge and Iron Hill. The vanguard of his forces, Hessian jaegers under the command of Lieutenant Colonel Ludwig Johann Adolph von Wurmb, at 9 a.m., were the first British troops that day to engage Maxwell's new light infantry. Maxwell stationed his men in the woods along the road to Cooch's Bridge. The Americans first surprised a dragoon unit under Captain

Johann Ewald. Ewald reported, "The Quartermaster General gave me six dragoons and ordered me to march at once to the left, where I should follow for five to six hundred paces a road which led to Iron Hill and Christiana Bridge. I took the dragoons with me to find the road that I had to take, and had not gone a hundred paces from the advanced guard when I received fire from a hedge, through which these six men were all either killed or wounded. My horse, which normally was well used to fire, reared so high several times that I expected it would throw me. I cried out, 'Foot jagers forward!' and advanced with them to the area from which the fire was coming. My horse followed the men, but I did not observe that the good animal, which had carried me the whole day, was wounded in the belly; it died in the evening. At this moment I ran into another enemy party, with which I became heavily engaged. Lieutenant Colonel von Wurmb, who came up with the entire Corps assisted by the light infantry, ordered the advanced guard to be supported."[23]

For two miles Maxwell's men fired from behind trees, retreated to other defensive locations, and fired again upon the British. Von Wurmb formed his men and returned fire. "The battalion of British light infantry brought their field-pieces into play, and, while Von Wurmb shifted a detachment into a patch of woods on the right of the road and made a spirited attack on Maxwell's left flank, Wurmb charged with the bayonet. The Americans withdrew up the road, taking cover again and renewing their fire. The enemy came on, the Americans stood fast and for a time held their position. But again they were forced to retreat, this time across the bridge."[24]

While von Wurmb was forcing Maxwell to retreat to the bridge, Howe sent light infantry troops of the Second Battalion under the command of Lieutenant Colonel Robert Abercromby to flank the Americans' right line. Abercromby became entangled in the woods and was stopped as he came upon "Purgatory Swamp," a section of land impossible to traverse. Abercromby doubled back to Cooch's Bridge in an attempt to aid in the attack on Maxwell, but arrived too late to help. Captain Carl August von Wreden and some Hessian grenadiers had better luck on the American left. After firing cannons von Wreden made a bayonet charge which broke Maxwell's defense, and the rebels, running low on ammunition, fled in great disorder. Purgatory Swamp saved Maxwell's new light infantry from a severe trashing.

Montresor described September 3, 1777, in his journal as, "Weather is fine but cool early. At daybreak the whole army under march except 2 Brigades with Major-Genl. Grant took the lower road to Christeen by the way of Aiken's Tavern, in order to avoid Iron Hill. At this Tavern we were to be joined by the troops under Lieutenant-General Knyphausen....About a mile beyond the Country is close—the woods within shot of the road, frequently in front and flank and in projecting points towards the Road, here the Rebels began to attack us about 9 o'clock with a Continued smart irregular fire for near two miles. The body of the Rebels consisted of 120 men from 6 brigades making 720 men of what they call their regulars, together with 1000 militia and Philadelphia Light Horse, but the 720 men were principally engaged were opposed by the Chasseurs and 1 Battalion of Light Infantry only the other Battalion of Light Infantry which was sent to surround the rebels through some mistake was led so far on our Right as to find an impassable swamp between them and the Army, which prevented this little spirited affair becoming so decisive. The rebels left about 20 dead among which was a Captain of Lord Sterling's Regt. We had 3 men killed and 20 wounded. The rebels' deserters since come in, say they lost 5 Captains. General Maxwell commanded this body of the enemy. From the Iron Hill the waters of the Chesapeake and Delaware are seen. At 2 the whole encamped. Head Quarters Aiken's Tavern. The Guards on Iron Hill, Dunop, the Hessian Grenadiers, together with the British, and all the Light Troops on the opposite side of the creek about 1 mile. Two or three shots exchanged in the night. Total amount of cattle amounts to 500 Head of Horned Cattle, 1000 sheep and 100 horses but not above forty of these Horses fit for Draught."[25]

Cooch's Bridge, where Maxwell was ordered by Washington to harass the British as much as possible, turned into a bloody skirmish. As with most Revolutionary War engagements, the exact number of casualties is impossible to determine and varying numbers have been reported. American losses were between 40 and 60 men with a majority of them killed. Captain Friedrich von Muenchhausen, aide de camp to Howe, wrote in his diary, "We buried 41 of the rebels, among them several officers, including a captain who was still alive when I rode by. He asked me to get him something to drink. Since I could not do it at the time, I hurried back to him, but I found him already dead. We do not know the number of rebel wounded because they carried them away. We have only taken four prisoners. They can run so fast that one can not catch them without taking a chance on being cut off."[26]

The British losses were less than the Americans'. Howe reported 3 dead and 21 wounded in a report to Germain from Germantown on October 10, 1777. A British camp follower told the Americans that Howe sent nine wagonloads of wounded back to Head of Elk. Depending on the size of the wagons and the number of wounded per wagon, the number of wounded reported by Howe appears to be close to the total his army received. Muenchhausen reported the English losses to be 3 officers and 9 rank and file wounded, 1 non-commissioned officer killed. He said the Hessians lost 14 wounded and 2 killed.

By 2 p.m. Cornwallis's division was encamped on the battleground while Knyphausen remained at Aiken's Tavern where Howe made his headquarters. Cornwallis stayed in the home of Thomas Cooch. On September 4, 1777, Howe thanked the Jaeger Corps for their work at Cooch's Bridge. He issued an order saying, "The courageous manner in which Lieutenant Colonel Wurmb, all the other officers, and the entire personnel of the Jaeger Corps, defeated yesterday the picked troops of the enemy army on the mountain near Cooch's Mill, deserve the highest praise and the fullest acknowledgment of the Commander in Chief, and has attracted the greatest admiration of the entire army."[27]

The march to Brandywine would be slow and take a week. Montresor described in the diary the next three days, "(September) 4th: Weather charming, morning now may be said to be cold in so much that fires are both agreeable and necessary. The great want of Horses prevents our moving this day. The People that come in say the Rebels lost yesterday 12 officers. (September) 5th: A man came in who slept in the rebel Camp at Chad's Ford on the Brandywine last night, where he left Major-Genl. Sullivan and 2000 men and 3 field pieces. Three Rebel Light Horse deserted to us—all Irishmen—some with the clothing of our 8th Reg. On—taken from us by their Privateers and each covered with a rifle shirt. (September) 6th: The whole army moved 2 hours before daylight—a remarkable borealis. March this day about 12 miles but 3 or 4 shots fired. A great deal of rebel cattle collected."[28]

Howe found few Americans willing to join his cause and one member of the 42nd Royal Highland Regiment, known as the Black Watch, reported that Howe changed from wanting to liberate the region to wanting to destroy Washington's army. For Washington, he was ready for a major engagement with Howe. Washington issued a General Order on September 5, 1777, saying should the British push their design against Philadelphia the enemy would put the outcome of the campaign on a single battle, and if they are defeated they are "utterly undone,...one bold stroke will free the land from rapine, devastations and burnings and female innocence from brutal lust and violence.... If we behave like men this third campaign will be our last."[29]

Birmingham Meeting House

The Birmingham Meeting House was used as a hospital by both the British and American armies during the Battle of Brandywine. Heavy fighting took place around the building during the afternoon action.

Chester County Historical Society, West Chester, Pennsylvania

Four

Quaker Country

The overwhelming show of support for the British monarchy and aid for his army that General William Howe had counted upon from the local citizens didn't materialize when his troops landed at Head of the Elk and later moved into Pennsylvania. Many of the citizens were indifferent to the two armies as the bodies of soldiers warily kept track of each other's movements in early September 1777 during their march to Brandywine. Some loyalists, however, did lend a hand to Howe, and the British general had far better intelligence concerning the country's terrain because of their efforts.

One such loyalist was Curtis Lewis. Lewis lived in Chester County with his wife, Hannah, and "from the commencement of the late ruinous war in America (Lewis) conducted himself as a good subject to His Majesty's government."[1] He joined the British army as soon as it arrived at Head of the Elk and then acted as a guide during the Battle of Brandywine. He died in New York City in 1781 while still serving the British army. John Watson, another loyalist from New Castle, Delaware, settled in America after departing Scotland in 1767. He was a physician, surgeon, and apothecary. An American regiment forced Watson, under the threat of jail, to join its unit. Watson eventually escaped from the rebels and joined Howe's forces on August 24, 1777. He served with the British army during the rest of the war and served with Captain Patrick Ferguson's riflemen during the Battle of Brandywine.[2]

Another Chester County resident, Jacob James, "ever firmly attached to his majesty's government, did seize the first opportunity of manifesting his loyalty by joining the Royal Army at the Battle of Brandywine and did there offer himself to Sir William Howe, to be employed in any capacity that the Commander-in-Chief should please to suggest."[3] Howe accepted the offer of his services and James was constantly employed as a guide to the British army in procuring good intelligence as a result of his knowledge of the country. Jacob Buffington, a carpenter from West Bradford in Chester County, waited until after the Battle of Brandywine when the British occupied Philadelphia to join Howe's troops. Buffington "zealously opposed the measures of the American Congress" and had his property confiscated because of his support of the British army.[4] Likewise, William S. Moore, who lived at Moore Hall in Chester County and was a member of a prominent local family, "always had the greatest zeal for the Royal cause...and offered his services to Howe....Rebel leaders threatened to take his life if captured."[5]

The most important Loyalist to come to Howe's aid was Joseph Galloway. Galloway was a leading Philadelphia lawyer, a politician, an officer of the American Philosophical Society, and a friend of Benjamin Franklin. In 1774 Galloway suggested to the First Continental Congress the problem of home rule be solved by giving American colonies status akin to a dominion. The plan at first drew support but failed by a single vote. He declined to be a delegate to the Second Continental Congress. Galloway, fearing a mob, left his Philadelphia home as Franklin tried and failed to change Galloway's allegiance. In December 1775 Galloway was with Howe during the British army's advance through New Jersey.[6] In September 1777 Galloway was with Howe once again, this time at Brandywine. "Fortunately for Howe, he had, some time before, made an important accession to his staff from the standpoint of gaining intelligence. Joseph Galloway, a dyed-in-the-wool Tory from Philadelphia, who was widely familiar with the Brandywine area, had arrived in Chester

County with the British general. Galloway's intimate information had much to do with the shape of Howe's tactics in the
imminent conflict. A Quaker by the name of Parker, whom
Howe had commandeered as a guide, likewise gave the British general a close familiarity with the country on the British
front."[7]

As a member of the Society of Friends, such members are
called Quakers, Parker belonged to a religious group that exerted a great amount of influence in Chester County, Pennsylvania as a whole and Delaware. The founder of the Commonwealth
of Pennsylvania, William Penn, became a Quaker in his 20s.
George Fox founded The Society of Friends (Quakers) in England in the 17th century. The Society of Friends is a pacifist
Protestant sect with roots in the period of the English revolution. They professed to be non-violent even though many
Quakers joined Washington's army. One of the rebel officers
who acted valiantly at the Battle of Brandywine was General
Nathanael Greene, a Quaker. Greene, who Washington in 1776
said was the best officer to succeed him as commander in chief[8]
was an unlikely war hero.

Rhode Islander Greene had no military experience when
he joined George Washington's army in the summer of 1775 in
Cambridge, Massachusetts. As a Quaker Greene opposed the
war for religious reasons, but when England's colonial poli-
cies became unbearable he discarded his pacifism, joined a
military association, and threw himself wholeheartedly into
the struggle for liberty and independence.[9] He first ran afoul
of the Quakers when he attended a military parade and was
"put from under the care of the Quaker meeting on September
30, 1773."[10] The dilemma Greene faced was present in every
Quaker household as the Revolutionary War spread. At what
point, if ever, should a Quaker abandon the teachings of his
faith and take part in the war? Some, like Greene, joined the
rebel army and others offered aid, such as food and material,
to the troops.

As for the Quaker leaders, there was no dilemma. Their
Peace Testimony made it clear that Quakers were not to aid

either side and they were not to follow any of the directives of the new rebel government sitting in Philadelphia. The Quakers felt "the setting up and putting down kings and governments is God's peculiar prerogative, for causes best known to himself, and that it is not our business to have any hand or contrivance therein."[11] In fact, the Philadelphia Yearly Meeting on September 1, 1777 — just 10 days before the Battle of the Brandywine — issued a directive to meetings within its sphere of influence which began: "In this time of deep probation and affliction the Philadelphia Yearly Meeting finds it necessary to give our sense and judgment to the monthly meetings so that our conduct is uniformly consistent with the Spirit of our Religious Principles. The fate of our Religious Society in these provinces hath now been very mightily considered and we pray for divine Wisdom in our solemn deliberations of these important subjects."[12]

The directive went on to note the "sorrowful account" of the "deviation of many in our Society from our Ancient Testimony Against War." Quakers were warned against joining the "Multitude in warlike exercise nor instruct themselves in the Art of War. Friends are advised to avoid all acts, including being spectators at training grounds, which might in any way compromise the Principles upon which this Society was founded."[13] Society of Friends leaders also objected to the Constitutional Convention's adoption of an ordinance requiring a payment of 20 shillings per month for those conscientiously opposed to bearing arms in lieu of military service. They forbid their followers, children, servants, or apprentices to pay the tax. They also advised that all Quakers should withdraw from being active in "Civil Government due to its founding in the Spirit of War and Fightings."[14]

Disobeying the directive brought Quakers the dire punishment of disownment, being dismissed from the Society. Members were expected to "earnestly labour on the Strength of God's love for the reclaiming of those who have thus deviated from our ancient Testimonies. A united effort must be maintained to strengthen each other in the way of truth and righteousness."[15] The directive concluded with the following plea for peace: "The great effusion of human blood and the loss of the lives of men since the commencement of the present tumults induce us to pray for the restoration of peace to our colonies. Our Meeting now being near closing, we again salute you in a degree of the Love of the Gospel and are, Your affectionate Friends and Brethren."[16]

Chester County's population at the time of the Battle of Brandywine was approximately 30,000 — the two armies almost doubled the population — with many being Society of Friends members. The local inhabitants all suffered the same injustices, such as taxation without representation and the imposition of tariffs, inflicted by England as other citizens of the colonies. Many supporters of the new American government believed the Quakers were Tories because of their pacifist beliefs. Others believed differently: "if the preferences of those Friends who violated the discipline of the Society by taking up arms is any indication of the prevailing sentiment we might conclude that at least ninety percent of Friends secretly favored independence."[17] Many Quakers were disowned, that is forced from the church, for such transgressions as joining the military, both British and American; driving a team to collect forage for the armies; paying taxes to support the war; working as a smith for the armies; holding a slave; driving a team for the armies; paying for substitutes; becoming a tax collector; keeping a tavern; and marrying outside the faith.[18]

The records of the various Chester County Monthly Meetings are replete with names of Quakers disowned by their faith for violating their directives involving war and other matters. As an example, Joshua Buffington was complained of by the Bradford Meeting for entering into military exercise on June 14, 1776. "He that declined the practice but offers no satisfaction. Disowned July 12, 1776."[19] James Sheward was complained of by the Bradford Monthly Meeting for driving a team to collect forage for the army and was disowned on September 18, 1778.[20] And, William Kinzer was disowned for two violations on March 3, 1779, for taking part in military exercise and for holding a slave.[21] In all, the monthly meeting records detail more than two hundred cases of Chester County Quaker men and women who were charged with violations of the Society of Friends directives. Some acknowledged their transgressions and were allowed to remain a Quaker. Among the women was Ann Hayes who was "complained of on March 17, 1790, for sending a Creture to exchange for one the collector had taken for a substitute fine for her husband." She admitted helping her husband escape military service and stayed a member of the Friends.[22] Isaac Rees was disowned for accepting and acting as Constable on November 10, 1780.[23]

Soldier and Quaker James Pyle ran into problems with the Kennett Monthly Meeting on October 17, 1776. They complained that Pyle was married by a priest to a young woman without her parents' consent. Pyle also enlisted as a soldier and took it upon himself to entice others to join the army. He was disowned by the Society of Friends on December 12, 1776.[24] Isaac Taylor of the Kennett Meeting managed to stay within the faith despite "attending a disorderly marriage." The definition of a disorderly marriage was not disclosed. Samuel Greave was not so lucky. He was disowned on August 12, 1779, for encouraging horse racing and having married outside of the meeting.[25] Encouraging discord within the Society of Friends was also not tolerated as Isaac Gray of the New Garden Meeting discovered. He was disowned on December 10, 1778, for "having a pamphlet published without the leave and contrary to the advice of Friends, the tendency of which Pamphlet is to spread discord and disunity in the Society."[26]

Richard Buffington was complained of by the Bradford Meeting for having "removed some time ago without taking a certificate reported to have gone to Nova Scotia." (While it does not appear that he took up arms he evidently sympathized with the Mother Country. He returned from Nova Scotia prior to February 17, 1786, and later took the "test" of loyalty offered by the new American government as shown by the following document): "I do certify that Richard Buffington of West Bradford, Chester County, hath voluntarily taken and subscribed the affirmation of Allegiance and Fidelity, as directed by an Act of General Assembly of Pennsylvania, passed the Fourth day of March, Anno Domini 1786. Witness my Hand and Seal, the Tenth day of October Anno Domini, 1786. THOS. CHEYNEY (Seal)."[27] The Thomas Cheyney who witnessed Buffington's affidavit was the same Squire Cheyney who rode to General Washington with the news that the British army had flanked him during the Battle of Brandywine.

George Gilpin was disowned by the Concord Monthly Meeting on October 4, 1775, for taking up arms in the Rebel army. He later served as colonel of the Fairfax militia in Virginia.[28] Another Gilpin, Gideon, was disowned by the Concord Monthly Meeting on January 6, 1779, for setting up a tavern. The home of Gideon and Sarah Gilpin, which later became the tavern, was the headquarters of General Marquis de Lafayette during the Battle of Brandywine. When Lafayette and his son, George Washington Lafayette, visited Chadds Ford in July 1825 they stopped at the house and visited Gideon Gilpin, who was on his deathbed.[29] Some dispute that Lafayette actually slept in Gilpin's home during the battle. Also, George Washington's headquarters at Brandywine was also owned by a Quaker, Benjamin Ring. And, one of the most important eyewitness accounts of the Battle of the Brandywine came from a Quaker, Joseph Townsend.

To illustrate the pacifists' beliefs of the Quakers, one local tale has a Quaker woman confronting General Knyphausen as he led his troops to meet Washington at Chadds Ford. She urged Knyphausen not to proceed and to stop the killing. The story has her saying, "Oh, my dear man, do not go down there, for George Washington is on the other side of the stream, and he has all this world with him." Knyphausen is said to have replied, "Never mind, madam, I have all the other world with me."

While each side received some support from the Quakers, for the most part they did stay neutral. Both armies were disappointed with the Quaker stronghold of Pennsylvania, the Americans for the minimum numbers of militia, the British for the lack of widespread Tory enthusiasm.[30] Washington had his own way of getting back at the Quakers for their lack of support. In the days before the Battle of Brandywine, Washington told his troops "if there should be any mills in the neighborhood of the enemy, and which might be liable to fall into their hands, the runners (millstones) should be removed and secured," making the mills useless. This was a frequent American practice wherever the British went.[31] After the British threat passed, the millstones would be replaced, except those owned by Quakers.[32] The ability of Quakers to survive and prosper was greatly diminished by the withholding of the millstones. Howe protested Washington's orders concerning the millstones. A month after the battle while Howe was gaining control of Philadelphia, he said the rendering useless of the grist mills inflicted untold hardship upon the civilian population of the city, whose only source of flour lay outside the urban limits.[33] Once flour made its way into Philadelphia, it also made its way to the tables of the British army.

Many of Washington's officers and enlisted men were not fond of the Quakers, as evidenced in a letter from Valley Forge on March 17, 1778, from Alexander Scammell of Massachusetts. Scammell, who succeeded fellow Bay Stater Timothy Pickering as Washington's adjutant general, wrote the letter to Pickering. "Dear Sir, I have now sit down to fulfill my promise of writing a long Letter, if these milk & water, white livered, unsancify'd Quakers don't interrupt me in Behalf of their Friend in ye provost. I am apprehensive that I shall imbibe an inveterate Hatred against the whole sect, or rather against those who make a Cloak of that profession to perpetrate the blackest Villanies."[34] Scammell was killed in 1781 at Yorktown. Pickering became a United States senator in 1803 and died in 1829.

Without substantial support from the populace of Pennsylvania, and especially Chester County Quakers, both sides prepared to fight the Battle of Brandywine.

*   *   *   *   *

After the British forced the retreat of Maxwell's light infantry at the engagement of Cooch's Bridge, Washington had to find a place to stop the British advance to Philadelphia. He also needed to have his troops properly conditioned, including having sufficient food and medical supplies available for them. Provisioning his army was proving to be a problem. Washington issued an order on September 4 at Wilmington, which said in part, "The Army is to be furnished with soft bread or flour which the commissarys are enjoined to do with more punctuality than they have done....The Commander in Chief can no longer excuse the neglects in that department....Much Injury having been done to the soldiers and some lives lost by their being taken by their officers from the Hospitals too soon without the concurrence of the superintending physician, that practice is absolutely forbid."[35]

Washington ordered Maxwell and the militia to keep an eye on the British, and before long he was receiving reports of Howe's army moving north. "The enemy," wrote General John Armstrong to President of the Pennsylvania Executive Council Thomas Wharton, Jr., on September 5, 1777, from Wilmington, "as far as we yet learn, appear to be spread over some considerable space of country, but in a detached way...to Nottingham (in southern Chester County)."[36] Armstrong went on to say that at the skirmish of Cooch's Bridge the losses on each side appeared to be nearly equal.

Howe also sent out scouts to find information on the movements of the rebel army. On September 5, 1777, the 1st Battalion of the British light infantry conducted a scouting expedition and came away with misleading information. Local residents told the British that the rebels were either at Brandywine or at Newark, Delaware. The rest of the British army stationed at Head of the Elk was ordered to join the main force. An advance by the British army on September 8 led them to Brigadier General George Weedon's brigade. At 3 a.m. the general alarm was given and the tents of the American army were struck. Six hours later three alarm guns were fired, bringing the Americans into line of battle on the eastern side of the Red Clay Creek to await the British attack. None came as Howe moved his army from Iron Hill to Newark and on to a road leading to Gap and Lancaster in Pennsylvania. Even though Howe had stolen a march, that was moved without being detected, on the rebels and could have launched a surprise attack on them, he continued on his way to New Garden in Chester County. Failing to turn on the Americans "was another of Howe's inexplicable errors."[37]

Washington certainly was aware that Howe was about to change positions. On September 7 from Wilmington, Weedon recorded, "The General has received a confirmation of the intelligence mentioned in the after orders of last night that the enemy have disencumbered themselves of all their baggage, even to their tents....This indicates a speedy and rapid movement....All baggage which can be spared, both of officers and men be immediately packed and up and sent off this day to the other side of Brandywine....The whole army is to draw two days cooked provisions....The tents of the whole army to be struck and packed in the wagons tomorrow morning an hour before day and the horses tacked....No more sick to be sent to Concord but to Birmingham."[38] The American army had taken over the Birmingham Meeting House and planned to use it as a hospital. On the afternoon of September 11, 1777, that Quaker meeting house would also be the site of one of the fiercest segments of the battle. On September 9, Weedon reported, "Intelligence having been received that the enemy instead of advancing towards Newport have turned another way and appear to have a design of marching northward.... Such of the troops as have not been served with rum to day are as soon as possible with one Gill per man."[39]

In the early morning hours of September 9 Washington began moving his troops on the Kennett Road that led from Wilmington to Chester County. Washington's army forded the Brandywine at Pyle's Ford below Chadds Ford. Washington proceeded north and made camp in the area where he would fight the Battle of Brandywine. While Washington was marching that morning, Howe had not put his troops on the road. At 2 p.m. General Knyphausen put his force in motion, but General Grant and Lord Cornwallis did not get under way until almost sunset. The coming darkness masked Howe's movements from rebel scouts. The dark also caused some confusion as British officers reported trouble finding the proper roads. Grant only made it to the Hockessin Meeting House, where he encamped for the night. Grant's troops would join Howe at Kennett Square, six miles from Washington's army at the Brandywine, during the day of September 10.

From Chadds Ford on September 10, the Quaker general, Nathanael Greene, took time to write to his wife, Catherine Littlefield Greene. Catherine Greene was a favorite of Washington and during one party Washington is said to have "danced with her all of three hours without stopping."[40] In his letter to his wife on the eve of the battle, Greene wrote:

> The enemy marched out day before yesterday. They took post in a position to turn our right flank, the Christiana being on our left. The General (Washington) thought our situation too dangerous to risque a battle as the enemy refused to fight us in front. The General ordered the army to file off to the right and take post at this place. A general action must take place in a few days. The army (is) in high spirits and wish for action....
>
> Here are some of the most distressing scenes imaginable. The inhabitants generally desert their houses, furniture moving, cattle driving and women and children traveling off on foot. The country all resounds with the cries of the people. The enemy plunder most amazingly. The militia of this country (is) not like the Jersey militia, fighting is a new thing with these, and many seems to have a poor stomach for the business.
>
> I am exceedingly fatigued. I was on Horse back for upwards of thirty hours and never closed my eyes for near forty. Last night I was in hopes of a good nights rest, but a dusty bed gave me...very little sleep the whole night.

Greene and the soldiers on both sides of the Brandywine would need their sleep that night. The final troops were gathering. By the time the battle would begin, Washington would have between 11,000 and 12,000 troops fit to fight out of the estimated 16,000 under his command in the area. Howe's strength would be about equal to Washington's command. Howe decided not to concentrate his force into one grand army. In a bold move he would divide his army into two sections with Knyphausen commanding about 5,000 soldiers while Cornwallis would have 7,500 under his direction during the crucial Battle of Brandywine.

Washington's Headquarters

General George Washington and his staff made plans for the Battle of Brandywine in his headquarters. The home belonged to Quaker Benjamin Ring.

Chester County Historical Society, West Chester, Pennsylvania

Five

A Peaceful Valley

During the days following the skirmish of Cooch's Bridge, British General William Howe directed the slow, but steady movement of his army away from the banks of the Chesapeake toward Philadelphia. Between Howe and the rebel capital city were positioned General George Washington's army and a body of water known as the Brandywine. Washington was well aware he needed to immediately engage and defeat Howe's army or risk the loss of Philadelphia. As John Marshall, future United States Supreme Court Justice and a captain in a Virginia unit of the American army, said, "It is impossible to protect Philadelphia without a victory."[1]

As the British army continued its march, officers took every opportunity they could to replenish the horses lost on the sea voyage. On the day following the action at Cooch's Bridge, Captain Friedrich von Muenchhausen, aide de camp to Howe, wrote in his diary that the 120 horses so far obtained in Maryland didn't make up for the 400 lost at sea. "I was more lucky than most officers since I did not lose a single horse at sea, but two of mine have died since we landed." He also reported that night "two of our patrols fired on each other by mistake; one dragoon was wounded, and two horses were lost. The rebel patrols, which usually consist of 10 to 15 dragoons and 20 to 30 infantrymen, now appear more often, and they fire at our posts occasionally....They were on patrol in search of information on enemy positions, as well as to round up horses. They returned without horses and without seeing the enemy."[2]

Rebel dragoons, some willingly, helped the British replenish their horse supply. The American dragoons were on patrol for days at a time in small groups. Some were captured and their horses taken and others offered to sell their horses to the British. "Many dragoons of the rebels have deserted. Undoubtedly the amount of money they get from us for their mounts is the reason." Another British officer reported he "bought three horses, and rather cheaply for local conditions, since I paid no more than 113 guineas for them."[3]

During the afternoon of September 9 General Knyphausen began his march toward the small farming village of Kennett Square by way of New Garden. With him were the Third Division of the British army and two additional British brigades. The other British divisions under Lord Charles Cornwallis and General Grant marched later in the day. That afternoon Howe received information that Washington had withdrawn from Newport and Wilmington in Delaware and had taken up a position along the Brandywine at Chadds Ford. The following day at 6 a.m. Cornwallis made his final push toward Kennett Square, six miles away, and arrived around noon under a hot midday sun. Knyphausen, who had arrived at 11 p.m. the previous night, had taken position on strong defensive ground on the east end of the village, and the army went about the business of gathering cattle and horses while the inhabitants of Kennett Square stayed in their homes. "On Wednesday, the tenth, Royal forces were collected around the Quaker meeting house at Kennett Square, a well-chosen rendezvous, distant enough from the enemy to baffle observation and near enough for early and decisive action."[4]

* * * * *

The invasion of Pennsylvania had commenced and the citizens and leaders of the Commonwealth were ready for Washington's army to take a heroic stand, defeat their hated foe, defend their freedom and stop the atrocities that the

British were supposed to have inflicted on other Americans. In fact, they insisted that Washington engage Howe. On September 10 the Supreme Executive Council of the Commonwealth of Pennsylvania issued the following "Proclamation concerning movement of British army":

> The time is at length come in which the fate of ourselves our Wives, children & Posterity must be speedily determined; Gen'l Howe, at the head of a British Army, the only hope, the last resource of our Enemies' has invaded this State, dismissing his ships & disencumbering himself of his heavy Artillery & baggage, he appears to have risked all upon the event of a movement which must either deliver up to plunder & devastation, this Capital of Pennsylvania & of America, or forever blast the cruel designs of our implacable foes. Blessed be God, Providence seems to have left it to ourselves to determine, whether we shall triumph in victory & rest in freedom and peace, or by tamely submitting or weakly resisting, deliver ourselves up a prey to an enemy, than whom none more cruel & perfidious was ever suffered to vex & destroy any people. View then on the other hand, the freedom & independence, the glory & the happiness of our rising States, which are set before us at the reward of our courage. Seriously consider on the other hand, the wanton ravages, the Rapes, the Butcheries, which have been perpetrated by these men in the State of New Jersey, & on the frontiers of New York; above all consider the mournful prospect of seeing Americans like the wretched inhabitants of India, stripped of their freedom, robbed of their property, degraded beneath the brutes & left to starve amid plenty, at the will of their lordly Masters, and let us determine once for all, that we will Die or be Free.
>
> The foe are manifestly aiming either by force to conquer, or by Stratagem & Stolen marches to elude the vigilance of our brave Commander; Declining a battle with our Countrymen, they have attempted to steal upon us by surprise. They have been hitherto defeated,

but numbers are absolutely necessary to watch them on every quarter at once.

The neighboring States are hurrying forward their Militia & we hope by rising as one Man & besetting the foe at a distance from his Fleet, we shall speedily enclose him like a Lion in the toils.

The Council therefore most humbly beseech and entreat all Persons whatsoever, to exhort themselves without delay, to seize this present opportunity of crushing the foe now in the bowels of our Country, by marching forth instantly under their respective officers, to the assistance of our great General, that he may be enabled to environ & demolish the only British army that remains formidable in America, or in the World. Animated with the hope that Heaven, as before is has done in all times of difficulty & danger, will again crown our righteous efforts with success, we look forward to the prospect of seeing our insulting foe cut off from all means of escape & by the goodness of the Almighty, the Lord of Hosts & God of Battles, wholly delivered into our hands.

Attest, Tho's Wharton, jun'r, Presid't
Timothy Matlack, Secretary.
God Save The People.[5]

* * * * *

Lieutenant James McMichael of the Pennsylvania Line was one of the Americans on the march to Brandywine. Not all of McMichael's comrades were willingly marching to meet Howe. On September 8, McMichael reported in his diary that one of the officers of his unit deserted his post while on picket duty and was immediately arrested. The next day, at 4 a.m., McMichael and the rest of his unit received marching orders and proceeded in an east-northeasterly direction on the road from Wilmington to Lancaster and through Kennett Township in Chester County and crossed the Brandywine. He reported camping in the Township of Birmingham and "being extremely fatigued for want of rest and severe marching."[6]

Washington and his army departed Delaware and began to make arrangements to defend Philadelphia from behind the banks of the Brandywine. Washington arrived at Chadds Ford — at least one member of the army believed the place was named shads Ford — during the afternoon of September 9 and began selecting the ground to position his army. He selected the land just east of the Brandywine and took over the home of Quaker Benjamin Ring for his headquarters. A neighboring home, owned by Quaker Gideon Gilpin, was to become the base for Lafayette. While Ring and Gilpin didn't protest the use of their homes for the American army, neither one openly offered his home. They both escaped censure from their fellow Quakers for aiding the American army. One of Washington's first orders was to scout the adjoining area and post sentries to ensure the security of the camp. General Nathanael Greene became senior officer of the day and Brigadier General Peter Muhlenberg became his assistant for the next 24 hours, the crucial period where Washington's army had time to scout out the land picked for the coming battle and to make sure Howe would not have an opportunity to spring a surprise on the American army. They would have 1,500 men, taken from all divisions of the army, for the guard and picket duties.

During the late afternoon hours of September 9 Washington assembled a meeting of his senior staff members. His division commanders included Greene, John Sullivan, William Alexander (known as Lord Stirling), Adam Stephen, John Armstrong, Anthony Wayne, and Henry Knox. Lafayette, Colonel Thomas Pickering, and Lieutenant Colonel Robert Hanson Harrison, Washington's military secretary, were at the Chadds Ford camp along with a number of other important officers, including Lieutenant Colonel Alexander Hamilton and Casimir Pulaski. A report of that crucial meeting has not survived and the list of the officers attending isn't known, but since the rooms in the Ring house, Washington's headquarters, weren't large, the attendance would have been limited.

The most important persons attending the meeting were not Washington's officers that afternoon, but several local residents. They were trusted by the rebel army leaders to give advice on the terrain and possible fording places for the British army. Washington and his officers all knew the importance of stopping Howe from flanking their army—the memory of Long Island was burned into their minds. Sullivan, who would have the responsibility of defending the right flank of Washington's army, especially was concerned about the possibility of Howe repeating the tactics he used at Long Island a year earlier and outflanking the Americans. One of the local patriots, whose identity has not been recorded, gave Washington information concerning the fords. He said that north of Buffington's Ford, which was located below the forks of the Brandywine, "there were none within twelve miles to cross at which the enemy must make a long Circuit through a very bad road."[7] Heavy rain had swollen the Brandywine to the height of a man's chest at various places and made a mess of the dirt roads. Any attempt at a flanking movement by the British would be hindered by the conditions of the road and river.

Sullivan, if the local residents were correct in their assumption, could protect the crossings north to Buffington's Ford and not worry about the Brandywine above that point. If the local man mentioned Jeffries Ford, the location Howe and Cornwallis used on September 11 to ford the Brandywine and outflank Washington (above Buffington's Ford but well within the 12-mile distance mentioned), none of the officers attending the meeting mentioned it in any post-battle report. Washington, Sullivan, and the rest of the staff would have a whole day preceding the battle to verify the information. They didn't do so. Historian and author Douglas Southall Freeman, in his study of Washington, criticizes the planning for Brandywine and comments, "Besides the usual factor of unskilled leadership and ill discipline, there was on the part of the Americans a most discreditable ignorance of the ground. Little or no reconnaissance was undertaken on the 10th of September.

Neither Washington nor any of his staff or division commanders or Colonels of cavalry appears to have known the correct names and locations of the fords." This failure to obtain valuable information before the battle on the terrain is even more perplexing since Washington had two battalions of local Chester County militia and men of at least two Pennsylvania Line regiments with knowledge of the area. Also, a number of officers, including Wayne and Persifor Frazer, were from Chester County.

Washington's battle plans might have been deficient, but he made it plain to his officers during that meeting that he was determined to fight Howe along the banks of the Brandywine. Later in the evening of September 9, members of the American dragoons were interviewed about their patrols of the day and ordered to continue their reconnaissance of the area. The information was given to Lieutenant Colonel Tench Tilghman, Washington's aide, to review. From these reports Washington learned that Howe was on the march toward his army and had spent the night at Hockessin. With reports that Knyphausen was already in Kennett Square, Washington issued orders to prepare his army for the coming fight. One order read, "No baggage is to be kept upon this ground that can possibly be dispensed with; and what cannot is to be loaded an hour before day and in readiness to remove....The men are to be provided with cooked provisions, for tomorrow at least; for two days would be still better, if they can get such kinds that will keep. The light horse, except those on duty, may lay quartered a little to the rear of Head Quarters. A total stop is to be put to all loose, disorderly firing in camp, as otherwise it will be impossible to distinguish guns fired for an alarm."

Washington's order was timely as he was informed of Cornwallis' arrival at Kennett Square and at noon the Americans' alarm guns summoned the rebel army to positions along the Brandywine to await the expected advance of the British. Captain William Beatty of the Maryland Line was one of those soldiers summoned by the alarm. "The whole army got under arms. However, the enemy did not approach. The army extended its right higher up the Brandywine at the same time a battery was began by the park of artillery opposite shads Ford, our division being on the right of the army, we extended to large stone mill about a mile above the ford in the position we lay all night," Beatty reported in his journal.

Acting upon the information from the local residents, Washington positioned his army to defend the eight fords on the Brandywine that he believed the British could use to attack his army. The most unlikely place for a British assault was to the south at Gibson's Ford. The Pennsylvania militia was perceived to be the weakest component of Washington's army and they were positioned at that ford. Armstrong had almost 2,000 troops and some artillery. He would watch not only Gibson's Ford, but also Pyle's Ford and Corner Ford, the southern most fords of the Brandywine in the area of Chadds Ford.

The fords at Chadds Ford and Chads Ferry were the points where Washington expected and wanted Howe to attack. The divisions of Greene, about 1,800 men, and Wayne, approximately 1,600 soldiers, were positioned to defend these points on the elevation south of Harvey Run. Wayne's men were slightly to the north and east of Greene near the battery of Colonel Thomas Proctor's artillery. Proctor's cannons commanded the fords and were strategically placed to contest any British crossing. They would become the focal point of a charge by Knyphausen's units during the afternoon of September 11. Stephen's division was the reserve force available to Greene and Wayne, and that unit was positioned to the east nearer to Washington's headquarters at the Ring House. Brigadier General Francis Nash had his 1,500-member North Carolina brigade positioned to also aid Greene and Wayne.

The right flank of Washington's army was entrusted to Sullivan and he placed his main force at Brinton's Ford. Behind Sullivan's men were those of Stirling, who were ready to aid Sullivan where needed. General Stephen's division was in a position to move to the support of either Greene and Wayne or Sullivan. Sullivan and Washington were concerned about three lesser fords north of Brinton's Ford and sent 80 men of Colonel Hall's Delaware Regiment to Jones's Ford. Colonel Moses Hazen, a former British army officer in the 44th Foot Regiment, was stationed near Wistar's Ford, near Plum Run with about 200 men, and a second unit of 200 men were at Buffington's Ford, below the forks of the Brandywine. Hazen commanded the 2nd Canadian Regiment, known both as "Congress's Own" and "Hazen's Own." The regiment was recruited near Albany, New York, and was composed mostly of Canadians. Responsibility for patrolling the area north of Buffington's Ford on both sides of the Brandywine was assigned to the light horse under the command of Colonel Theodorick Bland, who reported directly to Washington's headquarters. Even though Sullivan later would insist he was worried about the British flanking his position, he undertook no solid exploration of the land north of his position.

Washington did post elements of the 3rd Continental Dragoons on the west bank of the Brandywine, along with Maxwell's light infantry. Some of the dragoons explored the regions north of Sullivan. Included in Maxwell's unit were 200 men of local Chester County militia under Colonel Patterson Bell. Many of the soldiers had prior experience fighting with Bell in New York at Long Island. Maxwell's force would be the first American unit to contest the British at the Battle of Brandywine during the morning of September 11. After receiving reports that the enemy had not posted troops between Welch's Tavern, just east of Kennett Square, and Chadds Ford, Maxwell deployed his force and waited for the dawn and the expected assault by the British.

Back at the Ring House Washington wrote a note to General Israel Putnam. It said, "By Light Horsemen just come in, they are advancing upon us. We are preparing to receive them and should they come on, I trust, under the smiles of Providence and thro' our own conduct, that we shall give them a repulse or at the most, that they will have to enjoy a painful and dear bought victory."[8]

* * * * *

Flying at Washington's headquarters were several flags, including the new American flag authorized by the Continental Congress on June 14, 1777. The resolution by Congress said: "That the flag of the thirteen United States be thirteen stripes alternate red and white; that the union be thirteen stars, white in a blue field, representing a new constellation." The flag, commonly known as the Betsy Ross flag, was first flown on August 23, 1777, by Washington's army as it departed camp at Neshaminy and headed toward Philadelphia. A few hours after Washington wrote Putnam, the flag would come under fire at Brandywine for the first time. The design of the American flag and the place where it first came under fire has sparked controversy for more than two centuries. Elizabeth Griscom Ross and Francis Hopkinson, New Jersey Congressman and signer of the Declaration of Independence, both have been given credit for the flag's design.

One account has the flag coming under fire first at the Battle of Bennington on August 16, 1777, but there is no historical reference to a flag of stars and stripes being carried at Bennington, especially not one that was red, white and blue. A green, blue and white flag with stars, known as the Green Mountain Boys flag, is said to have flown at Bennington. Another claim has the Stars and Stripes being flown during the siege of Fort Stanwix in New York during August 1777. Likewise, no conclusive proof exists that the flag was flown at Fort Stanwix, and one diary says the flag at Fort Stanwix had blue stripes.

The most serious claim that the new American Stars and Stripes flag was under fire before Brandywine comes from Cooch's Bridge. The skirmish in Delaware came eight days before Brandywine and involved Maxwell's light infantry of Washington's army. Again, there is no record of Maxwell's men carrying the new American flag and since Maxwell's unit was formed just a few days before Cooch's Bridge, there is no guarantee that Maxwell was issued the new American flag and its actually being fired upon by the British. An address given by John P. Nields on September 9, 1927, at Cooch's Bridge in connection with the 150th anniversary of the Battle of Brandywine dealt with the flag issue. Nields said, "On yonder stone are inscribed the words, 'The Stars and Stripes were first unfurled in battle at Cooch's Bridge, September 3, 1777.' We are reasonably certain that the Stars and Stripes were carried by Maxwell's corps in the engagement here on September 3rd." Nields went on to list five facts that he said were certain. Those facts included the resolution by Congress creating the flag, that Washington had the flag when his army marched through Philadelphia, that Maxwell's corps was formed before the battle of Cooch's Bridge, that Maxwell was ordered to engage the enemy and, finally, "that in such an engagement it was appropriate that a standard with colors be carried." Nields' five facts don't prove the flag appeared at Cooch's Bridge.

All of the facts listed by Nields applied to Brandywine. The crucial difference was that Washington, himself, was at Brandywine and not present at the Cooch's Bridge skirmish. Also, the Reverend Jacob Trout made reference to the flag at Brandywine in the sermon he preached to troops on the night before the battle.

A flag known as the Brandywine flag was named as a result of the battle. Captain Robert Wilson's company, 7th Pennsylvania Regiment, carried the flag which was red bearing a stars and stripes canton, 7 white stripes and a white canton bearing 13 red eight-pointed stars in rows of 4-5-4.

* * * * *

While Washington was at his headquarters in the Ring home making plans to meet Howe, the British general took up residence at a tavern, at one time known as the Kennett Hotel, and mapped his final strategy with the aid of his officers and Loyalists from the region. Upon arriving at Kennett Square in midday, Howe wanted to immediately begin the assault on Washington. But when orders were given for the advance, staff officers advised Howe that a night's rest would greatly enhance the likelihood of victory, and the order was immediately cancelled. When Grant's troops, arrived he decided to divide the men and strengthen Knyphausen's division by adding the 1st and 2nd British brigades. Knyphausen was ordered to position his men to the east so he would be ready for the next day's action. This was the movement that caused the Americans to fire their alarm guns and move troops into positions along the Brandywine.

Howe made his usual pre-battle preparations for casualties, as he ordered 20 empty wagons to be available for each of the two columns. Knyphausen's column included four regiments of Hessians; the 1st brigade of the 4th, 5th, 23rd, and 49th Foot; the 2nd brigade of the 10th, 27th, 28th, and 40th Foot; 72nd Highlanders; a squadron of the 6th Light Dragoons; the Hessian mounted jaegers; the Queen's Rangers and Ferguson's Rifles. The column commanded by Cornwallis included two squadrons of the 15th Light Dragoons; mounted and dismounted Chasseurs; the 3rd brigade of the 15th, 33rd, 44th, and 55th Foot; the 4th brigade of the 17th, 37th, 46th, and 64th Foot; two battalions of Foot Guards; two battalions of light infantry; two battalions of Grenadiers, and three battalions of Hessian Grenadiers. Each column also had units of the Royal Artillery.

Howe's staff did take time to relax. "The evening was pleasant for many of the British and Hessian officers. The little town in which they were quartered was the first urban stop the army had made since Head of Elk. Local inns, though few and unpretentious, did a rousing business."[9]

* * * * *

Across the Brandywine the American army staff prepared for battle and they didn't have time to visit the local taverns. Its preparations and dispositions did result in damage to property owned by the local residents. General George Weedon's orderly book records a reference on September 10 from Birmingham concerning complaints being filed by residents about the destruction of fences and fields of grain and grass. The armies, both sides, would take a toll on property owned by the residents as a result of the battle. The orderly book also gives details of other preparations for the battle, including the cooking of provisions and the posting of pickets. Washington was to be informed of the posting of the pickets as soon as it was completed. The American dispositions on the east side of Brandywine were complete by the evening of September 10.

Washington's correspondence to Congress on the evening before the battle included the following, "The enemy are now lying near Kennett Square and in a tolerably compact body.... I hope notwithstanding that we shall be able to find their real route, and to defeat their purposes."[10] This correspondence, again, indicated Washington's concern over the roads and fords to be used by the British to cross the Brandywine and attack his army.

As the American army prepared for a night's rest, the Reverend Jacob Trout offered a sermon to the troops he gathered about him near Washington's headquarters, promising that the "doom of the British is near." The sermon was meant to ready the soldiers for the coming battle and possible death, to remind them of the atrocities of the British and their allies, and to remind them that their families were counting on their bravery. The new American flag was also used as inspiration for the troops.

Trout began:

Soldiers and Countrymen: We have met this evening perhaps for the last time. We have shared the toil of the march, the peril of the fight and the dismay of the retreat alike; we have endured the cold and hunger and the contumely of the infernal foe and the courage of the foreign oppressor. We have sat, night after night, at the campfire; we have together heard the roll of reveille, which called us to duty, or the beat of tattoo, which gave the signal for the hardy sleep of the soldier, with the earth for his bed and the knapsack for his pillow.

And now soldiers and brethren, we have met in the peaceful valley on the eve of battle, while the sunlight is dying away, behind yonder heights, the sunlight that tomorrow morn, will glimmer on scenes of blood. We have met amid the whitening tents of our encampment in time of terror and gloom, we have gathered together—God grant it might not be for the last time.

It is a solemn moment. Brethren does not the solemn voice of nature seem to echo the sympathies of the hour? The flag of our country drapes heavily from yonder staff; the breeze had died away along the green plain of Chadd's Ford, the plain that spreads before us in the glittering in the sunlight—the heights of the Brandywine arising gloomy and grand beyond the waters of yonder stream— all nature holds a pause of solemn silence on the eve of the uproar, the bloodshed and strife of tomorrow.

They that take the sword shall parish by the sword.

And have they not taken the sword?

Let the desolated plain, the blood-sodden valley, the burned farm house; blackening in the sun, the sacked village, and the ravaged town, answer—let the whitening bones of the butchered farmer strown along the fields of his homestead, answer—let the starving mother, with her babe clinging to her withered breast that can afford no sustenance, let her answer, with the death-rattle mingling with the murmuring tones, that mark the last struggle of life—let the dying mother and her babe answer.

It was but a day past and our land slept in the quiet of peace. War was not here—wrong was not here. Fraud and woe, and misery and want, dwelt not amongst us. From the eternal solitude of the green woods, arose the blue smoke of the settlers cabin, and golden fields of corn looked forth from amid the waste of the wilderness, and the glad music of human voices awoke the silence of the forest.

Now, God of Mercy, behold the change! Under the shadow of a pretext, under the sanctity of the name of God, invoking the Redeemer to their mid, do these foreign hirelings slay our people! They destroy our towns;

they darken our plains, and now encompass our posts on the plain of Chadd's Ford.

They that take the Sword shall parish by the Sword.

Brethren, think me not unworthy of belief when I tell you the doom of the British is near! Think me not vain, when I tell you that beyond the cloud that now enshrouds us, I see gathering, thick and fast, the darker frown and a blacker storm of Divine indignation!

They may conquer tomorrow. Might and wrong may prevail, and we may be driven from this field — but the hour of God's own vengeance will come!

Aye, if in the vast solitude of eternal space, if in the heart of the boundless universe, there throbs the being of an awful God, quick to avenge and sure to punish guilt, then will the man George; of Brunswick, called King; feel in his brain and his heart, the vengeance of the eternal Jehovah! A blight will be upon his life — a withered brain and a cursed intellect: a blight will be upon his children and upon his people. Great God, how dread the punishment!

A crowded populace, peopling the dense towns where the man of money thrives, while the laborer starves; went striding among the people in all of its forms of terror; an ignorant and God-defining priesthood, chuckling over miseries of millions; a proud and merciless nobility adding wrong to wrong, and heaping insult upon robbery and fraud; royals corrupt to the very heat, an aristocracy rotten to the core; crime and want link hand in hand, and tempting men to deeds of woe and death — these are a part of the doom and retribution that will come upon the English throne and English people!

Soldiers — I look around upon your familiar faces with a strange interest! Tomorrow morning we will all go forth to the battle — for need I tell you that your unworthy minister will march with you, invoking God's aid in the fight, to fight for your homesteads, for your wives and children.

My friends, I might urge you to fight by the galling memory of British wrong. Walton—I might tell you of your butchered father in the silence of the night on the plains of Trenton. I might ring his death shriek in your ears. Shellmire—I might tell you of a butchered mother, a sister outraged, the lonely farmhouse and night assault, the roof in flames, the shout of the troopers as they dispatched their victims, the cries for mercy, the pleading of innocence for pity. I might paint all of this again, in vivid colors of the terrible reality if I thought your courage needed such wild excitement.

But I know you are strong in the might of the Lord. You will march forth to battle on the morrow with light hearts and determined spirits, though the solemn duty—the duty of avenging the dead—may rest heavy on your souls.

And in the hour of battle, when all around is darkness lit by the lurid cannon's glare, and the piercing musket flash, when the wounded strew the ground, and the dead litter your path, then remember soldiers, that God is with you. The eternal God fights for you—he rides on the battle cloud—he sweeps onward with the march of the hurricane charge—God, the awful and the infinite, fights for you and will triumph.

They that take the Sword shall parish by the Sword.

You have taken the sword but not in the spirit of wrong and ravage. You have taken the sword for your homes, for your wives, for your little ones. You have taken the sword for truth, for justice and right, and to you the promise is—be of good cheer, for your foes have taken the sword in the defiance of all that man holds dear, of blasphemy of God—they shall perish by the sword.

And now, Brethren and soldiers, I bid you all farewell. Many of us may fall in the battle of tomorrow. God rest the souls of the fallen—many of us may live to tell the story of the fight tomorrow, and in the memory of all will ever rest and linger the quiet scene of the autumnal night.

Solemn twilight advances over the valley; the woods on the opposite heights fling their long shadows over the green of the meadows; around us are the tents of the continental posts, the suppressed bustle of the camp, the hurried tramp of the soldiers to and fro among the tents, stillness and all marks the eve of battle.

When we meet again, may the shadow of twilight be flung over a peaceful land. God in Heaven grant it.[11]

In a few hours Brandywine would be anything but a peaceful valley.

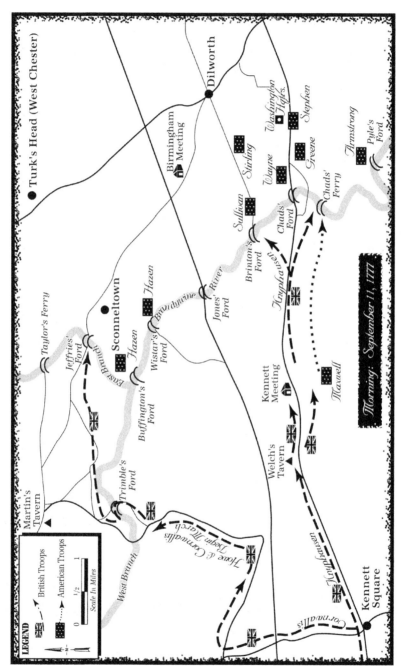

Turk's Head (West Chester)

Dilworth

Birmingham Meeting

Washington Hdqrs.

Stirling

Stephen

Sullivan

Wayne

Greene

Armstrong

Pyle's Ford

Chads' Ferry

Brinton's Ford

Chads' Ford

Knyphausen

Jones' Ford

Brandywine River

Taylor's Ferry

Hazen

Sconneltown

Hazen

Wistar's Ford

Jeffries' Ford

East Branch

Buffington's Ford

Kennett Meeting

Maxwell

Martin's Tavern

Trimble's Ford

Welch's Tavern

Howe & Cornwallis Begin March

West Branch

Knyphausen

Cornwallis

Kennett Square

Morning: September 11, 1777

LEGEND
British Troops
American Troops

Scale In Miles
0   1/2   1

N

Diane Cirafesi of Cirafesi Designs
West Chester, Pennsylvania

Six

Washington Escapes Death

Captain John Marshall was 13 days away from celebrating his 22nd birthday when he advanced with General William Maxwell's light infantry toward the British at Kennett Square on the morning of September 11. For the soldiers in the American army, and especially Colonel Thomas Marshall of the 3rd Virginia, young Marshall's father, a full day of hard fighting was ahead. Late in the day Thomas Marshall would play a pivotal role in delaying the British and allowing the beaten American army to retreat from Brandywine. John Marshall, a Virginian and future chief justice of the United States Supreme Court, was already an army veteran on that day as he had previously served with Daniel Morgan and commanded a company of the Virginia Line. Marshall would fight the whole day at Brandywine.

In the American army at Brandywine were actually two captains named John Marshall. Captain John Marshall of the 13th Pennsylvania was from Washington County, Pennsylvania, and was wounded during the morning advance by Maxwell's light infantry when it came into contact with British General Wilhelm Knyphausen's forces, according to the diary of Lieutenant James McMichael of the Pennsylvania Line. McMichael reported that Marshall was wounded as early as 7 a.m., the time the sun had burned through the early morning fog, during the day's first skirmishing. McMichael served in Captain Marshall's Pennsylvania rifle company.

Virginian John Marshall's experience in the American army fortified his belief in the principles of the new nation, and he witnessed first-hand the spirit of the new nation. On the soldiers of the Revolutionary War in the American army, he later wrote that he served "with brave men from different states who were risking life and everything valuable in a common cause." The experience, Marshall continued, confirmed his "habit of considering America as my country, and congress my government."[1] As for the fighting at Brandywine, Marshall gave the following opinion of his officers and fellow soldiers, "As must ever be the case in new-raised armies, unused to danger and from which undeserving officers have not been expelled, their conduct was not uniform. Some regiments, especially those which had served the preceding campaign, maintained their ground with the firmness and intrepidity of veterans, while others gave way as soon as they were pressed."

Early in the morning of September 11 in Kennett Square, British General William Howe and his officers and men were poised to exploit the shortcomings of George Washington's rebel army.

* * * * *

The British army was ready to move well before dawn. The order from Howe on the evening before battle said, "The army will March in two Columns at 4 o'Clock to-morrow morning, and receive their Orders of March from their respective Lieutenant Generals—His Excellency Lieut.-Gen. Knyphausen and Lieut.-Gen. Earl Cornwallis."[2] Howe and Lord General Charles Cornwallis set off on the Great Valley Road with their division of approximately 7,500 men at 5 a.m., almost an hour before the sun was to rise. "Our column," said Captain Friedrich von Muenchhausen, aide de camp to General Howe, "consisted of two battalions of English light infantry, two battalions of English grenadiers, two battalions of English Guards, two brigades of English infantry, two squadrons of dragoons, the Hessian jaegers and the Hessian grenadiers. Since our column had no baggage, but did have a number of sappers in the van, we moved forward quickly in spite of the great heat."[3] In that heat and heavy early morning fog, Howe's troops began a march of 17 miles that would conclude with a bloody battle with the Americans on the hills of Birmingham.

"At six o'clock in the morning Lieutenant-General Knyphausen set out to march with his column, which consisted of four regiments of Hessians, two brigades of Englishmen under General Grant, the 71st regiment of Highland Scots, one squadron of dragoons, the Hessian mounted jaegers, and 350 Provincials, as well as the English riflemen, plus all the baggage, including cattle. His route was towards Chads Ford by way of Welch's Tavern."[4] The soldiers under Knyphausen's command amounted to about 5,000, little fewer than the number in Howe's force.

Leading the British advance towards Chadds Ford were the Queen's Rangers under the command of Captain James Wemyss in their distinctive green uniforms, and the riflemen of Captain Patrick Ferguson. The Queen's Rangers unit was organized a year before Brandywine and later in the war would be led by John Simcoe, who was severely wounded during the Battle of Brandywine. At Brandywine the Queen's Rangers would gain fame, as the following passage from the unit history of the Queen's Rangers indicates, but that fame came at the expense of a number of lives. The British report of casualties lists 14 killed, 57 wounded, and 1 missing for the Queen's Rangers and 2 killed and 6 wounded for Ferguson's command.

> The adventures of the Queen's Rangers during the Revolutionary War in America lend a flavour of romance to the dull annals of military history. Tales of their daring exploits, of the Puckish tricks which they played on the enemy in the heart of the American wilderness, are strangely suggestive of the deeds of Robin Hood and his Merry Men of Sherwood Forest. Indeed, the very uniforms of the Rangers, green, like the attire of the genial outlaws...—in sharp contrast to the dignified red and white of the regular British uniform—would have heightened

the illusion. But there the similarity ends, for no regiment of either army could boast of better discipline in its ranks, and no other single regiment played so conspicuous a part in the campaigns of the Revolution.

It was under Major Wemyss at Brandywine Creek in September, 1777, that the corps won its first laurels....Lord Howe planned a circuitous march for the purpose of attacking the enemy in the rear, and while General Cornwallis was commissioned to undertake the march, Lieutenant-General Knyphausen in whose division the Queen's Rangers were included, was authorized to divert the attention of the Americans from Cornwallis' division, by making feigned efforts to cross the river at Chad's Ford. In the contest that ensued the fighting was desperate, and the brunt of it fell upon the Queen's Rangers. The affair at Brandywine was one of the most significant battles of the war, and had Lord Howe been quick in pursuit of the Americans, Washington's army would have been totally destroyed.

For their share in the encounter, the Queen's Rangers received warm praise from their General, and they were commended also by the Commander-in-chief of the British forces. Their loss was heavy, about one-fifth of the total British loss, but their reputation was made.... 'I must be silent as to the behaviour of the Rangers,' Lieutenant-General Knyphausen wrote to Lord Howe, 'for I want even words to express my own astonishment to give him an idea of it.' Henceforth the Rangers were placed in the vanguard of service, and the eyes of the entire army followed their activities with envy and admiration.[5]

As the Queen's Rangers and Ferguson Rifles advanced to Welch's Tavern, they met members of Maxwell's light infantry for the first time. Elements of Baylor's Light Horse had stopped at Welch's Tavern, near present-day Longwood, to take early morning refreshments. "Glancing out the window, one of the Americans saw the green uniforms of Knyphausen's lead units, and a rapid exodus followed after a wild exchange of shots. The

British hit nothing, but the Americans hit one of their own horses left tied to the inn's hitching rail. The Battle of Brandywine had begun."[6] The Americans escaped by the back door of the house and fled, leaving their horses for the British, toward Maxwell's main force. They crossed the fields east of Welch's Tavern and headed toward the woods. The firing gave Maxwell warning that the expected British advance had begun. Maxwell formed his first line of defense behind stonewalls at the Kennett graveyard next to the Kennett Meeting House with Captain Charles Porterfield, a company commander, in charge of the Americans.

Inside the meeting house the Quakers were holding their mid-week meeting. "One of those who attended, Jacob Pierce, noted that there was an engagement of some sort between the forces of Knyphausen and Maxwell outside on the lawn of the meeting house, but 'while there was much noise and confusion without, all was quiet and peaceful within.'"[7] The Quakers, true to their beliefs, were not about to allow the fight for Independence taking place a few yards outside their walls to disturb their prayers and meditation.

Porterfield's orders were to fire upon the British and then fall back to the second defensive position held by Maxwell. Porterfield followed his orders as the Queen's Rangers and Ferguson Rifles approached the meeting house at 9 a.m. After one volley Porterfield retreated with the Queen's Rangers in close pursuit. Maxwell selected with extreme care the positions from which to challenge Knyphausen, especially since Knyphausen's force outnumbered his by about seven to one. Even though he had been in command of the light infantry less than a month, Maxwell had mastered the tactics that made light infantry effective. Hills, woods, and small streams all played a part in Maxwell's plan to harass and delay the British march towards Chadds Ford, the Brandywine and General George Washington's main army.

After abandoning the meeting house's stone wall, Maxwell's men next used a stone house and trees to form a defensive line. Hard fighting by the Queen's Rangers and

Ferguson's Rifles was needed to dislodge the Americans as Maxwell's men poured accurate fire upon the oncoming British. About this time some of the English soldiers claimed an American unit under Porterfield hoisted a white flag as if to surrender. "It was a hoax. When the Queen's Rangers came close to the Continental position to accept the surrender they were fired upon and lost heavily."[8] The deception led to the killing and wounding of about 30 of the Queen's Rangers. The Americans immediately fled and continued their tactic of firing and retreating all the way to the Brandywine. Colonel Josiah Parker and Lieutenant Colonel William Heth commanded the next area of defense. Captain John Marshall, the future Supreme Court justice, was part of this unit. Wemyss approached the Americans with some caution, and after sporadic fire the Americans withdrew to form with the rest of the light infantry. They were reinforced from General Nathanael Greene's troops at Chadds Ford and three six-pound cannons were then under Maxwell's direct command.

Maxwell was on the east side of a deep gorge positioned near a marsh surrounding Ring Run. Knyphausen brought up his main force to aid the Queen's Rangers and Ferguson's Rifles in dislodging the Americans and personally surveyed Maxwell's positions. After seeing the American cannons, he ordered his own to be brought forward. Hessians from Major General Johann Stirn's brigade helped out Wemyss and Ferguson. Dragoons and a detachment of the 71st Foot went on a flanking mission as Ferguson's soldiers made their way to a house and were reinforced by Stirn. Knyphausen then placed the 28th and 49th regiments of the 1st brigade as support for his cannons and ordered the 4th Foot to cover his left flank and they moved to almost the banks of Brandywine opposite American General John Sullivan. They exchanged fire before the British took stronger positions to the west of the Brandywine.

Knyphausen used his cannon to pound Maxwell's position and sent the 28th Foot forward to slip around Maxwell's left flank and attack. The outnumbered Americans were forced to withdraw. "Soon the rebels, who had been shouting 'Hurrah' and firing briskly from a gorge in front of us, were quickly put to flight."[9] By 11 a.m. Maxwell was back across the Brandywine with Washington. Facing the Americans were Knyphausen with a strong British force and all of the army's wagons and supplies. Knyphausen's orders were to hold Washington at Chadds Ford and make Washington believe that the whole British army was before him making ready for an attack. Major Carl Leopold Baurmeister, who was with Knyphausen, wrote that at that time "the small-arms fire ceased entirely, although our cannon fired from time to time, each shot being answered by the enemy. The purpose of our gunfire, however, was only to advise the second (Howe's) column of our position."

* * * * *

Knyphausen described the morning's action in a letter he authored on October 21, 1777, while in camp near Philadelphia. It said:

> My Lord: The Commander in Chief Sir W. Howe having honored me with the Command of the Right Column of the Army at the attack upon the Enemy on the Brandywine Hills on the 11th of Sept., I took upon it was my duty to relate to your Lordship the particulars thereof.
>
> At V o Clock in the Morning I moved the column from Kennett's Square. Advancing on the road to Chads's Ford I had hardly come up to Welche's Tavern, when the advanced Corps fell in with about 300 riflemen of the Enemy. These were driven back by my advanced Party from one advantageous Post to another behind the Defilee to the westward side of the Brandywine Creek, before which there was a strong Morass.
>
> At 11 o'clock the Enemy were driven back over the Creek evacuating their very advantageous posts on this side. The most obstinate resistance they gave was on the road to Brandywine Creek's Bridge, but the gallant and Spirited Behavior of the 4th and 5th Regiment forced them to leave their Ground.

On this I ordered the Troops to halt and keep their position waiting for the Commander in Chiefs Attack on the right of the Enemy.[10]

A German officer authored another letter giving more details of the morning's action. He said:

This column marched along the main Chester road, which, between Welch's Tavern and Chad's Ford, has many defiles between hills and woods. When our van-guard, the Riflemen and the Queen's Rangers, arrived at Welch's Tavern, it encountered the first enemy troops. It drove them back and became master of the defile without delaying the march of the column. The skirmishing continued to the last hills of Chadd's Ford.

Heretofore the enemy had been repulsed by our van-guard alone, but now the engagement became more serious. The van had arrived at a place where the road passes through some swampy land. On both sides of this lowland are hills and woods, and beyond it a road turns off to the left from the main road and runs through this lowland for about half a mile. This road, which leads to a ford on Brandywine Creek, was enfiladed by an enemy battery situated beyond the creek. All the woods were full of enemy troops. Captain Ferguson posted his Riflemen behind a house beyond the lowland and was supported by a hundred men under Captain Long from Stirn's brigade. The English 49th Regiment, two heavy guns and two 3-pounders were detached to the right of the column and occupied an elevation directly above the riflemen. In the meantime the Queen's Rangers had proceeded to the left and after a short but very rapid musketry-fire, supported by the 23rd English Regiment, which had been detached to the left of the column, quickly drove the rebels out of the woods and straight across the lowland.

Under cover of a continuous cannonade, the 28th English Regiment went off to the right of the column, and soon the rebels, who had been shouting 'Hurrah' and firing briskly from a gorge in front of us, were quickly put to flight. Meanwhile the Riflemen and the Queen's Rangers had also advanced toward the left flank of the enemy, who were constantly yielding ground. The 28th, 23rd, 55th, and 40th English Regiments, the Leib Regiment and Mirbach's were formed in line on the height beyond the lowland and the road to the ford; the Combined Battalion and Donop's took position in column formation along this road, and the 5th, 49th, 27th, and 4th English Regiments this side of the lowland on the heights along the creek. All these movements were covered by the gunfire of the English artillery, the various pieces being mounted with all possible haste in strategic places on the high ground.

The enemy's fire was also heavy, especially that from the battery of four guns and one howitzer situated beyond the ford. However, though the balls and grapeshot were well aimed and fell right among us, this cannonade had little effect—partly because the battery was placed too low. We pushed our light troops and outposts close to the creek, for the enemy on this side were completely dispersed. Then we straightened our line, posted one battalion of the 71st Regiment and the Queen's Dragoons (16th of Light) on the height on our right flank where the enemy troops had held a fleche and the baggage under cover of the two other battalions of the 71st Regiment on the rising ground where we first skirmished with the enemy. These movements were completed by half past ten. The musketry ceased entirely. Our cannon fired from time to time, each shot being answered by the enemy; but the purpose of our gunfire was only to advise the second column of our position.

The enemy apparently thought that we were maneuvering to approach their formidable position and perhaps thinking of fording the creek. Hence, they directed their attention to the fords between them and us, especially to one very strategically situated, in front of which the 4th English Regiment was posted and which was covered by two guns on the nearest hill.[11]

* * * * *

Lieutenant Colonel Robert Hanson Harrison wrote to John Hancock from Chadds Ford at 8:45 a.m.: "Sir, The Enemy are now advancing. Their present appearance indicates a disposition to pursue this Route. If they do, I trust, they will meet with a suitable reception and such as will establish our Liberties. They are now advanced near the Brandywine & have fired several pieces of Artillery."[12]

From the American perspective, the advance of Knyphausen's professional troops was slowed by the hard fighting of citizen soldiers of Maxwell's light infantry and the tactics Maxwell employed.

> Maxwell fell back slowly down the road, taking cover from time to time and keeping up his fire, until he reached the Ford. Reinforced, he advanced again to the high ground and again engaged he enemy....the British deployed; Ferguson threw out his riflemen on the right, a hundred Hessians supporting him. But Porterfield and Waggoner's Virginians had come across the river; they drove the Riflemen and Hessians back to the shelter of William Harvey's stone house. The 49th English Regiment, with two heavy guns and two three-pounders, taking position on an elevation behind him, backed up Ferguson's forces and opened fire. The Queen's Rangers, led by Captain Wemyss, and the 23rd English regiment filed off to their left, flanked Maxwell, whose men 'had been shouting Hurrah!' and firing briskly and drove him out of the woods. The 28th regiment went into action and Maxwell was forced back across the upper branch of Chadd's Ford. The Rangers now joined the Riflemen and Hessians at the stone house; they swept down on Porterfield and Waggoner and cleared that side of the stream, the Virginians retreating to the other side by the lower of the two fords.

> The 28th, 23rd, 55th and 40th English regiments and the Leib and Mirbach Hessian regiments now formed a line on the heights overlooking the Ford, and the Combined Battalion and Donop's Hessians held the road, and

the 4th, 5th, 27th and 49th English regiments took position on the slope from the heights down to the lowland along the stream. These movements were all completed by 10:30 a.m.[13]

Commanding the artillery for the Americans from the eastern banks of the Brandywine was Colonel Thomas Proctor. Proctor's cannons pounded away at the British army and Royal Artillery. A home belonging to Quaker William Harvey Sr. was not spared as it was directly in the line of fire. Harvey had planned to stay at his home, protecting his belongings. A neighbor, Jacob Way, came to Harvey to plead with him to escape the danger. "As they exchanged words, a twelve-pound cannon-ball came from Proctor's battery directly for the house, passed through both walls of the kitchen and plunged along the piazza floor, tearing up the boards and barely avoiding William's legs, until, a little farther on, it buried itself six feet deep in the earth. It is recorded that William hesitated no longer, but sought a safer place. His house was thoroughly despoiled when the British came up."[14]

* * * * *

Captain Patrick Ferguson, who would later in the war be promoted to major, and his corps were armed with his new breech-loading rifle and they stood beside the Queen's Rangers during the morning engagement in the van of Knyphausen's column. They helped to drive the American light infantry to the Brandywine. As Ferguson, known as an expert shot, placed his men in defensive positions along the western bank of the river, he had an opportunity to change the course of the history of the United States and the world. The 33-year-old Ferguson had a high-ranking American general in his rifle's sight and well within the distance where Ferguson could have easily killed the gallant officer. "It was not pleasant to fire at the back of an offending individual who was acquitting himself very coolly of his duty, so I let him alone," Ferguson wrote. The officer Ferguson spared has been identified, but not conclusively, as General George Washington, the rebels' military leader and future first president of the United States.

Ferguson was born in 1744 in Scotland and was the second son of James and Anne Murray Ferguson. His father was a judge and Ferguson, known as Pattie by his friends and family, had two brothers and three sisters. They lived near Edinburgh. He attended a military academy at age 14 and began his military career at age 15 as a Cornet in the Royal North British Dragoons and received encouragement from his uncle, General James Murray. Ferguson served in the Seven Years' War in Germany until an illness weakened his health. He returned to Britain and spent time on garrison duty before he purchased a captaincy in the 70th Foot and spent three years in the Caribbean, including time in Tobago to put down a slave rebellion. He retuned home in 1772.

Inventors were developing forms of breech-loading rifles for a number of years before the American Revolution and some were being used as sporting weapons at the time, but the British had not converted the rifle into a military weapon. Ferguson developed a military model, known as the Ferguson Rifle, at his own expense. A breech-loading rifle would give soldiers the ability to fire more rapidly and to reload without standing up and exposing themselves to enemy fire. "Ferguson's rifle was fitted with a breech-plug which passed perpendicularly through the breech of the barrel and was opened on a smoothly-moving screw thread by a single horizontal revolution of the trigger guard. An opening was left at the top. A ball was inserted and powder was poured into the opening behind the ball. A turn of the trigger guard caused the breech plug to rise, closing the head of the barrel. The rifle was ready to fire after the powder spilled into the pan."[15] The weapon had a range of three hundred yards and could be loaded and fired as many as seven times by an expert where the musket in current use could be fired only three or four times a minute. The Ferguson Rifle weighed seven and one-half pounds, half of the weight of the musket.

A century after the battle, James Ferguson wrote about his famous relative:

> At the outbreak of the war with the revolted Colonies found him intent on the invention of a new species of rifle, with which to counteract the superiority as marksmen of the American backwoodsmen....The first exhibition of the new invention was made before Lord Townshend, then Master-General of the Ordnance. During 1776, Ferguson was then with the 70th Regiment. The weapon was credited for the first time for small arms to 1. fire at a target, at 200 yards distance, at the rate of four shots each minute. 2. He fired six shots in one minute. 3. He fired four times per minute, advancing at the same time at the rate of four miles in the hour. 4. He poured a bottle of water into the pan and barrel of the piece when loaded, as to wet every grain of the powder, and in less than half-a-minute fired with her as well as ever without extracting the ball. He also hit the bull's eye at 100 yards, lying with his back on the ground.
>
> Before long (the rifle) was exhibited before the King at Windsor, by Ferguson. The patent was dated March 17, 1776. Its main peculiarities were the loading at the breech by means of an ingenious contra-balance, by which the trigger-guard, acting as a lever, dropped a perpendicular plug or fine threaded screw, from flush with the top of the barrel to flush with the bottom of the bore, thus opening access to the chamber, and the provision of an elevating sight....The length is 50 inches, the weight is 7½ lbs. The bayonet is 25 inches and 1½ inches wide. (The rifle is) adept at ranges 100 to 500 yards.[16]

Among those witnessing the demonstrations of the new weapon were Lord Townsend and Lord Amherst, commander in chief of his Majesty's Army. Townsend ordered 100 breech-loading firearms, and four gun makers, William Grice, Benjamin Willets, Mathias Barker, and Alton and Son, were each asked to manufacture 25 weapons. A special corps of riflemen

was formed and sent to America in March 1777. A major problem developed because General Howe, the British commander,
was not consulted about Ferguson's joining his army, the use
of Ferguson's new weapon, or the company of riflemen to be
assigned to his army. When Ferguson arrived in New York,
Howe greeted the young officer personally and commented,
"I look forward to great things from this corps commanded
by so intelligent an officer."[17]

* * * * *

Knyphausen placed Ferguson's unit, numbering approximately 90 men on the morning of September 11, in the van-
guard of his column along with the Queen's Rangers. They
were ordered to make contact with the enemy and halt any
American counterthrust.

They stayed off the main roads. About a mile from
the Brandywine he encountered Maxwell's light infantry
and a fire-fight developed and the Americans withdrew.
Ferguson's men encountered stiffer resistance from a far
larger force. With support from a unit of the Queen's Rangers armed with muzzle-loading muskets, Ferguson gained
the advantage by a flanking movement.

With the enemy outflanked, he (Ferguson) ordered
his riflemen to fire from the prone position—an unheard
of manoeuvre since it was very difficult to reload a muzzle-
loading gun while lying down—but the Major's men experienced no difficulty in doing it since they possessed a
firearm quite capable of being handled in this fashion. The
British kept up a withering fire and again the Americans
were forced to fall back. Ferguson resumed the advance
and once more came under intense enemy fire with telling effect. Not one British rifleman had fallen but the
Queen's Rangers had suffered a 15 percent casualty rate.
As Ferguson remarked, "Such is the great advantage of
an army that will admit of being loaded and fired on the
ground without exposing the men....I through my people
on the ground under some pretty smart firing six times

that morning without losing a man." A tactical innovation, to say the least. But such a manoeuvre can only be effectively performed if the soldiers are suitably armed. The hard facts were that Ferguson's men possessed the proper weapon, while the Queen's Rangers did not.

Ferguson ordered a halt and waited for Knyphausen after seeing the rest of the Americans. Knyphausen came under fire from a large body of rebels concealed at the edge of a woods. On his own initiative, Ferguson drove his troops across an open stretch of land, firing as they moved. An advance such as this, where the unit provides its own continuous covering fire as it charged, was a startling feat, and one that could not be duplicated with a muzzle-loading gun. Americans withdrew and British advanced.[18]

Ferguson, writing to Dr. Adam Ferguson from Philadelphia on January 31, 1778, on the Battle of Brandywine, wrote:

General Howe made a Circuit with the Gross of the Army while Lieutenant-General Knyphausen, with whom we were, led a Column by the direct road to attack the Rebels at Brandywine, and the Rebels who were ignorant of General Howe's movement employed all their Light Troops to the Amount of Some Thousands to retard the Progress of our Column, & as the Country was very strong they would have found no difficulty in interrupting our march had they shown firmness equal to the ingenuity of their dispositions. But if their theory was good their Practice was the reverse for they seemed capable but of two motions: discharging their pieces in the air and running in a direct line behind them, for they remained planted like Cabbages whilst our parties divided, gained their flanks, turned their breast works, and then after throwing away their fire, would run off leaving Arms, hats, blankets, &c. and when we were once necessitated to advance to their breast work in front, although they kept a good Countenance until within 12 yards, they gave an ineffectual fire and turned their backs to the tenth part of their own numbers, wherefore I will make bold to say that Gen. Maxwell who commanded them had better begin his prenticeship as a corporal and that their Light troops (who by the by have seen three times the service of the rest of their army) have learnt to rely upon their heels.

Whilst Knyphausen was forming the Line within a Mile of the Rebel Camp to wait for G. Howe's attack, their Rifle men were picking off our men very fast by random shots from a wood some hundred yards in front as it is easy to do execution upon such large objects. I had only 28 men with me (a few having been disabled by the Enemy the rest from Fatigue) who however proved Sufficient for my Lads first dislodged them from the skirts of the Wood then Drove them from a breast work within it after which our purpose being answered we lay down at the furthest skirt of the wood—not unnecessarily to (provoke) an attack being so few with Support....[19]

At this point Ferguson reported seeing a rebel officer, believed to be Washington. Because of description of Washington's uniform and the timing of the incident, it is likely that the officer was Washington, even though the identification of the officer has been disputed. Ferguson wrote:

We had not lain long when a rebel officer, remarkable by a hussar dress, passed towards our army, within a hundred yards of my right flank, not perceiving us. He was followed by another dressed in dark green or blue, mounted on a bay horse, with a remarkably large cocked hat. I ordered three good shots to steal near to them and fire at them; but the idea disgusted me. I recalled the order.

The hussar in returning made a circuit, but the other passed again within a hundred yards of us, upon which I advanced from the wood towards him. On my calling, he stopped; but after looking at me, proceeded. I again drew his attention, and made signs to him to stop leveling my piece at him, but he slowly continued on his way. As I was within that distance at which, in the quickest firing I have seldom missed a sheet of paper and could have lodged half-a-dozen of balls in or about him before he was out of my reach, I had only to determine but it was not pleasant to fire at the back of an unoffending individual, who was acquitting himself very coolly of his duty so I let him alone.

The day after I had been telling this story to some wounded officers who lay in the same room with me, when one of our surgeons, who had been dressing the wounded rebel officers, came in and told us they had been informing him, that General Washington was all the morning with the light troops, generally in their front and only attended by a French officer in a hussar dress, he himself mounted and dressed as above directed. The oddness of their dress had puzzled me and made me take notice of it. I am not sorry that I did not know at the time who it was.[20]

The French officer has never been positively identified, but possibly could have been Polish cavalry officer Casimir Pulaski. The identification of Washington rests on the testimony of those unnamed wounded officers treated by the British on the day after the battle.

After passing up a shot at the American officer, Ferguson's Rifles were again called into action to halt an American drive to retake the woods. Two more assaults took place before Ferguson's unit was outflanked. As Ferguson removed his men, an American bullet shattered his right elbow. Despite intense pain and profuse bleeding, Ferguson managed to rally his men and lead them to another covered area. Firing from the prone position, the riflemen held the Americans in check until another Knyphausen division arrived. Ferguson was evacuated from the field and taken to a dressing station behind the British lines.

The wound not only put Ferguson out of action for months, but it also led to the disbanding of Ferguson's Rifles and the packing away of the breech-loading rifle despite its outstanding debut at Brandywine. "Ferguson's rifle had withstood the test: Yet, out of this victory came a shocking defeat for Ferguson—and quite possibly for the maintenance of Britain's American empire. While he convalesced, Howe disbanded and disarmed the rifle corps. The rifles were packed up and placed in storage—for good. The motives for these actions are not fully understood; but many believe that the British General (Howe) took umbrage at the formation of the rifle corps without his having been previously consulted and took opportunity to destroy the work."[21] Howe was not convinced of the reliability of the weapon and some reports had the weapon malfunctioning after repeated use and in bad weather.

The day after the battle, Ferguson received the following:

> Headquarters 12th September, 1777
> Sir,
> The Commander-in-chief has received from Lt. Gen. Knyphausen the most honourable report of your gallant and spirited behaviour in the engagement of the 11th, on which his excellency has commanded me to express his acknowledgements to you and to acquaint you, sir, that he shall, with great satisfaction, adopt any plan that can be effected to put you in a situation of remaining with the army under his command. For the present he has thought proper to incorporate the rifle corps into the light companies of the respective regiments. I am very happy to be even the channel of so honourable a testimony of your spirited conduct, and of that of your late corps. And I am, sire, with perfect esteem and regard,
> Your most obedient, humble servant, J. Paterson, Adjt.-Genl.[22]

Ferguson's wound was slow to heal as documented in letters from Sir James Murray, a British officer who concluded his career as a lieutenant colonel, who was also wounded. Murray was a first cousin of Ferguson, his mother being Janet Murray, one of Ferguson's maternal aunts. On October 30, 1777, Murray wrote his wife from Philadelphia, "...suffered a wound to the ankle at Brandywine and said would recover in a few days....Pate Ferguson has received a shot in the arm which will prove more tedious but he is getting better." On November 29, Murray reported, "I have got the better of my wound and fever. Pate Ferguson is likewise recovering though slowly." And on March 5, 1778, Murray wrote, "Pate Ferguson is far from being well yet, tho' his arm has lately taken a favourable turn and there is every reason to hope that it will continue to do well. He is otherwise in good health and in good spirits, though he has been particularly unfortunate, not only in the pain which he has suffered, but in being incapacitated from acting so early in the campaign, other wise tho' he laboured under many disadvantages I am sure that he must have distinguished himself, and recommended his rifle to the notice which it certainly deserves."[23]

Ferguson did recover from his severe wound; he underwent several operations to remove bone splinters and at times surgeons considered amputation. In time Ferguson learned to use his left hand much as he did his right before Brandywine. Ferguson, who would gain the nickname of "Bulldog," went on to fight in the southern theater of the war and on October 7, 1780, he led a group of Loyalists at King's Mountain. Ferguson, the only member of the British military involved in the battle, was shot from his horse and killed.

* * * * *

The hours immediately following Ferguson's being wounded and his decision not to fire upon the brave American officer would be crucial for the rebel army. Fighting diminished as an ineffectual long-range artillery duel was fought. Soldiers in both armies were sheltered from harm by thick woods. The exchange of shells did notify Howe that Knyphausen was in position and ready to attack. Washington would have to decide if the force that Maxwell fought all morning contained the whole of the British army. Or, if a part of the enemy forces had disappeared, where would they appear? The fate of Philadelphia, the young nation's center of government, rested on the decisions Washington was about to make.

Jeffries House

Wilmington merchants shipped a large quantity of wines and liquor to Chester County to keep the alcohol safe from the British army. The liquor was stored in this house and found by Howe's army as the troops marched to Osborne's Hill.

Chester County Historical Society, West Chester, Pennsylvania

Seven

Howe Disappears into the Fog

American General George Washington closely monitored the morning action of his light infantry as General William Maxwell contested the British advance upon his main line of defense at Chadds Ford. For several hours the British, under the direction of General Wilhelm Knyphausen, fought their way to the Brandywine and eventually took defensive positions across the river from Washington's army. The engagement settled into an exchange of cannon and small arms fire as the morning hours of September 11, 1777, faded, along with the fog, and the afternoon segment of the largest land battle of the American Revolution began.

Washington was prepared for a British frontal assault on his forces and he knew from the morning fighting that at least a large portion of the enemy army was arrayed before him. Was General William Howe's whole army facing him across the Brandywine or had Howe split his army as he did at Long Island a year earlier? Was Washington in danger of being outflanked and his army whipped or were the British troops across the Brandywine vulnerable to an attack by his army? Maybe the bulk of Howe's army was making a dash for Philadelphia or the supply depots around Downingtown and Reading. These were the crucial questions that needed immediate answers. Washington desperately required accurate intelligence.

Conflicting reports of British movements made it impossible for Washington to determine Howe's location. The contrary and incomplete intelligence caused Washington to hesitate and keep his troops in place on the eastern side of the Brandywine for several hours. He did not shift troops to meet a possible impending attack and even though he at one point ordered an assault on Knyphausen's troops, he immediately withdrew that order before it was fully executed. The lack of intelligence can be directly tied to Washington's not sending out enough dragoons to gather the vital information and not properly exploring the ground on the day before the battle.

"Washington conducted the Brandywine operation as if he was in a daze. The general who always had stressed the necessity of procuring the fullest intelligence and of analyzing it correctly had failed to do either or to employ his light horse adequately when the price of error might be the loss of Philadelphia."[1] Washington lost contact with more than 7,000 enemy troops for several hours even though he knew the location, Kennett Square, of Howe's whole army on the eve of the battle. Howe had disappeared into the early morning fog.

Major John Jamison of Colonel Theodorick Bland's 1st Continental Dragoons was dispatched to look for the British. While Washington was at Chadds Ford, near the American artillery, he received a report from General John Sullivan. The report said, "Maj. Jamison came from the right of the army, and I might depend there was no enemy there."[2] The message was deficient as to the exact time and place Jamison made his observations. The report reached Washington at 9:30 a.m. Later reports would also lack those same crucial pieces of information and Washington was unable to determine what areas were scouted and when the observations were made.

Sullivan said he immediately ordered Jamison "to Send an officer over to the Lancaster Road," about two miles north of Buffington's Ford, and that the officer "Returned & Said no Enemy had passed that way."[3] About an hour after Jamison's report to Washington, Sullivan sent another message to Washington. The message, relayed by Major Lewis Morris Jr., said Colonel Moses Hazen reported that Howe was on the march and attempting a flanking maneuver. Hazen had seen Howe's troops near the forks of the Brandywine. So, by noon Washington had two clearly conflicting messages — one saying the flank was clear and the other saying the enemy was in the midst of a flanking movement.

Earlier, Bland and a patrol of his command also went looking for the enemy on the right flank of the American army. As Washington was evaluating the conflicting reports, he still had not heard from Bland. Colonel Thomas Pickering, Washington's adjutant, was with Washington that morning near Proctor's battery of artillery. Pickering wrote that as late as "11 or 12 o'clock (Washington) bitterly lamented that Col. Bland had not sent him any information at all, and that the accounts he had received from others were of a very contradictory nature."[4] Charles Pinckney backed up the report as he wrote he was near Proctor's battery on the heights above Chadds Ford with Washington when he heard Washington "bitterly lament that Col. Bland had not sent him any information at all, & that the accounts he had received from others were of a very contradictory nature."[5]

Washington sent a note to Bland about 11:20 a.m. that said, "I earnestly entreat a continuance of your vigilant attention to the movements of the enemy, and the earliest report not only of their movements, but of their numbers and the course they are pursuing. In a particular matter I wish to gain satisfactory information of a body confidently reported to have gone up to a ford seven or eight miles above this. It is said the fact is certain. You will send up an intelligent, sensible officer immediately with a party to find out the truth, what number it consists of, and the road they are now on. Be particular in these matters."[6] Bland did not discover the British until after 1 p.m.

By noon the elements were in place for a major American defeat. For seven hours Howe's main force had been on the march around Washington's right flank, and the American general had not received solid information on the movement. Washington had not attacked Knyphausen's force and he had not shifted his forces to meet the flanking movement. As each minute passed, Washington's chances of victory lessened and defeat increased. Strategic defensive positions near Birmingham Meeting House, the site of an American hospital, were left undermanned. Also, by noon the time had passed when Washington could order a successful attack on Knyphausen. There was not enough time for the Americans to cross the river, attack, and defeat Knyphausen's veteran British and German troops before Howe would have been attacking the rear of Washington's army.

At noon Washington received a report from Lieutenant Colonel James Ross, son of George Ross II, of Lancaster County and signer of the Declaration of Independence. Ross was a member of the 8th Pennsylvania and his report made it clear that Howe was flanking Washington. "Sept. 11, 1777, Great Valley Road Eleven o'clock A.M. Dear General, A large body of the enemy from every account 5000, with 16 or 18 field pieces, marched along this road just now. This road leads to Taylor's and Jefferies ferries on the Brandywine and to the Great Valley at the Sign of the Ship on the Lancaster Road to Philadelphia. There is also a road from Brandywine to Chester by Dilworth's Tavern. We are close to their rear with 70 men. Capt. (Michael) Simpson lay in ambush with 20 men, and gave them three rounds within a small distance, in which two of his men were wounded, one mortally. I believe Genl. Howe is with this party, as Joseph Galloway is here known by the inhabitants with many of whom he spoke, and told them that Genl. Howe is with him. Yours, James Ross, Lieut. Col. D.P. Regt."[7]

Ross's report made it clear to Washington that the enemy force facing him at Chadds Ford was only a portion of the British army and his own American army outnumbered those commanded by Knyphausen. Washington ordered Sullivan across the Brandywine to attack the left flank of Knyphausen's forces and General Nathanael Greene to do the same on Knyphausen's right. The order was an ill-advised one. The veteran British forces would not have been easily dislodged from their positions behind the Brandywine. Washington was about to abandon his defensive positions to attack the British. Knyphausen, planning an attack on the rebels, would await the Americans behind defensive cover. The British artillery, posted on the heights overlooking the Brandywine, was poised to inflict losses on the American army if a crossing was attempted. Washington's forces would have precious little time to dislodge Knyphausen before Howe's army would arrive and sandwich Washington between Howe and Knyphausen.

Greene and Sullivan received their orders to advance and set their troops in motion. Sullivan reported that Washington sent "word to cross the Brandywine with my Division & attack the enemy's left while the army crossed below me to attack their Right. Lt. Col. Samuel Smith of the 4th Maryland Regiment, who was in Sullivan's division, says in his autobiographical account that (Lieutenant-Colonel Nathaniel) Ramsay, of the Maryland line, crossed the river, and skirmished with and drove the jaegers."[8] Just as the attack began, Sullivan was approached by Major Joseph Spear of the 8th Chester County militia. Spear, according to Sullivan, reported that he had come "from the upper country, that he had come in the road, where the enemy must have passed to attack our right, and that there was not the least appearance of them in that quarter."[9] Sullivan sent a report to Washington and ordered Spear to report to Washington in person. "Dear General — Since I sent you the message by Major Moore, I saw Major Spear of the militia, who came this morning from a tavern called Martin's at the fork of the Brandywine. He came from thence to Welsh's tavern and heard nothing of the enemy in that quarter; so that Colonel Hazen's information must be wrong. I have sent to that quarter, to know whether there is any foundation for the report, and shall give your Excellency the earliest information. I am. John Sullivan."[10]

Spear's account was confirmed by Sergeant William Tucker of the 1st Continental Dragoons, whom Sullivan had sent out "'on purpose to make discoveries & had passed on as he said to Lancaster Road.' Sullivan hesitated, however, before sending Spear's report to Washington. Sullivan later claimed that he doubted the truth of Spear's information and forwarded it only for fear that he would be blamed if it should prove correct and Washington's planned attack on Knyphausen be defeated. 'Had the General,' Sullivan wrote on October 6, 1777, 'crossed over (the Brandywine); left his own advantageous post...& found the whole British army well posted in his front & his Army put to the rout having a river unfordable in rear, except in one or two places & most of his troops pushed into it,...& he had afterwards found out that I had received & withheld the intelligence, which might have prevented this misfortune & demanded my reasons I believe I never shou'd have been able to give on[e] which wou'd be Satisfactory to him to congress or to the world.' Whatever Sullivan's doubts about Spear's information, he did not discuss them in his letter to Washington. Left to draw his own conclusions, Washington gave Spear's report too much weight, being induced by it 'to suppose that the [flanking] movement of the Enemy was a feint, & that they were returning to reinforce Knyphausen at Chad's Ford.' Any idea of attacking Knyphausen was abandoned. Washington later lamented that Spear's 'intelligence was no doubt a most unfortunate circumstance; as it served to derange the disposition that had been determined on in consequence of prior information, of the enemy's attempt to turn and attack our right flank, which ultimately proving true, too little time was left us, after discovering its certainty, to form a new plan, and make adequate arrangements to prevent its success.'"[11]

During the heat of the Battle of Brandywine Washington, once again, faced a serious dilemma. How did the Ross report fit with the Spear report? Which officer should Washington believe? Because of the lack of specifics of time and place in the reports, both men could have been correct. Spear's information was gathered in the morning hours; a notation on Spear's report indicated the observations might even have been made the night before the battle, long before Howe reached the forks of the Brandywine. Spear reported being at Martin's Tavern, which was a mile north of the route taken by Howe, thus he wouldn't have seen the British army. Spear's report offered another possibility, that Howe had feigned the flank-ing movement and was marching back toward Chadds Ford to join Knyphausen.

Colonel Pickering said Washington came to the conclusion that Howe indeed was on his way back to join Knyphausen. Washington wisely called off the assault on Knyphausen, if for the wrong reason. "Unresolved conflict of intelligence — rash to assume the offensive. Enemy might be waiting. Orders re-voked," Washington wrote.[12] Washington even dismissed a report from Sullivan, a brief time after the attack was cancelled, that Sullivan was convinced that Howe was flanking Wash-ington. By 2 p.m. Squire Thomas Cheyney made his impas-sioned plea to Washington concerning Howe's advance and Bland soon after confirmed Cheyney's report. "A quarter past one o'clock. Sir: I have discovered a party of the enemy on the heights, just on the right of the two Widow Davis's, who live close together on the road called the Fork Road, about half a mile to the right of the Meeting-house. There is a higher hill in front. — Theodorick Bland."[13] Washington knew for sure his army was in serious danger of being outflanked and destroyed.

"On the morning of the 11th Sept. 1777, we were apprised that the enemy was advancing; and soon after heard the en-gagement between our light troops and their advanced par-ties. Whilst their main design was in front to our right, the cannon ceased firing except now and then; and small detach-ments of our troops were constantly skirmishing with them. But in a short while, we found that they had crossed the Brandywine near the forks, and were coming in flank of our right wing," wrote Colonel James Chambers of the 1st Regi-ment of the Pennsylvania Line.[14] Chambers' command opposed Knyphausen at Chadds Ford and during the battle Chambers received a wound, a ball in his right side that would bother him the rest of his life.

* * * * *

Captain John Montresor, chief engineer of the British army, was with Howe as the long march began from Kennett Square.

He wrote, "At daybreak this morning the Commander in Chief with their body of the Army marched, consisting in this column, about 7000 men....A thick fog contributed greatly to favor our march. Passed the forks of the Brandywine Creek at Trumbull's Ford and at Jeffries' Ford and arrived upon an open clear height at ½ past 2 and halted and refreshed ourselves for an hour, during which time observed the Gross of the rebel army forming upon an opposite height, one mile and ½ from us and 2½ miles from Chad's Ford on the Brandywine."[15]

The Papers of George Washington at the University of Virginia report that Howe's column consisted of about 8,200 men and it departed Kennett Square at 5 a.m. and marched north along the Great Valley Road, avoiding settlements and initially enjoying the cover of fog. Howe's column consisted of two battalions of British light infantry, two battalions of British and three battalions of Hessian grenadiers, two battalions of British Guards, the 3rd and 4th British brigades, two squadrons of British dragoons, and mounted and dismounted German jaegers. Knyphausen's column, which contained about 6,800 men, set out an hour later. It consisted of a Hessian brigade, the 1st and 2nd British brigades, the 71st Regiment of Highland Scots, Capt. Patrick Ferguson's British riflemen, the Queen's Rangers, and a squadron of British dragoons. Both columns were accompanied by field artillery.

Captain Friedrich von Muenchhausen, aide de camp to Howe, described the morning's march in his diary and the sounds of the fighting between Maxwell and Knyphausen. He wrote:

> At five o'clock in the morning General Howe marched off to his left, up the Brandywine....Since our column had no baggage, but did have a number of sappers in the van, we moved forward quickly in spite of the great heat. During the march, we heard some small arm firing about 10 o'clock in the morning, and later, cannon shot, which continued almost during the whole march. At noon our vanguard came upon 200 rebel dragoons, who

wounded some of our men by their fire, but they soon retreated.

We crossed the Brandywine seven miles up from Chads Ford, where the river is divided into two branches; the bridges were destroyed. The men had to cross these two branches in up to three feet of water. We then continued our march a short distance straight ahead, and then suddenly to the right down along the Brandywine toward the region of Chads Ford.[16]

Howe placed in his front the German jaegers and light infantry companies from the 17th and 42nd Foot. The total number of troops was about 250 with Lieutenant Johann Hagen in charge of 15 mounted jaegers, and the Highlanders of the 42nd under Captain James McPherson while Captain William Scott led a company of light infantry. McPherson was in overall command while Captain Johann Ewald commanded the jaegers. The British didn't find any opposition from Washington's army and encountered only a few civilians during the march to Trimbles Ford on the West Branch of the Brandywine. By 11 a.m., the British army had completed the crossing at Trimbles Ford. The three-mile march between the two branches was also uneventful, but when the British reached Jeffries Ford on the East Branch of the Brandywine, they found three feet of water. Since the crossing was uncontested, the British took their time crossing and then dried out their equipment and clothing in the hot midday sun that had long ago burned off the last of the fog that helped cover Howe's advance. During the rest, British foragers discovered liquor stored in a barn, placed there by Wilmington merchants who thought that the spirits would be safer in a country barn than a city warehouse.[17] The alcohol and other goods of the Wilmington merchants were in the possession of Emmor Jefferis and "casks were rolled out, the heads knocked in, and the officers, quaffing the old Madeira, drank to its rebel owners."[18]

Ewald took his mounted troops to scout the next portion of the road while the soldiers rested in the sun. Ewald discovered an area that would be perfect for an ambush and reported his findings to Lord Cornwallis. Ewald wrote, "I was ordered to march as slowly as possible, and to use all caution in order not to fall into an ambuscade, as the area was traversed by hills, woodlands, marshes, and the steepest defiles....where the road ran up along a deep and winding precipice...I was astonished when I had safely reached the end of this terrible defile, which was over a thousand paces long, and could discover nothing of the enemy....The pass had been left wide open for us, where a hundred men could have held up either army the whole day."[19] Guiding Ewald during the dangerous march was a local man. Ewald was impressed with Chester County loyalist Curtis Lewis of East Caln Township, near present-day Downingtown. Ewald wrote that Lewis was a "veritable geographical Chart....I was often amazed at the knowledge that this man possessed of the country."[20]

As the British army moved slowly through the narrow defile, Ewald continued his advance scouting of the land. It was during this period that patriots Squire Cheyney and Colonel Hannum of the local militia spotted the British crossing the Brandywine at Jeffries Ford and that Bland's unit of the American army spotted and skirmished with the British. Bland reported the fighting took place at 1:15 p.m. After more than eight hours of marching undetected through the heartland of the rebel army's country, finally Americans who would convince Washington of the British advance detected Howe's flanking movement. Bland immediately asked Sullivan for help and reported that he saw dust kicked up by the British army rising in the country for about an hour. The discovery of the British troops by the Americans lessened Howe's chances of a total victory over Washington's forces. To survive September 11, 1777, Washington would quickly have to shift troops to stop Howe's advance while delaying Knyphausen's crossing of the Brandywine at Chadds Ford, thus allowing an orderly retreat toward Philadelphia.

* * * * *

Thursday, the day of the battle, was a day of meeting for the local Quakers. The Birmingham Meeting House was being used as a hospital for American soldiers, and members of the religious sect needed a place to gather and selected a wheelwright's shop in the small village of Sconneltown. The place the Quakers selected was on the direct route of Howe's army as the British soldiers marched to meet the Americans on the hills of Birmingham. Attending the meeting that day was a young Quaker, Joseph Townsend, who later wrote an account of what he witnessed of the Battle of Brandywine. Townsend was born on February 26, 1756, in East Bradford Township, near West Chester, then called Turk's Head, and was the seventh child of John and Joanna Townsend and a grandson of Joseph Townsend, who was born in Berkshire, England, in 1686 and immigrated to America in 1714. Joseph Townsend, the witness to the Battle of Brandywine, later moved to Baltimore and was a member of that city's Board of Health. He married three times and had 23 children before his death in 1841.

Commenting on the Quakers and Chester County at the time of the battle, Townsend wrote, "Several persons in the neighborhood, who had manifested a disposition to support the Americans, now thought it advisable to remove their families, stock and furniture to a distance, that it would be the consequence if left in their way. Others being of a different opinion, were disposed to remain at home and risk the danger that they might be exposed to, let the consequence be what it might. A majority of the inhabitants were of the Society of Friends, who could not consistently with their principles take any active part in the war, and who generally believed it right to remain in their dwellings, and patiently submit to whatever suffering might be their lot, and trust their all of a kind protecting Providence, who had hitherto protected and prospered their undertaking in an extraordinary manner, ever since their first settlement of the country under the proprietor and governor William Penn."[21]

On the morning of the battle Townsend decided to do a little exploring before attending the meeting. He wrote:

> Possessed of curiosity and fond of new things, my brother William Townsend and myself with some others, rode along side of the Brandywine for some distance, to discover the approach of the British army, in case they should attempt to cross any of the fords on the creek between Jefferis' and Chadd's; we fell in with many like ourselves, but no intelligence could be obtained. We then returned to the aforesaid wheelwright shop to assemble with Friends in holding our weekday meeting, being near the hour appointed. While we were sitting therein some disturbance was discovered near the house and about the door, which occasioned turning, and the uneasiness not subsiding, suspicions arose that something serious was taking place, the meeting accordingly closed.
>
> On our coming out of the house, and making some inquiry of what had happened, found it to be an alarm among some of the neighboring women, that the English army was coming, and that they murdered all before them, young and old. Some of us endeavored to quiet their fears by telling them it was not likely to be the case, and that they had better compose themselves than to make further disturbance, and that while we were reasoning with them, our eyes were caught on a sudden by the appearance of the army coming out of the woods into the fields belonging to Emmor Jefferis, on the west side of the creek above the fording place. In a few minutes the fields were literally covered with them, and they were hastening towards us. Their arms and bayonets being raised, shone as bright as silver, there being a clear sky and the day exceedingly warm.
>
> Recollecting that there was no one at our dwelling except some of our sisters, we concluded it advisable to return home as expeditiously as possible.[22]

Townsend's parents were at a daughter's home near Kennett Square caring for a sick grandchild. Townsend went home but immediately returned to the British army.

The space occupied by the main body and flanking parties was near half a mile wide. They inquired what sort of a man Mr. Washington was. My brother had a knowledge of him by being with him at his quarters at Chadd's Ford, and replied that he was a stately well proportioned, fine looking man, of great ability, active, firm and resolute, of a social disposition, and was considered to be a good man....One soldier said 'that he might be a good man, but he was most damnably misled to take up arms against his sovereign.'...Another said, 'You have got a hell of a fine country here, which we have found to be the case ever since we landed at the head of Elk.' Cornwallis passed by and he was on horseback, appeared tall and sat very erect. His rich scarlet clothing, loaded with gold lace, epaulets & c., occasioned him to make a brilliant and martial appearance. The advanced part of the army made a halt at this place, and refreshed their horses by hastily cleaning off some of the corn patches that were within their lines. It may be observed that most or all of the officers who conversed with us, were of first rank, and were rather short, portly men, were well dressed and of genteel appearance and did not look as if they had ever been exposed to any hardship; their skins being as white and delicate as is customary for females who were brought up in large cities or towns.

We reached the advanced guard, who were of the German troops. Many of them wore their beards on their upper lips which was a novelty in that part of the country. They were then between the dwelling of Richard Strode and Osborne's Hill.[23]

Townsend went along the road and came across soldiers forming for battle. A fence had to be removed and a German officer ordered Townsend to help with the aid of a drawn sword. "On the removal of the second rail, I was forcibly struck with the impropriety of being active in assisting to take the lives of my fellow beings, and therefore desisted proceeding any further in obedience to his commands."[24] Townsend later joined some friends on Osborne fields.

> It was now some time of seriousness and alarm among them....little was to be heard but the firing of the musketry and the roaring of cannon....It appeared those on horseback were some of the principal officers of the British army with their aides, who had collected together to consult respecting carrying on the engagement to the best advantage. Among them was General Howe. He was mounted on a large English horse much reduced in flesh, I suppose from their being so long confined on board the fleet between New York and the Head of the Chesapeake Bay, which was about six weeks, occasioned by contrary winds. The general was a large, portly man, of coarse features. He appeared to have lost his teeth, as his mouth had fallin in. As I stood alongside I had a full opportunity of viewing him as he sat on horseback, and had to observe his large legs and boots, with flourishing spurs thereon.
>
> While we remained on Osborne's hill, we had the opportunity of making many observation, the engagement of both armies, the fields in front of us containing great heaps of blankets and baggage of the British army, consisting of horse and foot, artillery, baggage and provision wagons, arms and ammunition, together with a host of plunders and rabble that accompanied the army.[25]

* * * * *

As Townsend watched, Howe and Cornwallis halted the advanced van of the British army and allowed them time to rest and take tea and nourishment. The break, after a 17-mile march, was needed. As the British enjoyed the rest, the American army began forming on the hills near the Birmingham Meeting House. Washington's papers placed the British one mile south of Osborne's Hill. They were less than three miles from his headquarters at Chadds Ford.

"Cornwallis knew when to hurry, and when to take his time. He had passed the pace for ten consecutive hours over sixteen miles of rough and unexplored country; and then he halted till the rear of his column had closed up, and deployed his whole force as coolly and methodically as if he were in Hyde Park....In front were the Guards, the grenadiers and light infantry, and the Hessian Chasseurs; while eight English battalions, twelve hundred Germans and two squadrons of cavalry followed in support, or in reserve. Cornwallis gave the word. His troops charged, and at both extremities of the line they charged home."[26]

As Washington's troops rushed to form lines to meet the enemy, the British army began its assault in three columns. The time was almost 4 p.m. on September 11, 1777.

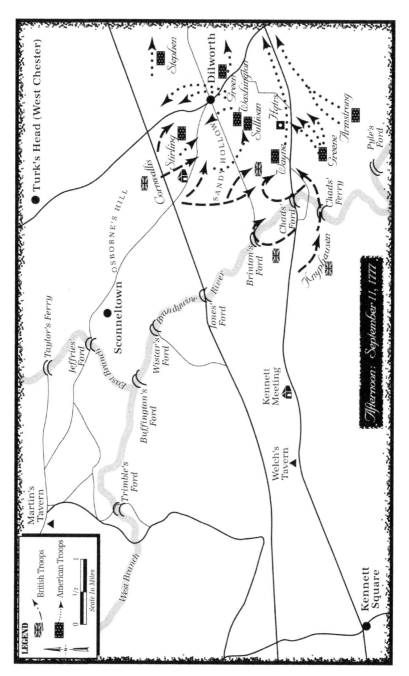

Turk's Head (West Chester)

Stephen

Dilworth

Green

Washington

Sullivan

Hetry

Cornwallis

Stirling

SANDY HOLLOW

Wayne

Greene

Armstrong

Pyle's Ford

OSBORNE'S HILL

Chads' Ferry

Brinton's Ford

Chads' Ford

Knyphausen

Taylor's Ferry

Sconneltown

East Branch

Brandywine River

Jones' Ford

Jeffries' Ford

Wistar's Ford

Buffington's Ford

Kennett Meeting

Trimble's Ford

Welch's Tavern

Martin's Tavern

West Branch

Kennett Square

Afternoon: September 11, 1777

LEGEND

British Troops

American Troops

Scale In Miles

0   1/2   1

N

Diane Cirafesi of Cirafesi Designs
West Chester, Pennsylvania

Eight

The Most Grand and Noble Sight Imaginable

With receipt of reliable intelligence as to the positions of the two sections of the British army, American General George Washington faced a crisis that threatened not only the survival of his army but also the future of the United States of America. Facing Washington across the Brandywine was General Wilhelm Knyphausen with at least 5,000 British and German soldiers and to Washington's north were General William Howe and Lord Cornwallis with about 8,000 more enemy troops completing a flanking movement that would pinch Washington's whole army between the two forces.

Washington ordered the divisions of William "Lord Stirling" Alexander and General Adam Stephen to move to the Birmingham Meeting House area to meet Howe's threat. At first Washington believed only two brigades were opposing him to the north per a communication from General William Sullivan. The troops of Stirling and Stephen set off at a trot; Stirling's division was at Brinton's Ford and reached the battleground before Stephen, who had a longer distance to travel. Washington decided to stay at Chadds Ford with General Nathanael Greene, still believing that the majority of the British forces were with Knyphausen. After dispatching the first two divisions, Washington ordered Sullivan to move his troops from Brinton's Ford to meet the enemy's threat and take command of the forces at Birmingham. Sullivan reported

117

receiving this order at 2:30 p.m. and beginning his march within five minutes.

"I...had not marched a mile," Sullivan later wrote, "when I met Colo. Hazen with his Regiment which had been Stationed at a Ford three miles above me who Informed (me) that the Enemy were Close upon his Heels & that I might Depend that the principal part of the British army were there: altho I knew the Reports Sent to head Quarters made them but two Brigades as I knew Colo. Hazen to be an old officer & a good Judge of Numbers I gave Credence to his Report in preference to the Intelligence before Received."[1] Sullivan wrote he was not sure of the exact position of the enemy but took the "most direct road for the enemy." With Hazen's troops leading his column, Sullivan advanced a mile and saw the advanced British troops. Sullivan ordered this troops to form on a hill and as he did so he saw the divisions of Stirling and Stephen on Birmingham Hill, almost a half mile to his right, and slightly to the rear, of his position.

The position of the American defenders didn't suit Sullivan, especially the large gap between the two units, and he rode to Birmingham Hill to consult with Stirling, Stephen, Brigadier General William Woodford, and other American officers. Stirling and Stephen were ordered to shift to the right as Sullivan ordered his troops to move to close the half-mile gap. Brigadier General Preudhomme de Borre insisted his troops should be given the honor of holding the extreme right of the line. De Borre pulled his men from their positions and marched them to the right, forcing a quick reorganization of the whole American line as Howe was poised to begin his assault. A portion of de Borre's division, a German regiment under his command, would be the first to break during the British assault, and de Borre would make no effort to stop them or rally them. Because of his conduct during the Battle of Brandywine, de Borre resigned from the American army rather than face a court of inquiry. Woodford of Stephen's division was ordered to shift his troops behind the hill to the American right, but the order was too late to adjust the position of

Colonel Thomas Marshall and the 170 men of his 3d Virginia Regiment. Marshall had been positioned in the woods to the right of the American line, near the Birmingham Meeting House, to protect the flank and several artillery pieces. The shifting lines left Marshall in advance of the American main line.

* * * * *

British Captain John Montresor wrote in his journal that at 2:30 p.m. his column "arrived upon an open clear height...and [we] halted and refreshed ourselves for an hour, during which time [we] observed the Gros(s) of the rebel army forming upon an opposite height."[2] The line formed by the Americans impressed Lord Cornwallis as he commented, "The damned rebels form well."[3] As the British prepared for the advance, officers encouraged their men and pointed out their objectives. Lieutenant Colonel William Meadows told the 1st Battalion of Grenadiers, "Grenadiers, put on your caps; for damned fighting and drinking I'll match you against the world."[4] The advance was organized, according to Major John Andre, the adjutant general of the British army, with the Guards forming upon the right, the British Grenadiers in the center, and the Light Infantry and Chasseurs on the left. The Hessian Grenadiers supported the Guards and British Grenadiers, and the 4th Brigade supported the Light Infantry on the right of the Grenadiers. The 3rd Brigade under General James Grey was the reserve. "At 4 p.m. with British regimental bands playing the 'Grenadiers March,' Cornwallis struck the American right with fury."[5] The assault was "the most Grand and Noble Sight imaginable, the Grenadiers beating their March as they advanced contributed greatly to the dignity of the Approach to battle."[6]

The Americans had a little fury of their own as the batteries of Sullivan's forces opened fire on the British and Marshall's 3rd Virginians began a fierce battle with their enemy. Sullivan remained in the center of the American line to take command and did not rejoin his units during their movement to the right. Montresor's journal described the initial action at Birmingham

Hill as follows, "Some skirmishing begun in the valley in which the enemy was drove, upon gaining something further of the ascent the enemy began to amuse us with 2 guns, the ground on the left being the most difficult the rebels disputed it with the Light Infantry with great spirit, particularly their officers, this spot was a ploughed hill and they covered by its summit and flanked by a wood....The British Grenadiers and Guards at the same time laboring under a smart and incessant fire from the Rebels out of a wood and above them, most nobly charged them without firing a shot and drove them before them, they covering their retreat with their Light Troops from one patch of woodland to another firing upon us, as we advanced into the cleared intervals until our Cannon surmounted the summits from one to another which effectually drove them."[7]

The first two British companies tested Marshall's men positioned in the orchard. The British halted their advance behind a fence. Then, as Sullivan was adjusting his lines to close the gap between the American forces, Howe adjusted his lines. "The sharp eyes of General Howe," Captain Friedrich von Muenchhausen, Howe's aide, wrote, "noticed (the movement of American troops) and at once ordered the 4th brigade to advance from the second to the first line, on the left wing. At the same time, the 3rd brigade, which at first was in reserve, was ordered to take the place of the now advanced 4th brigade."[8] As the British Guards swung too far to the right, a mistake that would eventually aid the British attack on American General Anthony Wayne's defense at Chadds Ford later in the day, Howe ordered the Hessian Grenadiers into the first line to fill the gap between the British Guards and Grenadiers. The British march across the fields of ripe wheat and corn was slow and uneven as numerous fences had to be torn down or climbed by the British forces. The American cannons opened fire as the British were almost halfway between Osborne's Hill and Birmingham Hill. The fire did not deter the British as the army continued its advance, even when the Americans changed from solid shot to canisters filled with deadly small missiles. The concentrated fire did drive the advancing British units to cover for a period of time. "The trees (were) crackling over ones head. The Branches riven by the artillery....The leaves falling as in autumn by the grapeshot."[9] Some of the American cannons used the stone walls near the Birmingham Meeting House's cemetery for protection.

While the Americans were inflicting casualties on the British, the Americans were also losing men. The 1st Maryland under Colonel John Stone was leading Sullivan's division and suffered when they moved from the left of the American line to the right. When de Borre's brigades broke and fled, a gap in the center of the American line couldn't be permanently filled and the Americans eventually gave way to the oncoming British. A British soldier reported that he and his fellow troops "ascended the hill and had a glimpse of the enemy's line as far as the eye could reach to the right and left....(The) enemy's guns were too far back on the heights to annoy us but, their line advancing on us, we were compelled to throw ourselves on our knees and bellies, and keep up a fire from the slope of the hill....The British light infantry captured five guns, the enemy running away from us with too much speed to be overtaken."[10]

The ensuing fighting on and around the hill was intense. " 'When we got close to the rebels,' Howe's aide-de-camp Captain von Muenchhausen, wrote in his diary entry for this date, 'they fired their cannon; they did not fire their small arms till we were within 40 paces of them, at which time they fired whole volleys and sustained a very heavy fire. The English, and especially the English grenadiers, advanced fearlessly and very quickly; fired a volley, and then ran furiously at the rebels with fixed bayonets.' Sullivan says in his account of the fighting: 'five times did the Enemy drive our Troops from the Hill & as often was it Regained....The General fire of the Line Lasted an hour & forty minutes Fifty one minutes of which the Hill was Disputed almost Muzzle to Muzzle in Such a manner that General Conway who has Seen much Service Says he never Saw So Close & Severe a fire.'"[11]

The British pressed their advance on the right of the American line and outflanked Stephen and Stirling. The Americans retreated and abandoned their cannons. As their right wing gave way, so did the American center, and a majority of the Americans, except for troops under Hazen, retreated to the second line of American defense southeast of Birmingham Hill. Some New Jersey regiments aided Hazen in keeping two cannons safe from the British, but the British reported taking nine cannons. The 1st Maryland, under Stone's command, had reached the left of Stirling's division when the Hessian Grenadiers attacked. The Maryland regiment was moving through a narrow lane when attacked and retreated to the top of the hill under a heavy fire by the British. Stone reported losing 23 men in the lane and Stone, himself, was thrown from his horse. Stone's retreat led to more divisions of the 1st brigade, the 3rd, 5th and 6th Maryland and the Delaware regiment to retreat. One Maryland officer reported he was told a retreat had been ordered. Another Maryland officer, Samuel Smith of the 4th Regiment, stayed in position with about 30 of his men until he was forced to withdraw.

Stone, who a few weeks later would be wounded at Germantown and would attain the rank of lieutenant colonel, wrote a letter two weeks after the battle which said:

> Washington did not know until 3 p.m. that enemy had crossed the Brandywine....their numbers were not known. Three divisions of our army were immediately ordered to march and meet them, but the enemy had got possession of the most advantageous grounds, and drawn within one and a half miles of our right before we marched, Genl Sullivan, Lord Stirling and Genl Greene's divisions marched to oppose the enemy, and perhaps might have routed them if things had been properly managed. Our division marched to join Lord Stirling who was on the ground where the enemy appeared, and where they seemed to intend their attack; by the time we reached the ground they had to cannonade the ground allotted to us, which was very bad, and the enemy within musket shot of it, before we were ordered to form the line of battle. I marched in front of Gen'l Sullivan's division,

when I received orders from him to wheel to the left and take possession of a rising ground 100 yards in our front, to which the enemy was marching rapidly. I wheeled off, but had not reached forming regularly, and by wheeling to the left it doubled our division on the brigade immediately in the rear of the other. Thus we were in confusion, and no person to undue us to order, when the enemy pushed on and soon made us all run off.

Of all the Maryland regiments only two ever had an opportunity to form, Gist's and mine, and as soon as they began to fire, those who were in our rear could not be prevented from firing also. In a few minutes we were attacked in front and flank, and by our people in the rear. Our men ran off in confusion, and were very hard to be rallied. Although my men did not behave so well as I expected, yet I can scarcely blame them when I consider their situation; nor are they censured by any part of the army. My horse threw in the time of action, but I did not receive any great injury from it. Lord Stirling's division, who were attacked at the same time we were, and routed at the same time. We retreated about a quarter of a mile and rallied all the men we could....[12]

The 33rd Foot was part of the British force attacking Stirling's forces. The unit history of the 33rd Foot reports, "There was no thought of fatigue in spite of the tiring march. The moment the word came the troops charged home. Soon the 33rd were in the thick of the fight and before long Sullivan's soldiers were in disorder. Lord Stirling, who was in Sullivan's center with some guns, fought with great determination, more than once driving back the attack. Being threatened vigorously on both flanks, to avoid capture he was compelled to retire to the stronger position afforded by the wood."[13] Stirling, while in England in the 1750s sought the earldom of Stirling, but failed to officially receive the title even though he was known as Lord Stirling. Sir George Otto Trevelyan wrote of Stirling and this action in his history of the American Revolution, "Two brigades, on the American right, broke and fled; and Sullivan's own division, after a short resistance, escaped in disorder to the rear. Lord Stirling, in the center, had come early on to the ground and had found time to plant his cannon, and drew up his battalions, in accordance with his own rigid notions of military perfection. He repelled the attacks delivered by the troops in front of him; and he made a stout fight of it even when some victorious British regiments, which had disposed of their own opponents, clustered in on him from several quarters. Sullivan, after vainly trying to rally the fugitives of his own division, exerted himself with desperate valour to maintain this last fragment of his line of battle. Two of his aides-de-camp were killed."[14]

Sullivan was trying to bring some order and discipline to the American line and dispatched four aides to rally them. The attempt failed, and except for Hazen, Sullivan's division of 1,300 men did not fight again that day. Hazen's forces were on the left of Sullivan's line and held off a charge by the Hessian grenadiers who were not supported by other nearby British troops because of American artillery fire. Colonel Thomas Marshall's 3rd Virginia continued to harass the British troops attacking toward Birmingham Meeting House as American artillery protected Marshall's forces without firing too closely to them because of a fear of endangering them. The 1st battalion of British light infantry advanced on Marshall's position and thus avoided artillery fire by Stephen's guns. The light infantry was joined by other British troops near the meeting house and they advanced on Marshall with the 17th light infantry on the right and 42nd Foot on the left. Marshall's unit fired and retreated to the Birmingham Meeting House where they took positions behind a stone wall and continued to fire upon members of the light infantry. Eventually, the regiments of the light infantry made their way around Marshall and the meeting house.

As the light infantry was attacking, General Cornwallis ordered Lieutenant Colonels William Meadows and Henry Monckton of the 1st and 2nd British grenadiers to attack. The jaegers, under Captain Ewald, joined Monckton. General Howe had advanced to join his troops as the British pushed the American lines at every point. As Stephen's troops were being driven from their positions near Birmingham Meeting House, Stirling's men exchanged volleys with the British grenadiers and stopped them for a moment. The delay in the British advance was brief as the grenadiers fixed bayonets and charged Stirling's men. Stirling and General Thomas Conway did everything they could to steady their men, but strong pressure on both flanks by the British caused a collapse. Hazen's regiment was protecting Stirling's left but was driven off by the charge of the Hessian grenadiers. "Four officers, and seventy three non-commissioned officers and rank and file of the regiment were killed, wounded and taken prisoner."[15] Woodford's brigade of Stephen's division were the only Americans now on Birmingham Hill. As the left of the American line crumbled, Marshall's 3rd Virginia was ordered to withdraw. Also, Marshall's men suffered additional casualties from friendly fire.

It was a battered regiment that finally reached Woodford's position by circling around the back of the hill. Colonel Thomas Marshall, father of future chief justice, John Marshall, was on foot, his horse having "received two balls...Captain (John) Chilton was killed, (Captain Philip) Lee mortally wounded...Lieutenants (William) White, (Apollos) Cooper, and ensign (Robert) Peyton were killed; lieutenants (John Francis) Mercer, (John) Blackwell and (John) Peyton wounded...Thirteen non-commissioned officers and sixty privates fell" out of 150 men in the regiment.

Even after Marshall had reached Woodford's position, Woodford held on in order to give the other parts of Sullivan's force time to regroup. But the British would not be denied the hill. They would bring up their cannon and fire grape shot. Woodford had not seen the enemy emplace these cannon, and suddenly the British artillery took them obliquely. With a flash, "Woodford's Capt. Of Artillery and 3 Lieuts were wounded and more than half his men killed." In addition "the horses were shot down," eliminating any chance of saving Stephen's "two field pieces."

Further, in this sudden cannonade, Woodford was wounded and retired from the hill to have his wounds dressed. Finally, the cannon fire ceased and the 1st light infantry could be seen by the men of Woodford's brigade charging at them. They were within twenty yards when the Woodford brigade gave way and plunged into the woods down the back of the hill, leaving Birmingham Hill totally in possession of the British, along with many prisoners and equipment.[16]

A Hessian officer described the action on Birmingham Hill: "At 4 o'clock the columns advanced to attack, the center column along the main road, and the other two on both sides through valleys and woods. When they had come close enough, they formed in line and advanced upon the enemy, who received them with a heavy fire of cannon and musketry. Our men, however, made a spirited attack with their bayonets and drove them back into the woods, following close upon their heels. Colonel von Donop with the Hessian grenadiers supported the English brigade of Guards throughout, as he had been ordered to do. Three companies of light infantry threw themselves against the flank of the enemy's right wing, which seemed to be outflanking our line, and after turning it back, rejoined their battalion. The Hessian grenadiers joined the English grenadiers in the line. General Agnew, however, in spite of great efforts, was unable to align completely the fourth brigade forming the left wing, because of the rough terrain. Thus the left flank of the 2nd English Grenadier Battalion was unsupported for some time and was compelled to fall back a little before the enemy's attack. However, General Agnew did arrive to support this battalion, the enemy withdrew all along the line from one height to another. Though they fought stubbornly all the way, they were compelled to escape towards Chester. By five o'clock in the evening the entire column had gained a victory and advanced far enough to join our column on the Brandywine hills at nightfall."[17]

After the firing on Birmingham Hill had concluded, Quaker Joseph Townsend and his friends followed the British army to the Birmingham Meeting House where wounded were being treated. He reported, "We hastened thither and awful was the scene to behold — such a number of fellow beings lying together severely wounded, and some mortally a few dead, but a small proportion of them considering the immense quantity of powder and ball that had been discharged. It was now time for surgeons to exert themselves, and divers of them were busily employed. After assisting in carrying two of them into the house I was disposed to see an operation performed by one of the surgeons, who was preparing to amputate a limb by having a brass clamp or screw fitted thereon, a little above the knee joint, he had his knife in his hand, the blade of which was of a circular form, and was about to make an the incision when he recollected that it might be necessary for the wounded man to take something to support him during the operation. The officer refused alcohol. No doctor, it is not necessary, my spirits are up enough without it."[18] Townsend and friends helped in the care of the wounded, and reported officers received attention before enlisted men.

* * * * *

Washington was aware Sullivan's forces were facing a strong British force and wrote to Congress in a note dated 5 p.m. from Chadds Ford: "There has been a scattering loose fire between our parties on each side of the Creek, since the action this morning which just now became warm, when Genl. Maxwell pushed over with his corps....At half after 4 o'clock the enemy attacked Genl. Sullivan at the Ford next above and the action has been very violent ever since. It still continues. A very severe cannonade has begun here too and I suppose we shall have a very hot evening. I hope it will be a happy one."[19] Washington would not get his wish this day.

Washington maintained his position near Proctor's batteries on the heights overlooking the Brandywine. When word was received that Sullivan had been pushed off Birmingham Hill, Washington ordered more troops diverted from Chadds Ford to aid Sullivan. General Greene's forces, acting as reserve for Wayne, were sent along with General Francis Nash's North Carolina brigade. At Germantown Nash had his thigh broken by a cannon ball and he died three days later. "Nash's North Carolina Brigade did not get into action that hot, dusty afternoon. It had been held in reserve, but had been near enough to the action to see the haze of battle and be stung by the pungent odor of burnt powder. Upon one occasion the men were within fifty yards of the enemy and were prepared to meet them with the bayonet when the British were driven back."[20] Greene was ordered to aid Sullivan and also keep the road to Philadelphia open for a possible retreat. A new volunteer American officer, Marie Joseph Paul Yves Roch Gilbert du Motier, Marquis de Lafayette, offered to rush to help Sullivan. This would be the first battle in the American Revolution for Lafayette, the young Frenchman who would be instrumental in obtaining French aid for the Americans.

Lafayette, the wealthy son of a French army officer, had married Marie Adrienne Francoise de Noailles when he was 16 and already a three-year veteran of the army. Lafayette, despite opposition from French rulers, joined the American army and was appointed a major general by the Continental Congress on July 31, 1777. Washington and Lafayette quickly entered into a close and lasting friendship. A few days after his 20th birthday Lafayette was at Brandywine, rushing to meet the British army. Lafayette arrived near Sandy Hollow, south of the Birmingham Meeting House, as the British 2nd light infantry was attacking Conway's forces. Sullivan, Stirling, and Conway had backed down Birmingham Hill, seeking a defensive position to stop the British advance and to give Woodford's brigade, including Marshall's 3rd Virginians, a chance to escape. Sullivan selected a four hundred-foot elevation southeast of Birmingham Hill, along Forks Road. Conway's brigade and two cannons were posted there while Hazen's regiment was sent to another hill, about seven hundred yards away on the east side of Forks Road.

Forks Road was being used as a route of retreat by American units, including Woodford and Stephen. They were aiming to regroup near the village of Dilworth, but a segment of the British army, including the 2nd Light Infantry battalion and the jaegers, attacked the retreating Americans. Some of the British troops had been delayed because of swampy land encountered along Radley Run and had fallen behind the rest of Howe's forces. A gap in the British line developed and Howe filled the hole with troops of the 4th brigade. As Stirling tried to protect his retreating compatriots, the British routed Stephens' men and they scattered. At this point Lafayette joined Conway, a fellow French volunteer, and fierce fighting, some hand-to-hand, took place in the woods west of Sandy Hollow. "Lafayette alighted (from his horse) and did all he could to make the men charge at the point of a bayonet...but the Americans, little used to this sort of fighting, did not care to do so, and soon this brigade fled like the rest of the army."[21]

* * * * *

While rallying his new comrades, Lafayette took a ball in the left calf of his leg. The wound would require two months of recuperation in Bethlehem, Pennsylvania, before he would be able to rejoin Washington's army. During that period he wrote several times to his wife to reassure her that his life was not in danger. The day after the battle Lafayette sent a letter to his wife from Philadelphia. "I send you a few lines, dear heart, by some French officers, my friends, who came here with me but have not obtained positions and are returning to France. I shall begin by telling you that I am well, because I must end by telling you that we fought in earnest yesterday, and we were not the victors. Our Americans, after holding firm for a considerable time, were finally routed. While I was trying to rally them, the English honored me with a musket shot, which wounded me slightly in the leg. But the wound is nothing, dear heart; the ball hit neither bone nor nerve, and all I have to do for it to heal is to lie on my back for a while—which puts me in very bad humor. I hope, dear heart, that you will not worry; on the contrary, you should be even less worried than before, because I shall now be out of action for some time....This battle will, I fear, have unpleasant consequences for America; we must try to repair the damage, if we can. You must have received many letters from me, unless the English are as hostile to my letters as to my legs....Last night was spent in our retreat and in my journey here, where I am very well cared for."[22]

Two weeks after the battle Lafayette wrote to Henry Laurens of South Carolina, "My leg is about in the same state and without your kindness would be in a very bad one."[23] Laurens, who would become president of Congress, began a close friendship with Lafayette on their journey to Bethlehem. In a letter of October 18, 1777, Lafayette wrote to Laurens from Bethlehem, "At length I go to camp, and I see the end of my so tedious confinement. My wound (thro' the skin is not yet quite over) seems to me in so fine a way of recovery that I judge myself able to play my part in our first engagement."

Lafayette attempted to calm his wife about his wound and assure her that he was not placing himself needlessly in danger. In a letter to Adrienne from Bethlehem on October 1, 1777, he wrote, "I wrote to you, dear heart, on the twelfth of September; the twelfth is the day after the eleventh. About that particular eleventh, I have a tale to tell you. To put the best face on it, I could tell you that mature reflection had induced me to remain in my bed for several weeks, sheltered from all danger. But I must admit that I was invited to stay there because of a very slight wound in the leg. I do not know how I received it; in truth, I did not expose myself to the enemy fire. It was my first battle, so you see how rare battles are.... But we are speaking of my wound; the ball passed through the flesh and touched neither bone nor nerve. The surgeons are astonished by the rate at which it heals; they are in ecstasy every time they dress it, and maintain that it is the most beautiful thing in the world. I myself find it very foul, very tedious, and rather painful; there is no accounting for tastes. But finally, if a man wished to be wounded just for his own amusement, he should come and see my wound and have one just like it. There, dear heart, you have the story of what I pompously call my wound, to give myself airs and to make myself interesting."[24]

A full year after the wound Lafayette wrote another letter to his wife concerning the wound. This letter was to Adrienne from Bristol near Rhode Island on September 13, 1778. "It is now more than a year since I dragged about at Brandywine with one leg in rather bad condition; since then there no longer seems to be even a (slight wound) there, and my left leg is almost as strong as the right. That is the only scratch I have had and the only one I shall ever have."

* * * * *

About 4:30 p.m., with the battle raging at Birmingham Hill and Knyphausen beginning his attack across the Brandywine, Washington decided to join Sullivan and allow Wayne to handle Knyphausen. Washington and his staff, which included Count Casimir Pulaski, Alexander Hamilton, aide John Laurens, and Colonel Charles Pinckney of South Carolina, rushed to Birmingham Hill. In seeking out the fastest route he enlisted an elderly farmer, Joseph Brown, to lead him to the battle. Brown declined but was forced into service. Legends, one printed more than 70 years after the battle, have an aide threatening Brown with death by the sword if he didn't lead the way to Birmingham. During the harrowing ride, which included jumping a number of fences at a gallop, Washington is supposed to have kept telling Brown, "Push along, old man. Push along, old man." This version is discounted by a number of historians, as Washington's actions don't match the future president's documented demeanor.

By the time Washington and officers and men of Greene's command reached Birmingham, the British had routed Sullivan's forces. The retreating American army was in danger of being destroyed. Greene's divisions under Muhlenberg and Weedon came upon the scene just in time to end the rout. Muhlenberg, son of a Lutheran missionary and himself a Lutheran clergyman, was educated in Germany and had served in the Prussian army. Greene wrote, "I marched one brigade of my division...between three and four miles in forty-five minutes. When I came upon the ground I found the whole of the troops routed and retreating precipitately, and in the most broken and confused manner. I was ordered to cover the retreat...." Lt. James McMichael of Weedon's brigade says in his diary entry for this date: "We took the front and attacked the enemy at 5:30 P.M., and being engaged with their grand army, we at first were obliged to retreat a few yards and formed in an open field, when we fought without giving way on either side until dark." Greene says in his account: "We were engaged an hour and a quarter, and lost upwards of an hundred men killed and wounded. I maintained the ground until dark, and then drew off the troops in good order."[25]

"Opening their ranks, the fresh Americans allowed their exhausted comrades to stagger through and re-form closing their ranks again to confront the flower of Europe. At first they held them, backed up by artillery. But the British pressure was too great, and Greene began a slow, fighting retreat. Coming to a narrow defile, flanked on both sides by thick woods, the Americans turned again—holding off their pursuers with a steady fire. Still the enemy pressed forward, resorting for the first time to regular volleys of musketry, launching repeated bayonet charges. The fighting raged so close, sometimes hand to hand, that the Anspachers recognized their old comrade, Colonel Muhlenberg, who had fought with them as an enlisted man. 'Hier kommt Teufel Piet!' they cried in delight. 'Here comes Devil Pete!' But the Americans doggedly held the pass for forty-five minutes. At last the sun went down, and Greene skillfully drew off his entire division. Exhausted, the British and Hessians made no attempt to follow."[26] One soldier in the 3rd New Jersey wrote, "We broke and Rallied and Rallied & broke from height to height till we fell on our main Army (Greene) who reinforced us & about sunset we made a stand."[27] Weedon's brigade, especially the 10th Virginia and Colonel Walter Steward's Pennsylvania regiment, bore the brunt of the attack.

Washington met with Generals Sullivan and Greene on Harvey Road where it was decided that Weedon's brigade would halt and take the British in the flank as they came down the road. Pickney was dispatched to tell Weedon of the plan and have the men under Colonel Alexander Spottswood and Colonel Edward Steven halt in the plowed field, the southern side of Sandy Hallow. The Delaware regiment was one unit saved by the arrival of Greene and Weedon. The Delaware men had withstood cannonading by the British for an hour and then close combat. "Cannon balls flew thick and many and small arms roared like the rolling of a drum. Finally, Stephen's division on the right, which took heavy fire, retreated. The order to withdraw was given....We had marched about half-a-mile and crossed a road at right angles when Lord Stirling rode up. Officer, says he, General Washington is in the rear. Face about! I did so, as the British were firing on us. I looked about for his Lordship to obey his further orders, but saw my Lord whipping and spurring down the road at a full gallop. Some of our soldiers were wounded. I thought 'Well, I have no business here fighting in this place. I can do no good'...with quick marching I fell back."[28]

As Muhlenberg advanced to attack the British, his men were hampered by Sullivan's retreating command. Sullivan was later able to re-form some of his soldiers. Helping to blunt the British attack on the American right was Pulaski. Pulaski took charge of about 30 horsemen and charged. Pulaski also helped to rally some of Sullivan's men and oppose the British under General James Agnew.

* * * * *

One of Pulaski's cavalry members years late wrote about the Battle of Brandywine:

> We had been in the saddle about an hour, under the intrepid Pulaski, who, with his own hands, examined our swords, pistols, and other equipments, as if assured that the struggle would be deadly and a long continued one. The day was one of the most beautiful that ever broke over the earth. We were about a half a mile from the main body, ranged along a green slope, facing the west, our horses, about four hundred in number, standing as patiently

as so many marble statues; until just as the eastern sky began to redden and undulate; and cloud after cloud to roll up, and heave like a great curtain up the wind; and the whole heaven seemed discharging all its beauty upon one spot.

I happened to turn about, and saw the tall Pole (Pulaski) bare-headed, tilting his horse, like some warlike presence come up out of the solid earth to worship upon the very summit of the hill behind us; it might be, (for the noble carriage of the man, the martial bearing of the soldier, would permit either interpretation) it might be in the awful employment of devotion or in the more earthly one of observation: But suddenly he reined up his charger, shook the heavy dew from his horseman's cap, replaced it and leaped headlong down the hill, just as a bright flash passed away on the horizon, followed by a loud report; and the next instant a part of our ranks were covered with dust and turf, thrown up by a cannon ball that struck near the spot he had just left.

Our horses pricked up their ears at the sound, and all at once, as if a hundred trumpets were playing in the wind, came the enemy in his advance. Pulaski unsheathed his sword, called out a select body, and set off at full gallop, to a more distant elevation, where we saw the enemy advancing in two columns; one under Knyphausen, which moved in tremendous steadiness, in a dark solid mass, towards the spot occupied by General Maxwell, the other under Cornwallis, which seemed to threaten the right flank of our main body. Intelligence was immediately sent to Washington, and reinforcements called in, from the spot we had left.

We kept our position, awaiting for a whole hour, the sound of conflict; at last a heavy volley rattled along the sky, a few moments passed, and then another followed, like a storm of iron upon drum heads. The whole air rang with it; another, and another followed; then gradually increasing in loudness, came peal after peal, till it resembled

a continual clap of thunder, rolling about under an illu-
minated vapor. But Pulaski, with all his impetuosity, was
a general, and knew his duty too well, to hazard any movement till he should be able to see with certainty the operation of the enemy in the vapor below.

Meanwhile, several little parties which had been sent
out came in, one after the other, with the intelligence that
Knyphausen had broken down upon Maxwell in magnificent style — been beaten back again; but that he had finally
prevailed, and that Maxwell had retreated across the river.
A thin vapor had risen from the green earth below us and
completely covered the enemy from our view. It was no
longer possible to follow him, except by the sounds of his
tread, which we could feel in the solid earth, jarring ourselves and our horses; and now and then, a quick glim-
mering in the midst, as some standard raised above it;
some weapon flourished, or some musket shot through it
like a rocket.

About an hour after, a horseman dashed through the
smoke on the very verge of the horizon, and after scouring the fields, for a whole mile in view, communicated
with two or three others, who set off in different directions; one to us, with orders to hurry down to the ford,
where the commander-in-chief was determined to fall on
Knyphausen with all his power, before Cornwallis could
come to his aid. It was noble but hazardous game. And
Pulaski, whose war horse literally thundered and light-
ened along the broken and stony precipice by which we
descended, kept his eye warily to the right as if not quite
certain that the order would not be countermanded.

We soon fell in with General Greene, who was posting, all on fire, to give Knyphausen, battle and the next
moment saw Sullivan in full march over a distant hill towards the enemy's flank. This arrangement would, doubt-
less, have proved fatal to Knyphausen, had not our
operations been unfortunately arrested at the very moment we were prepared to fall upon him, man and horse,

the intelligence that Cornwallis had moved off to another quarter. It was a moment of irresolution—doubt. It was the death blow to our brilliant hopes of victory. Greene was recalled, and Sullivan commanded to halt.

Hardly had this happened, our horses being covered with sweat, and froth, fretting in the bit like chained tigers, and ourselves covered with dust, it being an excessively hot and sultry day, when a heavy cannonade was heard on our right flank, and Greene, to whose division we had attached, was just into motion to support Sullivan who had left home some hours before. The truth now broke upon us like a thunderclap. The enemy had passed, concentrated, we supposed, and fallen on our right.

I shall never forget Greene's countenance when the news came; he was on the road side, upon an almost perpendicular bank, but he wheeled where he was, dashed down the bank, his face white as the bleached marble, and called to us to gallop forward, which such a tremendous impulse, that we marched four miles in forty minutes. We...on our way in a cloud of dust...met Sullivan all in disorder, nearly a mile from the ground, retreating step by step, at the head of his men, and shouting himself hoarse, covered with blood and sweat, and striving in vain to bring them to stand, while Cornwallis was pouring in upon them an incessant volley.

Pulaski dashed out to the right, over the broken fences, and there stood awhile upright in his stirrups, reconnoitering, while the enemy, who appeared, by the smoke and the dust that rolled before them in the wind, to be much nearer than they really were, redoubled their efforts; but at last, Pulaski saw a favorable opportunity. The column wheeled; the wind swept across their van, revealing them like a battalion of spirits, breathing fire and smoke. He gave the signal: Archibald repeated it, then Arthur; then myself. In three minutes, we were ready for the word.

When Pulaski, shouting in a voice that thrilled through and through us struck spurs into his charger; it was a half minute, so fierce and terrible was his charge, before we were able to come up with him. What could he mean!—Gracious heaven! My hand convulsively, like that of a drowning man, reined up for a moment when I saw we were galloping straight forward into a field of bayonets: yet he was the first man! And who would not have followed.

We did follow him, and with such a hurricane of fire and steel, that when we wheeled our whole path lay broad before us, with a wall of fire on the right hand and on the left; but not a bayonet or a blade in front, except what were under the hoofs of our horses. My blood rushes now, like a flash of fire through my forehead, when I recall the devastation that we then made, almost to the very heart of the enemy's column.

But Pulaski, he who afterwards rode into their retrenchments on horseback, sword in hand, was accustomed to it; and having broken over them once, aware of his peril if he should give them time to awake from their consternation, he wheeled in a blaze of fire, with the intention of returning through a wall of death, more perilous than that which shut in the children of Israel, upon the Rea Sea. But on! The wall had rolled in upon us; and we were left no alternative but to continue as we had begun.

The undaunted Pole rioted in the excess of his joy! I remember well how he passed me, covered with sweat and dust, riding absolutely upon the very points of their bayonets. But at last, they pressed upon him, and horseman after horseman fell from their saddles; when we were all faint and feeble, and even Archibald was fighting on foot, over his beautiful horse, with Arthur battling over his head, we heard the cry of "Succor! Succor!" immediately we felt the enemy give way, heaving this way, then that, and finally concentrating beyond us.

"Once more! Once more!" cried Pulaski and away he went, breaking in upon them as they were forming;

and trampling down whole platoons in the charge, before a man could plant his bayonet or bring his gun to an aim; our aspect, as we came thundering round them, was sufficient; the enemy fled, and we brought off our companions unhurt.

I have been in many a battle, many a one that made my hair afterwards stand when I dreamed of it; — but never in one where the carnage was so dreadful: and firing so incessant as that which followed the arrival of Greene. But the enemy had so effectually secured his exposed points by ranks of men kneeling with planted bayonets, that we could make no impression upon them, although we rode upon them again and again, discharging our pistols in their faces.[29]

* * * * *

The British had the 2nd Light Infantry, 2nd Grenadiers and the 4th brigade ready to meet the reformed Americans. "As the new British line moved forward, it passed what is now Webb Road and suddenly 'ran into several American regiments.' Weedon's men who were under good cover, held their fire until the flank of the British line was almost directly in front of them. Then Weedon's men 'gave the Enemy such a check as produced the desired effect.' Captain Ewald was more specific regarding the effectiveness of Weedon's fire. He said 'there was terrible firing. And...nearly all of the officers of these two regiments the (46th) and 64th were slain.'"[30]

The 64th Foot pressed forward despite suffering a number of casualties, at least until it suffered additional losses from Muhlenberg's men. The British halted until reinforced. Captain John Montresor, chief engineer of the British army, reported, "We then pursued them through Dilworth Town and drove them for one mile and a ½ beyond it, to the skirt of the wood, where they had collected and from whence they fired on us particularly on the Guards and 4th Brigade, the heaviest fire during the action....At the Battle of Brandywine, 11th Sept. 1777, I directed the position and attack of most of the field train, and late in the evening when the action was near concluded a very heavy fire was received by our Grenadiers from 6000 Rebels, Washington's rear Guard, when Col. Monckton requested me to ride through it to Brigadier-General Agnew's Brigade, and his 4 twelve Pounders, which I did in time enough to support them and by my fixing the 4 twelve Pounders, Routed the Enemy."[31]

The unit history of the 64th Foot reported, "Cornwallis formed his men in two lines, and with the 4th Brigade as left support, and 3rd Brigade in reserve, advanced in the direction of Dilworth. He soon came on the enemy, whom he attacked with great impetuosity, and drove them into the woods in the rear; they however rallied and took up a second position in some woods near Dilworth, but were dislodged after a desperate resistance, by the 2nd Light Infantry. This corps, with the 2nd Grenadiers, and the 4th Brigade, now moved forward a mile beyond Dilworth, where they found a fresh body of the enemy, strongly posted to cover their retreat, whom they did not dislodge until after it was dark....The 64th lost Captain Nairne, and 4 men killed, besides Major Mackleroth, Lts. Jacob, Torianno, Wynward and Ensigns Freemand and Grant, five sergeants and 31 men were wounded."[32] The 46th Regiment, known as the South Devonshire Regiment of Foot "sustained but trifling loss," its unit history reported.

The heroic stands of the American army at Birmingham Hill, Sandy Hollow, and Dilworth stopped the mighty British army at times, but the British had many heroes of their own. The East Yorkshire Regiment, the 15th Regiment of Foot, ran short of ball ammunition during the fight. "They were in a thick wood, with the enemy advancing on them in large numbers, when the situation was reported to the commanding officer, Lt.-Col. John Bird. That resourceful man was quite equal to the occasion. 'Then snap and be damned,' he ordered — and snap the 15th did. That is to say all available ball ammunition was handed over to the best shots, and the rest of the battalion were ordered to keep snapping — fire small blank charges of powder — while running from tree to tree. The ruse worked, the American colonists were completely deceived and were successfully held in check until reinforcements arrived to make victory certain."[33] Bird died in the fighting at Germantown.

As Howe pressed the Americans on Birmingham Hill and beyond, Knyphausen's forces were forcing a crossing of the Brandywine at Chadds Ford against the troops of General Anthony Wayne. The British were attempting to trap and destroy Washington's army between their two advancing columns.

John Chad House

The home of John Chad, a ferryman, stood about a half mile north of the ford where General Knyphausen crossed the Brandywine to engage General Anthony Wayne's men during the late afternoon of September 11, 1777.

Chester County Historical Society, West Chester, Pennsylvania

Nine

Much Stained with Blood

General Wilhelm Knyphausen waited and watched until late afternoon from the cover of the western bank of the Brandywine River for the British force under General William Howe to complete its flanking movement and attack the Americans' right flank. When the Grenadiers' March was played and the attack on Birmingham Hill began, the first phase of Knyphausen's assignment successfully concluded. Knyphausen had held American General George Washington's troops at Chadds Ford and allowed Howe's force to gain an advantageous position to attack the rear of Washington's army.

In front of Knyphausen were American troops commanded by General Anthony Wayne, who was fighting on his home Chester County turf. Wayne's troops vigorously contested Knyphausen's crossing of the Brandywine. The result, as a sergeant in the British 4th Regiment of Foot said, was that the river was "much stained with blood."[1] Before the British units rushed across the Brandywine, Knyphausen subjected the Americans to an artillery bombardment and Colonel Thomas Proctor's American guns returned the fire.

Sir George Otto Trevelyan described the advance, "After hearing the cannon fire of Cornwallis, Knyphausen sent his infantry across Chads Ford in a dense succession of regiments, distinguished one from another by numerals which are all of them so many titles of honor in the estimation of an old-fashioned Englishman. The Fourth Foot, the Fifth

Foot, the Seventy-First Glasgow highlanders and the Twenty-Third Fusiliers, splashed through the water, scrambled up the bank, ran over the ditch and parapet and captured a hostile breast-work with many of the defenders, and all the cannon. They drove the Republicans before them in a running fight, from one enclosure to another; until the British Guards, who had lost their way in the thicket, but had kept their faces in the right direction, stumbled up against Anthony Wayne's retreating battalions and scattered them in a hopeless rout. Washington's army was now caught between two bodies of troops, advancing at right angles to each other from two widely separated points and meeting at last on the field of victory."[2]

Leading the advance at the Chads Ferry section of Chadds Ford at approximately 5:15 p.m. was the 4th Foot, known as The King's Own Regiment. A unit history says, "At 4 o'clock sounds of musketry warned the waiting troops that Cornwallis had reached his objective, and the King's Own and the 5th Regiment led Knyphausen's column across the river. Lt. Col. James Ogilvie commanded the King's Own as it led the attack in gallant style and rushed through the stream with fixed bayonets. They advanced under a heavy fire of round and canister shot, and overpowering all opposition, drove the Americans out of their entrenchments and captured three brass pieces and a five and a half inch howitzer. The King's Own pressed upon the retiring enemy, and at this moment the Guards came blundering through the woods, accidentally, but happily, upon the enemy's flank. The retreat now became general, but darkness came down before an attempt could be made to pursue and Washington's army escaped."[3]

Waiting for the attack by the British troops led by Ogilvie were members of the 1st Regiment of the Pennsylvania line led by Colonel James Chambers. During the battle Chambers received a wound to his right side that would later in life cause him frequent and troubling illnesses. In a letter he authored several days after the battle, Chambers wrote:

> The cannonade commenced, about three o'clock but
> soon gave way to small arms, which continued like an

incessant clap of thunder till within an hour of sunset, when our people filed off. Then the attack began with us on the left. But I must observe to you that while the right was engaged, the troops that were on the right of our brigade on the hill were drawn off...and left our right flank quite uncovered. The enemy kept an unremitted fire from their artillery (and ours too, played with great fury) until advancing under the thick smoke they took possession of the redoubt in front of our park.

As there were no troops to cover the artillery in the redoubt—the enemy was within thirty yards before being discovered—our men were forced to fly and to leave three pieces behind. Our brigade was drawn into line, with the park of artillery two hundred yards in the rear of the redoubt. Our park was ordered off then, and my right exposed. The enemy advanced on the hill where our park was, and came within fifty yards of the hill above me. I then ordered my men to fire. Two or three rounds made the lads clear the ground.

The General (Wayne) sent orders for our artillery to retreat—it was on my right—and ordered me to cover it....It was done but to my surprise the artillerymen had run and left the howitzer behind. The two field pieces went up the road protected by about sixty of my men, who had very warm work, but brought them safe. I then ordered another party to fly to the howitzer and bring it off. Captain Buchanan, Lt. Stimson and Lt. Douglass went immediately to the gun, and the men followed their example, and I covered them with the few I had remaining. But before this could be done the main body of the foe came within thirty yards and kept up the most terrible fire I suppose ever heard in America: though with very little loss on our side. I brought all of the brigade artillery safely off, and I hope to see them again fired at the scoundrels. Yet we retreated to the next height in good order, in the midst of a very heavy fire of cannon and small arms. Not thirty yards distant, we formed to receive them, but they did not choose to follow.

I lost Lieutenants Halliday and Wise killed; Captain Grier was badly wounded, Captain Craig and myself slightly wounded. I have, I suppose, lost six or seven killed, and about the same number wounded. We lost several fine officers out of the brigade.[4]

* * * * *

British Major Carl Leopold Baurmeister described the fighting at Chadds Ford in a letter a month after the battle, "Finally towards four o'clock we heard the attack of the left column. Lieutenant General von Knyphausen gave orders to advance; the artillery begun a fearful cannonade; the 1st Battalion of the 71st Regiment pushed toward the ford and crossed the stream; it was followed by the Riflemen and the Queen's Rangers, the 4th English Regiment led by his Excellency General von Knyphausen himself, the 5th and all the English regiments of this brigade according to their rank, and lastly Stirn's brigade. The crossing was affected on our right wing, about 250 paces from the enemy's battery, which lay a little to the left of the ford. After crossing, the troops attacked them furiously, partly with the bayonet. The enemy's left wing began to fall back and we took the battery. Our regiments gained one height after another as the enemy withdrew. They withstood one more rather severe attack behind some houses and ditches in front of their left wing. Finally, we saw the entire enemy line and four guns, which fired frequently, drawn up on another height in front of a dense forest, their right wing resting on the Chester road. By the time it grew dark, the van of the left column and General Howe had joined us."[5]

Hessian Captain Johann Ewald says in his diary that "the 4th and 5th regiments, along with the 71st Highland Regiment, Ferguson's, and the Queen's Rangers, waded through the creek at Chad's Ford, which is about fifty paces wide and a half-man deep, under grapeshot and small-arms fire from the enemy's first battery. They continued their march...in the best order without firing a shot, deployed with complete composure, attacked the battery and the escort with the bayonet, stabbed down all who offered resistance, and captured four cannon and a howitzer. A part of the enemy infantry took a new position behind the first fence or wall, defending itself from wall to wall in the best way possible, but was constantly attacked from post to post by our gallant troops and finally completely driven back over the hills toward Chester."[6] The Regimental Records of the Royal Welsh Fusiliers reported, "The ford was quickly traversed and the entrenchments carried....There they (Americans) made another stand, but after a further desperate resistance were dislodged, and utterly routed."[7] A short and precise description of the crossing of the Brandywine, from the British standpoint, was, "All efforts of the enemy to stop the advance of the British were futile, Wayne was defeated and his guns captured."[8] Dislodging Wayne's troops was not quite that easy.

* * * * *

Wayne's forces opposing Knyphausen had the Pennsylvania militia holding his extreme left flank while his men, Maxwell's light infantry, and Colonel Thomas Proctor's artillery commanded the center and right of the line, where the intense fighting took place. The militia, stationed at Pyle's Ford, would disengage without being involved in the battle at Chadds Ford. Wayne was defending his home turf, as his 380-acre family estate, his birthplace, was Waynesboro at the top of South Valley Hill in eastern Chester County. Wayne was born there on New Year's morning 1745.

Proctor was born in Ireland in 1739 and was eldest son to Francis Proctor, who immigrated to this country some years before the Revolution. Proctor raised and commanded the only regular organization of Pennsylvania artillery and on October 27, 1775, he was made a captain. "The efficiency of Proctor's artillery was so well demonstrated in the experiences of the last campaign that with the opening of the year 1777, General Knox, of the Continental Army, exerted his influence toward having Proctor's forces annexed to the Continental train artillery under his command."[9] On July 16, 1777, Washington asked Congress to attach Proctor's command to join his army "without loss of time." During Brandywine, Proctor "returned with spirit" the fire from Knyphausen's artillery. The black horse he rode was shot from under him and he received pay for this horse in the settlement of his accounts with Pennsylvania in 1793.[10]

The Americans put up a stiff defense but the determination of the British troops and a little luck doomed the defense of the Brandywine. The British Guards, part of Howe's troops, had strayed too far to Howe's right and got lost in Wistar's Woods and didn't participate in the battle on Birmingham Hill as intended. They emerged from the woods at the right place and right time to aid Knyphausen. "Knyphausen attacked the position at Chad's Ford in earnest, and the Fourth and Fifth regiments crossing the ford quickly stormed the first entrenchment and captured four guns. The Guards then came blundering through the woods — accidentally but most opportunely — upon the uncovered flank of the American center, and the retreat of the enemy became general; but darkness came on before Knyphausen and Cornwallis could join hands, and thus saved the Americans from absolute destruction."[11]

Some of the fiercest fighting took place by the Americans in defense of Proctor's artillery. Proctor's guns contested the British crossing and Knyphausen ordered his lead units to overtake the first battery. The British soldiers overran the position. "It was during this assault that Hercules Courteney, one of Proctor's captains, fled from his howitzer in what was described by one of his men as in a 'cowardly unofficerlike manner.' In this same encounter, 'Col. Thomas Proctor's horse was shot from under him.'"[12] Proctor's men fled, some of them being cornered in a nearby field by British troops. The British were putting their bayonets to good use as they drove Wayne's men from their entrenchments. Proctor ordered his men to abandon their positions and equipment and do what they could to save themselves.

Captain Courteney commanded Company B of the 4th Continental Artillery and at Valley Forge on December 28, 1777, "he was tried by court martial, the charge being 'leaving his howitzer in the field in the action at Brandywine in a cowardly, unofficerlike manner.' The court found him guilty, but 'as he has ever supported the character of a brave man' he was sentenced only to be reprimanded by the artillery brigade commander (Brigadier General Henry Knox) in the presence of all the Artillery officers.' Due to what Washington called 'the state of evidence,' however, the sentence was disapproved, with the direction that Courteney be 'discharged from arrest without censure.' He was later dismissed from service for neglect of duty on Feb. 28, 1778, for leaving camp while Officer of the Day."[13]

During the day of the battle, Proctor's guns were deployed on the high ground above Chadd's Ford.

British troops came driving down from the north and got to within thirty yards of the gun positions before they were seen. No infantry had been deployed to cover the American cannon, and the crews on the extreme right of the artillery position had to flee, abandoning three of their guns. The rest of Proctor's force took up a position about two hundred yards to the rear; but before long Gen. Wayne ordered the artillery to retreat, sending orders to the same time to Col. James Chambers, commanding the 1st PA, to cover the artillery's withdrawal. "But to my surprise," Col Chambers wrote, "the artillerymen had run and left the howitzer behind." Two fieldpieces were brought off, escorted by about 60 men of the 1st PA. Chambers then sent a party to bring off the howitzer while the rest of his regiment laid down covering fire. But before this could be done, the main body of the foe came within thirty yards and kept up the most terrible fire. Chambers reported "I brought all the brigade artillery safely off."

In all of this chaos, someone remembered to order the drivers to abandon their ammunition wagon and flee. However, one of the drivers belonging to Captain Courteney's company, a Negro named Edward Hector, refused to obey. Instead, he moved out with his wagon and team and as he passed abandoned muskets discarded by retreating infantrymen, gathered them up, eventually making his way safely to the army's rendezvous point in Chester. Despite Hector's achievement and efforts of Col. Chambers' men, the 4th Continental Artillery lost a number of its guns and the bulk of its available ammunition at the Battle of Brandywine.[14]

"Eleven guns were abandoned by the Americans, among them two brass three-pounders which had been captured from the Hessians under Gen. Gottlieb on Christmas Day 1776 at Trenton. A few wagon loads of ammunition and arms were brought off, such as those saved by Edward Hector, a black private in the 3rd PA Artillery."[15] Hector was a wagoneer and refused to abandon his horses and wagon. He gathered up some abandoned arms and made good his escape from the British. Hector fought in other Revolutionary War battles and died in 1834 at age 90.

With the loss of Proctor's guns, the British successfully across the Brandywine and the British Guards crashing his right flank, Wayne prepared to withdraw all of his forces. Maxwell's Light Infantry fought a delaying action on the main Chester Road. Wayne's troops moved down Ring Road to support Maxwell, and Armstrong's militia were ordered to retreat. By nightfall, all segments of Washington's army were on their way to Chester to regroup. "We marched all night until we neared the town when we halted, but not to sleep," Lieutenant James McMichael of the Pennsylvania Line reported in his journal. "This day for a severe and successive engagement exceeded all I ever saw. Our regiment fought at one stand about an hour under incessant fire, and yet the loss was less than at Long Island; neither were we so near each other as Princeton, our common distance being about 50 yards."

* * * * *

The British army commanded the battlefield as night fell and remnants of Washington's army made their way to regroup in Chester. Howe's men had a long day, up before dawn, marching 17 miles and engaging the American army for almost two hours at Birmingham. Knyphausen's portion of the British army had spent the early part of the day fighting Maxwell's light infantry troops from Kennett Square to Chadds Ford and then demonstrating in front of Washington to give Howe time to flank the American army. During the late afternoon hours of September 11, 1777, Knyphausen crossed the Brandywine and dislodged Wayne's troops from defensive positions. Howe had a major decision facing him. Should he continue to press the retreating Americans toward Chester? Howe had held troops in reserve at Birmingham and they had not seen action. Even though the Americans were vulnerable Howe decided to rest his army on the battlefield he conquered that day, with Howe making his headquarters about one mile south of Dilworth. "Night and the fatigue the soldiers had undergone prevented any pursuit," wrote British Major John Andre in his journal. "It is remarkable that after reconnoitering after the action, the right of General Howe's camp was found close on General Knyphausen's left, and nearly in a line, and in forming the general camp next day scarce any alteration was made."[16]

One of Howe's first reports on the Battle of Brandywine briefly described the day:

> On the 11th at Day-break the Army advanced in two Columns. The right commanded by General Knyphausen took the direct road to Chad's Ford and arrived in Front of the Enemy about Ten o'clock. The other Column under the Command of Lord Cornwallis marched about twelve miles to the Forks of the Brandywine, crossed the first branch at Trimbles Ford, and the second at Jeffery's Ford about two o'clock in the afternoon, taking the Road to Dilworth in order to turn the Enemy's Right at Chad's Ford.

> General Washington having intelligence of this movement detached General Sullivan to his right with near ten thousand Men, who took a strong Position on

the commanding ground above Birmingham Church. As soon as this was observed which was about four o'clock, the King's Troops advanced in three Columns under a heavy Fire of Artillery and Musquetry, but they pushed on by an Impetuosity not to be sustained by the Enemy who falling back into the woods in their rear, the Kings Troops entered with them, and pursed closely for nearly two miles.

The Army laid this Night on the Field of Battle.

With most perfect Respect, etc.

W. Howe

Knyphausen authored a more detailed report from his camp near Philadelphia on October 21, 1777. It said:

The Commander in Chief Sir W. Howe having honored me with the Command of the Right Column of the Army at the attack upon the Enemy on the Brandywine Hills on the 11th of Sept., I took upon it was my duty to relate to your Lordship the particulars thereof.

At V o Clock in the Morning I moved the column from Kennett's Square. Advancing on the road to Chads's Ford I had hardly come up to Welche's Tavern, when the advanced Corps fell in with about 300 riflemen of the Enemy. These were driven back by my advanced Party from one advantageous Post to another behind the Defilee to the westward side of the Brandywine Creek, before which there was a strong Morass.

At 11 o'clock the Enemy were driven back over the Creek evacuating their very advantageous posts on this side. The most obstinate resistance they made was on the road to Brandywine Creek's Bridge, but the gallant and Spirited Behavior of the 4th and 5th Regiment forced them to leave their Ground.

On this I ordered the Troops to halt and keep their position waiting for the Commander in Chiefs Attack on the right of the Enemy. At 2 o'clock great Movements were observed in the Enemy's Position on the opposite side of the Creek. Four Battalions of the Artillery from the Right fled off to where the attack on the Left of our army was to be made, and the Road to Chester was covered with Wagons going this Way and that Way. At 4 o'clock by an uninterrupted firing of Musketry, first we discovered the Commander in chiefs Approach & attack upon the right of the Enemy Whereupon I immediately formed my attack.

On a Hill at the Left of the Road which crosses Chads' Ford the Enemy had a battery which commanded and which kept up a constant Fire upon the Road and the Ford while the Troops went over. A little to the right of this Battery was a second Battery which they had already quited in the morning after an ammunition wagon of theirs had blown up. (The Troops) having passed the Ford which is about thirty paces broad, continued their March on the Road and when they came near the Battery drew up to the left and attacked the Enemy in such a manner as forced them to quit it notwithstanding the uninterrupted Fire of round and Grape Shot which continued ever since the Troops crossed the Creek.

The Enemy were in full Flight, and as soon as they had quitted the 1st Battery, they placed 4 ½-pounders on a height to the Right of the Road crossing Chads's Ford to cover their Retreat which they took towards Chester.

I have the Honor to be with great Respect. My lord, your most obedient humble Servant

Knyphausen

In a letter to Germain from his headquarters in Germantown on October 10, 1777, Howe did offer some more details. He wrote:

After this success, a part of the enemy's right took a second position in a wood about half a mile from Dilworth, from whence the 2nd lt. Infantry and chasseurs soon dislodged them, and from this time they did not rally again in force. The 1st British (Grenadiers), the Hessian (Grenadiers)

and Guards, having in the pursuit got entangled in very thick woods, were no further engaged during the day.

The 2nd Light Infantry, 2nd (Grenadiers) and 4th Brigades, moved forward a mile beyond Dilworth, where they attacked a corps of the enemy that had not been before engaged, and were strongly posted to cover the retreat of their army by the roads from Chads Ford to Chester and Wilmington; which Corps not being forced until after it was dark, when the troops had undergone much fatigue in a march of 17 miles, besides what they had supported since the commencement of the attack, the Enemy's army escaped a total overthrow that; must have been the consequence of an hour's more daylight.

The 3rd Brigade was not brought into action, but kept in reserve in the rear of the 4th brigade. Did not know how far Lt. General Knyphausen's attack had succeeded; nor was there an opportunity of employing the cavalry. Lt. General Knyphausen kept the enemy amused in the course of the day with cannon, and the appearance of forcing the ford, without intending to pass it, until this attack upon the enemy's right should take place....I conclude the strength of the enemy's army was not less than 15,000 men....The army laid this night on the field of battle, and on the 12th Major General Grant marched to Concord (on the road to Chester) and Cornwallis joined him the next day.

Captain John Montresor, chief engineer of the British army, reported in his journal, "Our army marched this day no less than 17 miles after which they gained a Complete victory over the rebels in this general action. Rebel orderly Books found to the 7th Instant inclusive, where Washington expected our attacking him at Wilmington and his Order respecting it particularly, this now was their time for their utmost exertions as their liberties and the fate of America depended upon one general action. Rebel returns found that their regular, Continental or standing army, consisted yesterday of 12,900 men, exclusive of their militia and 2 regiments Light Horse then present and fit for duty. This return by some supposed to be false, Ordnance taken, ten pieces of Cannon and one Howitzer. Killed of Rebel Army of Officers, non-commissioned and privates 450 and prisoners of the same 400."[17]

Writings by British officers are replete with victorious statements. Major Baurmeister wrote in letters about a month after the battle, "The British army, complete masters of the so-called Brandywine Hills, which the enemy had had infinite hope of holding and believed to be impregnable, took position on them in excellent formation. The enemy, however, gained the road to Chester in considerable confusion. Had not the darkness favored their retreat, we might have come into possession of much artillery, munitions and horses....By five o'clock in the evening the entire column had gained a victory and advanced far enough to join our column on the Brandywine hills at nightfall. The enemy's loss in killed, wounded, and prisoners is said to be more than 1,000. We had about five hundred killed and wounded in the two columns. Our first column captured six brass cannon, and the second, four more and one howitzer. The cannons were French 4-pound Couleuvrines made at Douay in 1737. The other two were new Hessian 3-pounders which the rebels had taken at Trenton, one of which had since been re-bored to make a six-pounder of it. We also obtained possession of some ammunition wagons, a quantity of muskets, most of which were made in the French style and had, perhaps, been furnished by French factories, and many entrenching tools. On the morning of the September 12th we buried the dead and transported the wounded to Dilworth, where we found a flour magazine, from which the army was provisioned for two days."[18]

* * * * *

Nightfall certainly saved Washington's troops as Howe wrote to Lord George Germain on October 10, 1777. "The enemy's army escaped a total overthrow that must have been the consequence of an hour's more daylight." A history of the

15th Foot said, "but darkness came on before Knyphausen and Cornwallis could join hands, and thus saved the Americans from absolute destruction."[19] American officers agreed. The journal of Colonel Timothy Pickering of Massachusetts described the conclusion of the fighting and the retreat, "Nevertheless, Weedon's brigade which got up a little before night, fought bravely and checked the pursuit of the enemy, and gave more time for the others to retreat. This engagement on the right began about half after three p.m. or four, and lasted till night....The whole army this night retired to Chester. It was fortunate for us that the night came on, for under its cover the fatigued stragglers and some wounded made their escape."[20] One of the units straggling into Chester that night was the 7th Virginia under the command of Major John Cropper. The unit had lost its flag, but Cropper "put a red bandanna handkerchief on a ramrod and marched into camp. Washington congratulated him for his conduct."[21] A member of the 3rd Philadelphia Associators recalled, "Our way was over the dead and dying, and I saw many bodies crushed to pieces beneath wagons, and we were bespattered with blood. As we marched directly under the English cannon, which kept up a continual fire, the destruction of our men was very great."[22]

Sergeant Major John H. Hawkins, a member of the unit commanded by Colonel Moses Hazen wrote of the severe fighting against a superior enemy and the difficulty he had in returning to the main army:

> The enemy were much superior to us in numbers, as but a small part of our army were engaged, and men of our regiment, Col. Hazen thought himself obliged to affirm, that no troops behaved better, nor any troops left the field in greater order. Four officers, and seventy-three non-commissioned officers and rank and file of the regiment were killed, wounded and taken Prisoners....In the engagement I lost my knapsack, which contained the following articles, 1 uniform Coat—brown faced with white; 1 shirt; 1 pr. Stockings; 1 sergeants sash; 1 pr. Knee buckles; ½ bar of soap; 1 orderly book; 1 mem Book, of Journal

and state of my company; 1 quire paper, 2 vials of ink; 1 brass Ink horn; 40 Morning returns, printed blanks; 1 tin gill cup; A letter and a book entitled Rutherford's Letters. I likewise lost my hat, but recovered it again.

The weather was very warm, and, thus my knapsack was very light, was very cumbersome, as it swung about when walking or running, and in crossing fences was in the way so I cast it away from me, and had I not done so would have been grabbed by one of the ill-looking Highlanders, a number of whom were firing and advancing very brisk towards our rear. The smoke was so very thick that about the close of the day I lost sight of our regiment and just at dark I fell in with the North Carolina troops, and about two o'clock in the morning (Sept. 12) arrived at Chester, just as the whole of the baggage wagons were leaving. I saw several regiments which had been halted for a rest. I searched around for tidings of my regiment, but could only find one officer and I heard that my regiment was coming. About 8 o'clock it reached Chester, when the whole body of troops that was there marched towards Darby. On a hill just beyond Darby, we halted and rested for two hours, and then marched until we came to the Lancaster road, near Gardner's Place, where we halted, and at the edge of a woods rested for the night.[23]

Units on both sides of the battle began constructing casualty reports. "Private Stacey Williams, of Humphey's Company of the 6th PA Reg. was wounded at Brandywine. And later (Williams) lived in Philadelphia until died in 1820 at age 76.... Finally, a pension application from John Francis identifies him as a Negro: he had served in Epple's Company of the 3rd PA Reg. until both his legs were 'much shattered' by grapeshot at the Battle of Brandywine."[24] Major John Hawkins Stone, of Smallwood's Maryland Regiment, wrote in a letter a month after the battle that he "lost 23 privates and 2 sergeants killed, wounded and taken, and one Captain (Ford) wounded; he will recover." Stone would later be wounded in the fighting at Germantown.

A copy of a letter from an American general officer written in camp near Schuylkill on Sept. 28, 1777, said, "I have only time to inform your Excellency that on the 11th inst. We had very nigh given the enemy a severe drubbing. The action commenced about 8 o'clock in the morning and with several intermissions, continued till night. About 5 o'clock it resembled an earthquake, far exceeding the loudest thunder. Lt. Co. Neaville of the 12th began the attack at Birmingham meeting house, and his regiment was the last that left the field; they behaved well. Col. Marshall, of the 3rd regiment, attacked the enemy's left column with his single regiment and at first repulsed them; but, overpowered by numbers, was obliged to retire, which he did in good order. In this contest, which continued violent for near three quarters of any hour, this brave regiment lost four officers on the spot, amongst them a brave young Gentleman, Lieutenant Peyton, and Captain Chilton, who, brave as Wolfe, imitated his manner in death, inquiring about the success of the day as he expired. The Colonels Nelson and Innis, and Major Richeson, distinguished themselves, and I suppose many other officers, whom I had not an opportunity of observing in the action."

The 33rd Foot of the British army in its history says, "The loss of the 33rd was small. Its light company had Captain Dansey wounded; the grenadier company had two officers wounded, Lt. Harris and Drummond; the battalion companies lost one rank and file filled, a sergeant and 11 men wounded, and a private missing."[25] A unit history of the 15th East Yorkshire Regiment, known as the Duke of York's Own, reported, "The Battle Companies of the Regiment did not suffer any loss, being with the 3rd Brigade in Reserve under General Grey, but the flank Companies, being formed in Grenadier and Light Infantry Battalions, and present with the 1st Battalions in the front line had Lt. Hon. William Falconer killed, and Capt. Andrew Cathcart wounded, both of the Grenadiers; and Capt. James Douglas and Lt. Charles Leigh, of the Light Company wounded. Capt. John Lockhart died during the month of September....The Regimental muster rolls give the names of

Privates James Wilson, of the Light Company, killed, and John Hogg, Edward Murray and Philip Peterkin, of the Grenadiers, and William Whittaker, of the Light Company, taken prisoners."[26]

The 10th Foot, the Lincolnshire Regiment, was with Knyphausen in the 2nd Brigade and fought in the morning action at Brandywine and also crossed during the evening's clash. "Grant, who commanded the brigade in which the Tenth was fighting, handled his troops so skillfully, that in spite of Washington's obstinate resistance, the Tenth's loss was small—two rank and file killed, and six men wounded....That night the Tenth lay on the battlefield, little comprehending the dismay which filled the hearts of the Americans throughout the country when news of the disaster came. While they slept after that hard day of fighting, the highways were thronged with fugitives, who were told lying tales of the barbarities practiced by the British troops."[27]

* * * * *

The long day of hard fighting and retreating from the battlefield didn't dampen the spirits of the American soldiers. They stood face-to-face for hours upon Birmingham Hill and in some instances fought hand-to-hand and didn't scatter in panic, even when they faced the feared British bayonet. Brandywine built upon the belief of the American soldier began at Trenton that the rebel army could indeed hold its own with one of the best professional armies of the time. A Delaware soldier wrote, "Through all these trying times, I saw not a despairing look, nor did I hear a despairing word. We had our solacing words always ready for each other—'Come boys, we shall do better another time'—sounded throughout our little army."[28]

Major John Hawkins Stone wrote of Brandywine, "Never was a more favorable opportunity for us; fortune seemed in the morning to count us to victory and honor, but the scene was much changed in the evening. Had our intelligence been as good as it ought to have been, or had we crossed the fords when Gen. Washington first ordered it, it is almost as certain as that two and two make four, that the whole British Army would have been routed and perhaps, this war ended....upon the whole, I do not think we have lost anything but the day. My manner of carrying on the war would be so different from the present system that I should frequently expect to be driven from the ground. We ought to attack them everywhere we meet them. By this method it would make our men soldiers, and be constantly reducing enemy and ensure us success in a few months."[29]

Not everyone, including Washington, was as confident after the day concluded. Colonel Timothy Pickering wrote, "But soon our retreat became general. I retired by the General's (Washington) side. We had not gone a mile when he said to me, 'Why, it is a perfect rout.' Daylight was departing, and, according to orders, the troops retreated to Chester."[30] A soldier reported, "Our misfortune at Brandywine occasioned some small depression of spirits in our army."[31] New Jersey Major Joseph Bloomfield wrote in his diary that September 11, 1777, was "an unfortunate day for our army." Washington, fatigued from the long and stressful day, had to report to Congress on the outcome of the battle and asked his aides to draft a note. Pickering drafted the letter, but Washington added a "word of hope of another day would yield a more favorable result."[32]

Octavius Pickering writes in his biography of his father Colonel Timothy Pickering that "General Washington and his staff arrived at Chester late at night (on 11 Sept.), and took up their quarters in a house in that town, all of them very tired. The General, however, said he must send to Congress a report of the engagement, and called upon his military secretary, Colonel Harrison, to prepare the dispatch. Colonel Harrison desired to be excused, on account of fatigue, and requested Colonel Pickering to write it. Colonel Pickering retired to another room, made a draft, and handed it to Washington. The General, having read it, said it was very well, but that some words of encouragement should be inserted, as that he hoped to give a better account of the enemy another time. Mr. (Jared) Sparks told me, that, in relating the circumstances to him, Colonel Pickering remarked, that this was a very proper and a very important suggestion."[33]

Washington's report, dated midnight on September 11, 1777, at Chester, to the president of Congress read:

> I am sorry to inform you that in this day's engagement, we have been obliged to leave the enemy masters of the field.
>
> Unfortunately the intelligence received of the enemy's advancing up the Brandywine, and crossing at a ford about six miles above us, was uncertain and contradictory, notwithstanding all my pains to get the best. This prevented my making a disposition, adequate to the force with which the Enemy attacked us on the right; in consequence of which the troops first engaged, were obliged to retire before they could be reinforced. In the midst of the attack on the right, the body of the Enemy which remained on the other side of Chad's Ford, crossed it, and attacked the division there under the command of General Wayne and the light troops under Gen. Maxwell who, after a severe conflict, also retired. The Militia under the command of Major Genl. Armstrong, being posted at a ford, about two miles below Chad's, had no opportunity of engaging.
>
> But though we fought under many disadvantages, and were from the causes, above mentioned obliged to retire, yet our loss of men is not, I am persuaded, very considerable, I believe much less than the enemy's. We have also lost about seven or eight pieces of cannon, according to the best information I can at present obtain. The baggage having been previously moved off, is all secure, saving the men's Blankets, which being at their backs, many of them doubtless are lost.
>
> I have directed all the Troops to Assemble behind Chester, where they are now arranging for this Night. Notwithstanding the misfortune of the day, I am happy

to find the troops in good spirits; and I hope another time we shall compensate for the losses now sustained.

The Marquis de La Fayette was wounded in the leg, and Gen. Woodford in the hand. Divers other Officers were wounded some Slain, but the number of either cannot now be ascertained.[34]

While the fighting at Brandywine had concluded, for soldiers and officers of both armies and the civilians of the region the aftermath of the battle would affect them for many months and in some cases years.

Dilworth

The village of Dilworth was the scene of the last sustained fighting of the Battle of Brandywine. Washington's army retreated to Chester, Pennsylvania, and Howe's troops remained on the battlefield.

Chester County Historical Society, West Chester, Pennsylvania

Ten

Fowls Unknown

The soldiers of the armies of General George Washington and General William Howe during the Battle of Brandywine were not the only ones to suffer. For many of the civilian residents of the once-peaceful community surrounding the river in Chester County, Pennsylvania, the war brought deprivations.

Many citizens reported to the Commonwealth government the losses they suffered and asked for reimbursements. A sampling of those losses included:[1]

- September 12, 77, British army cut down and destroyed 8 acres of corn, destroyed 20 bushels oats and six bushels rye. Burnt 1,000 rails took 2 horses.
- 1 mare, 27 sheep, yearling calf, potatoes and cabbage, Andrew Boon—taken by British
- A list of damage done by the British Army: Oats, rye, 3 pairs of new shoes, shirts, a pair of new buckskin britches, large iron pot, acre buckwheat, 15 sheep, 1 large hog, 30 turkeys and fowls unknown
- Sworn 11/16/1782: John Brown of Tredyffrin Township. An account of property taken or destroyed by the army of the King of Great Britain and their adherents under the command of General Howe from September 11 to the 16th 1777 belonging to George Brinton of Thornbury Township. 233 bushes of wheat, 5 casks of flour, 1 brown horse -12 years, 16 young cattle, cheese,

bacon, 12 blankets, 3 bedticks, tablecloth, 1 beaver mat, 6 shirts, linen, knives, forks and spoons.

- Charles Dilworth of Birmingham: 3 beef cattle, 2 heifers, 2 horse colts, 24 large fat hogs, 45 pigs, 10 sheep, wheat, hay.

The civilians of Chester County were a conquered population. Members of the British army and their followers took what they wanted from homes and burned contents at will. Furniture, woods, and fences were all used as fuel by the British army. Fields of crops and herds of cattle were consumed by the British. For many residents, years would pass before they would recover from the losses they sustained because of the Battle of Brandywine.

George Clymer, a member of the Continental Congress, signer of the Declaration of Independence, and one of the first Continental treasurers, had his Chester County home vandalized after the Battle of Brandywine. His wife and children hid nearby in the woods as the British damaged the home.

* * * * *

Many of the civilians had stories of their own to tell concerning the battle, including the Frazer family. Sarah Frazer, daughter of Colonel Persifor Frazer, had her own harrowing experience as she thought her father had been killed during the fighting. Her father, Colonel Frazer, was a local officer who fought under General Anthony Wayne. Frazer was a member of the committee of Chester County, the group chosen to carry out the resolutions of Congress. He was also elected a delegate to the Provincial Council, also known as the Committee of Safety. Colonel Frazer was one of the local officers Squire Thomas Cheyney named to verify his allegiance to the American cause when Cheyney reported to Washington in the early afternoon of September 11, 1777, about the movement of Howe's troops crossing the Brandywine. Sarah Frazer was born on January 11, 1769, and was eight years old when the battle took place.

Sarah and her brother, Robert, were at school when shooting from the area of Brandywine near Chadds Ford was heard between nine and ten o'clock in the morning. The teachers of the school abandoned their classrooms and went outside to listen to the sounds of the guns being fired. Since the battle was not far from the school, the teachers dismissed the students and told them to go home.

> As we returned we met our Mother on horseback going over towards the place of action, knowing that her husband our father must be in the midst of the affray. We heard musketry, with an occasional discharge of heavy artillery through the day but particularly towards evening. There was a continual discharge of small arms heard at our house.

> Father rode home that night....At early morning I got up and seeing my father's Regimental coat all stained and daubed with blood, I set up the murder shout as I thought he must be dead. He awoke and as soon as his horse was prepared mounted and rode off to the army. He was taken prisoner with Major John Harper four days afterwards in Edgemont Township while on a reconnoitering party.[2]

Sarah's mother, Mary Worrall Taylor Frazer, recorded her own memories of Brandywine. She was a Quaker and when she wed Persifor Frazer on October 2, 1766, the marriage was opposed by her stepfather since she was marrying "out of the meeting." Persifor Frazer, who was born in 1736, was the son of John Frazer, who emigrated from Scotland to Chester County in 1735. After her marriage, Mary became a Presbyterian. Persifor Frazer joined the American army on January 4, 1776, after his good friend, Anthony Wayne, called for officers. Frazer was made a captain and put in charge of Company A of the 4th Pennsylvania battalion. In the spring of 1777 he was promoted to major and later became colonel.[3]

The night before the Battle of Brandywine Colonel Frazer stayed with his family and on Thursday morning he rode off in a dense fog to join his troops as his children went to school.

As the children were returning home, Mary Frazer rode off to try to find her husband.

Frazer faced a frightening sight at Chadd's Ford as Knyphausen unleashed his infantry. The retreat from Chadd's Ford was not so rapid as to prevent Col. Frazer's lending a helping hand to a wounded Britisher. The soldier had taken a shot in his back, a fact that was to bemuse Col Frazer in his later recollections. He got the man on his horse and walked by his side to the Seven Stars Tavern. There he put the soldier in a wagon bound for Chester, where the retreating American army was to bivouac.

Col. Frazer did not go to Chester immediately. He rode directly for six miles from the Seven Stars to Thornbury. He left his coat hanging on the stair railing. His eight-year-old daughter later recalled getting up early the next morning and seeing 'my father's regimental coat all stained and daubed with blood; I set up the murder shout as I thought he must be dead. Oh, my daddy's killed, my poor daddy's killed,' she cried. Turning, she found her awakened father behind her.[4]

British troops and Tories were in charge of the neighborhood where the Frazer family lived. The Frazer home had been used to store military goods for Washington's army. Mary Frazer had taken the precaution to remove many of the family's valuables and placed them in the "vines" near the home. Colonel Frazer left to rejoin the army on Friday and again returned home that night. Two men had asked to stay at the Frazer home and Mary gave them permission. They rode off in the middle of the night and the enemy visited the next day. "British officers came to the Frazier home...'Where are the damned rebels?' an officer asked. 'So I said to him that I knew no Rebels—there was not a Scotchman about the place.' At this the fellow flew into a great rage, and used very abusive language."[5] The house was ransacked and a barrel of salt taken. Also, Mary Frazer wrote that some of the British soldiers were drinking and one was about to strike her when a British officer drove off the soldier with his sword. The British were looking for ammunition and other military items. They found soldier clothing and took 50 bushels of wheat. As the British officer was departing, the following exchange reportedly took place between the officer and Mary Frazer. The officer said, "I had orders to take Mr. Frazer prisoner and burn the house and barn, but these I give to you." Mary replied, "I cannot thank you for what is my own, and if those were your orders, you would not dare to disobey them."[6]

Mary Frazer lived until November 19, 1830, when she died at age 85. Her husband was captured by the British on September 16, 1777, while riding with another American officer in Aston townhip and mistaking British soldiers for Virginia riflemen. Frazer was taken to Philadelphia, but escaped on March 17, 1778, after some British guards became drunk. He served in the American army until October 9, 1778, when he resigned. He served as Register of Wills of Chester County and in 1782 he was appointed brigadier general of Pennsylvania. He died on April 24, 1792, of a heart attack at age 56.[7]

* * * * *

The family of Benjamin Ring also suffered at the hands of the British. Washington had used Ring's home as his headquarters during the battle. Ring's grandson wrote a letter to a family member concerning Brandywine:

> In about an hour the British begun to pour in, all the Brandywine hills appeared scarlet, in the meantime the booming of the cannon commenced, which shook the ground....In the morning some of the American spies informed grandfather that he and his family had better get away from the place, for it would not be safe to stay there, and if they had anything valuable they had better take it with them, and that they had no time to lose.
>
> A one-horse vehicle was rigged in a few minutes and things of the most value placed in it, in as quick time as possible, but time proved too short, grandmother and some of the girls took passage in carriages and I think, if I

mistake not, your father drove the horse but they had not proceeded far before they met the American soldiers. The road became completely blocked up and the horses and carriage with its contents of valuables was abandoned and grandmother, the girls, and grandfather made their escape across the field. In the chest there was about $900 in gold and silver, and plate to a considerable extent, and other valuables, in all amounting to $1,400 to $1,500, which of course they never saw or heard of after and glad to get away with life....He told me that grandfather favored the side of his colonies in every way, as far as his religion would permit, and many thought he went further in his politics than he ought, in taking sides with what was called the Rebel Congress and rebel Army, and the fact of General Washington having his headquarters for the time being at grandfather's. Whilst others were protected, he was pointed out as a rebel, and his property given over to the enemy for destruction."[8]

* * * * *

While the civilians dealt with the aftermath of the battle, Washington and Howe tended to the wounded. In an order issued the night of the battle from his headquarters at Dilworth Howe ordered "a small party, with a Surgeon's Mate and Waggon from each Corps, to be sent off by day-break in the morning, to Pick up their Wounded in the Woods and bring them to the General Hospital at Dilworth."[9] The day after the battle Howe wrote to Washington, "Sir, The number of wounded officers and men of your Army in this neighborhood, to whom every possible attention has been paid, will never the less require your immediate care, as I shall not be so situated as to give them the necessary relief. Any surgeon you may choose to send to their assistance upon application to me in consequence of your order shall be permitted to attend them. The officers paroled or will be taken and the men considered as prisoner of war. With due respect I am, Sir, Wm Howe Your most obed. Servant."[10]

On Saturday, Washington replied to Howe from his headquarters at Germantown. "Sir, I was this evening honoured with your letter of the 12th. The attention, which, you are pleased to assure me, has been paid to the Officers & privates of the Army under my command, who were unfortunately wounded in the Action on Thursday last, has a claim to my Acknowledgements. Agreeable to the permission you offer, I have directed the following gentn, Doctrs Rush, Leiper & Latimer, and Mr Willet, a Mate in the Hospital, with their Attendants, to wait upon you and to take them under their care. The Wounded will be considered in the light you place them. I am Sir with due respect Yr Most Obedt servt. G. Washington.

P.S. I have thought proper to add Doctrs Way and Coats to the Surgeons above mentioned, that the Wounded may have the earliest relief."[11]

British Captain John Montresor wrote in his diary on September 14 that "this evening the noted Dr. Rush, a rebel Doctor and Delegate with 3 Surgeons (came) to attend the wounded Rebels left scattered in the House about the field of Battle unattended by their Surgeons till now." The next day Montresor wrote, "Came in two more Rebel Surgeons to dress their wounded and two more on the road coming in....The rebel wounded sent off to the Turk's Head Tavern, 5 miles from Dilworth, Except Doctor Delegate Rush."[12] Benjamin Rush, who was born in 1746, was a physician and a signer of the Declaration of Independence. A graduate of Princeton, he also studied in Edinburgh and London before returning to Philadelphia in 1769. He volunteered to serve in the army in 1775 and on April 11, 1777, he became surgeon general of the Middle Department. He was critical of the handling of medical care for the soldiers and didn't stay in the army. In a letter on October 21, 1777, he wrote to John Adams, "Our hospital affairs grow worse and worse. There are several hundred wounded soldiers in this place who would have perished had they not been supported by the voluntary and benevolent contributions of some pious whigs."[13]

Rush rushed to Washington's army at the conclusion of the battle to attend to the soldiers in need. "While attending the wounded at the battle of the Brandywine, Rush nearly fell into the enemy's hands. Two days later Washington dispatched a letter to Lord Howe and sent Rush with several surgeons under a flag of truce to dress the wounded American soldiers who had been left on the battlefield. Rush was treated with great politeness by the British officers. Rush was much impressed with the discipline and order of the British Army as contrasted with the American army. Rush in his next letter to John Adams said: he was struck with the vigilance of the sentries saying that 'they spoke, they stood, they looked like the safeguards of the whole army.' He was impressed with their regard for secrecy and 'supreme regard to the cleanliness and health of their men.' After the battle the British soldiers were forbidden to touch any of the blankets belonging to the American dead or wounded for fear of contracting and spreading 'rebel distempers.'"[14]

Taking care of the wounded remained a concern for weeks. On September 21, 10 days after the battle, Howe again wrote to Washington: "Sir, There being some wounded officers and men of your Army at Howells Tavern and the neighboring homes with whom a surgeons mate is left, with orders to join me on the 23rd, if not sooner relieved by one of your surgeons. I am to request you will lose no time in sending whom you think proper for this purpose, with directions to give receipt for the wounded to delivered up as prisoner of war to be hereafter exchanged. With due respect I am Sir, Your most obedient servant Wm Howe."[15] Washington responded the same day, "Sir, Your favor of this day was received this evening, and agreeable to your request I have sent Doctor Wilson to take charge of the wounded officers and men of this Army under my Command, who have fallen into your hands at Howell's Tavern and the Neighboring houses. The Doctor has directions to give a receipt for all that are delivered, and they will be considered as your Prisoners. I am, Sir, With due respects Your most obedt. Servant G. Washington."[16]

Besides the problem of proper medical care, American prisoners kept in Philadelphia complained of the way they were treated by the British. In a letter written to Howe on November 17, 1777,[17] by American army and naval officers, they listed a number of complaints. They complained that they had been frequently denied the small privilege of walking in daylight in the enclosed yard adjoining the house where they were confined, thus affecting their health. They said visits by family members and friends were denied and that money sent to them had been "accidentally lost." Officers of the Delaware Frigate had received bad treatment since their surrender, the quantity and quality of their provisions were lacking, and their sick were not properly attended. Also, the letter noted that a watch had been taken from the home of Colonel John Hannum by the Light Dragoons after Brandywine and never returned.

* * * * *

While Rush was attending to the wounded men in Washington's army and Washington was trying to rally the troops near Chester, Thomas Paine, an acquaintance of Rush, was in Philadelphia writing about Brandywine on September 12, 1777, the day after the battle. Rush had earlier encouraged Paine to write a pamphlet encouraging Americans to support independence, and Paine authored the acclaimed series of essays, Common Sense. On Brandywine, Paine wrote about the inevitability of Howe's defeat and that Washington had come close to defeating Howe at Brandywine. He then closed by saying that Howe was the tool of a miserable tyrant. Paine wrote the day after the battle:

> Those who expect to reap the blessings of freedom, must, like men, undergo the fatigues of supporting it. The event of yesterday was one of those kind of alarms which is just sufficient to rouse us to duty, without being of consequence enough to depress our fortitude. It is not a field of a few acres of ground, but a cause, that we are defending, and whether we defeat the enemy in one battle, or by degrees, the consequences will be the same.

Look back at the events of last winter and the present year, there you will find that the enemy's successes always contributed to reduce them. What they have gained in ground, they paid so dearly for in numbers, that their victories have in the end amounted to defeats....His (Howe's) condition and ours are very different. He has everybody to fight, we have only his one army to cope with, and which wastes away at every engagement: we can not only reinforce, but can redouble our numbers; he is cut off from all supplies, and must sooner or later inevitably fall into our hands.

Shall a band of ten or twelve thousand robbers, who are this day fifteen hundred or two thousand men less in strength than they were yesterday, conquer America, or subdue even a single state? The thing cannot be, unless we sit down and suffer them to do it....Could our whole army have come up to the attack at one time, the consequences had probably been otherwise; but our having different parts of the Brandywine creek to guard, and the uncertainty which road to Philadelphia the enemy would attempt to take, naturally afforded them an opportunity of passing with their main body at a place where only a part of ours could be posted; for it must strike every thinking man with conviction, that it requires a much greater force to oppose an enemy in several places, than is sufficient to defeat him in any one place.

There is a mystery in the countenance of some causes, which we have not always present judgment enough to complain. It is distressing to see an enemy advancing into a country, but it is the only place in which we can beat them, and in which we have always beaten them, whenever they made the attempt. The nearer any disease approaches to a crisis, the nearer it is to a cure....

Thank God! Our army, though fatigued, is yet entire. The attack made by us yesterday, was under many disadvantages, naturally arising from the uncertainty of knowing which route the enemy would take; and from that circumstance, the whole of our force could not be brought up together time enough to engage all at once. Our strength is yet reserved; and it is evident that Howe does not think himself a gainer by the affair, otherwise he would this morning have moved down and attacked General Washington....

I close this paper with a short address to General Howe. You, sir, are only lingering out the period that shall bring with it your defeat. You have yet scarce begun upon the war, and the further you enter, the faster will your troubles thicken. What you now enjoy is only a respite from ruin; an invitation to destruction; something that will lead on to our deliverance at your expense. We know the cause which we are engaged in, and though a passionate fondness for it may make us grieve at every injury which threatens it, yet, when the moment of concern is over, the determination to duty returns. We are not moved by the gloomy smile of a worthless king, but by the ardent glow of generous patriotism. We fight not to enslave, but to set a country free, and to make room upon the earth for honest men to live in. In such a case we are sure that we are right; and we have to you the despairing reflection of being the tool of a miserable tyrant.[18]

Paine wasn't the only American patriot writing about the American army's performance at Brandywine. Benjamin Franklin, a signer of the Declaration of Independence, wrote about the conduct of foreign officers in the American army. The correspondence was printed in the *Boston Gazette* newspaper on October 2, 1777. He wrote, "A great Number of French Officers were in the Action. The Marquis de la Fayette, the most accomplish'd Youth, behaved with a Bravery equal to his noble Birth and amiable Character. The Polish Count Pulawski with a Party of light Horse rode up to reconnoiter the Enemy within Pistol-shot of their Front. The Chevalier du Plessis, who is one of General Knox's Family, had three Balls thro' his Hat. Young Fleuri's Horse was killed under him. He shew'd so much Bravery, and was so useful in rallying the Troops, that the Congress have made him a Present of another. I should not do Justice if I did not add that the French Officers in general behaved extremely well."[19]

* * * * *

While Americans such as Paine and Franklin were putting the loss at Brandywine in the best light, British soldiers wrote about their victory. One letter written on the field of battle the night of the conflict described part of the day's fighting. The letter said, "What excessive fatigue—a rapid march from 4 o'clock in the morning till four in the eve: When we engaged. Till dark we fought...There was a most infernal fire of cannon and musketry....Incline to the right! Incline to the left! Halt! Charge! The balls ploughing up the ground...the branches riven by the artillery. The leaves falling as in autumn by the grape shot—the effect was grand....The action was brilliant....Mr. Washington retreated (ran away) and Mr. Howe remained master of the field. We took ten pieces of cannon and howitzers."[20]

Another British soldier on the battlefield that night was Cornet Banastre Tarleton. Tarleton would gain an infamous reputation in America for the tactics he used fighting in the southern colonies later in the war. He served in the 16th Dragoons and participated in the Philadelphia campaign. Tarleton was at Brandywine as a cornet under Sir William Harcourt.[21] Tarleton survived the war and died in 1833.

In two orders issued by Howe on September 12, he began preparations for the next phase of the campaign and also thanked his troops for their efforts during the Battle of Brandywine. From the "Head Quarters, Camp on the Heights of Brandywine," Howe ordered:

> An Escort of a Captain, 3 Subalterns and 100 Infantry with an Officer and 20 Dragoons, to Parade immediately at Dilworth to attend the Commissary in Search of Flour. All Waggons and Horses taken Yesterday to be

given in to the Quarter Master General. All Sheep and Cattle to the Commissary General.

Patrols to be immediately sent from each Corps, into the Woods near their respective Encampments, to search for Wounded Men, Ordinance Stores, & c. One Day's bread and two days' fresh provision to be immediately Issued to the Troops at Chads's Ford. The Artillery Park to be at Dilworth, in the green field in front of the Public House, where all Ordnance and Stores taken yesterday are to be immediately sent by the Corps now possessed of them.

Returns of the Killed, Wounded, and Missing, to be immediately given to the Deputy Adjutant Generals at Head Quarters. The General Hospital is Established at Dilworth. One Battalion of the 42nd Regiment will immediately take up their Ground near the Hospital in the rear of the Army, where the Troops first engaged Yesterday afternoon.

Four Women from each Brigade British to be sent to the General Hospital to attend the Wounded; the Surgeons of the Hospital will dispose of them. All Orderly Books of the Enemy whatever, which are on or may hereafter be taken, to be given into Head Quarters, as soon as possible.

Two days' Rum for the Officers, Non-Commissioned Officers, and Soldiers doing duty, to be Issued immediately. The 1st. and 2d. Brigades British to receive theirs a Mile and a half on this side Chads' Ford, the (rest) of the Army at the Meeting house in the rear of the camp.[22]

On the evening of September 12, Howe had the following order issued to his troops, "The Acknowledgements and thanks of the Commander in Chief to the General Officers, and Soldiers of the Army in General and to advanced Corps, in particular, very weakly expresses the Sentiments he entertains of their very gallant and Spirited behaviour in the General engagement of Yesterday, by repeatedly charging and Routing, under a very heavy fire, the Enemy posted to the greatest advantage."[23]

* * * * *

Washington had his own general orders issued to his army from his headquarters near Germantown on September 13 and he too thanked them for their bravery, but he also tempered his enthusiasm and chastised those who fled from battle.

> The General, with peculiar satisfaction, thanks those gallant officers and soldiers, who, on the 11th instant, bravely fought in their country and its cause — If there are any whose conduct reflects dishonour upon soldiership, and their names are not pointed out to him, he must, for the present, leave them to reflect, how much they have injured their country — how unfaithful they have proved to their fellow-soldiers; but with this exhortation, that they embrace the first opportunity, which may offer, to do justice to both, and to the profession of a soldier. Altho' the event of that day, from some unfortunate circumstances, was not so favorable as could be wished, the General has the satisfaction of assuring the troops, that from every account he has been able to obtain, the enemy's loss greatly exceeded ours; and he has full confidence that in another Appeal to Heaven (with the blessing of providence, which it becomes every officer and soldier humbly to supplicate) we shall prove successful.

> The Honorable Congress, in consideration of the gallant behaviour of the troops on Thursday last — their fatigue since — and from a full conviction that every future occasion they will manifest a bravery worthy of the cause they have undertaken to defend — having been pleased to order thirty hogsheads of rum to be distributed among them, in such manner as the Commander in Chief should direct. He orders the Commissary General of Issues, to deliver to each officer and soldier, one gill per day, while it lasts.[24]

The order goes on to direct the gathering of straggling soldiers and have them taken to their brigades. Washington's stay at Germantown was to be brief as he ordered them to be ready to march at 9 a.m. the next day. Washington also ordered 40 rounds of cartridges to be given each member of the

Continental troops and clothes to those in need. Washington allocated tents for the soldiers and officers, made preparations for food and other supplies and ordered "no woman under any pretence whatsoever to go with the army, but to follow the baggage."[25]

As the armies of Washington and Howe prepared for the next segment of the Philadelphia campaign, both generals would be criticized for their generalship at Brandywine as they were blamed for missing opportunities and committing serious blunders. Other American officers, especially General John Sullivan, would be publicly castigated for their actions.

First Shots of the Afternoon

The first shots of the afternoon battle took place on the road from Osborne's Hill toward the Birmingham Meeting House. The house at the left sustained damage from a cannon ball during the battle.

Chester County Historical Society, West Chester, Pennsylvania

Eleven

Disasters and Disgrace

General John Sullivan found himself, as he did at the Battle of Brandywine, at the center of the action in the post-battle controversy. On September 11 Sullivan had the responsibility of guarding the right of the American army against a flanking movement by the British. Sullivan failed as the British turned his flank, forced the American troops led by Sullivan from Birmingham Hill, drove the whole American army toward Chester, and opened the route to Philadelphia where the members of the Continental Congress were located. A major mistake Sullivan made, and one he shared with General George Washington, was not doing his own investigation of the fords of the Brandywine to his north. Sullivan and Washington both relied on information from local sympathizers that the river couldn't be crossed by the British army for another 12 miles above his army. British Commander in Chief William Howe had, indeed, found a way across the Brandywine at both the east and west branches of the Brandywine within a short march of Sullivan's flank and attacked Washington from the rear.

Sullivan was the likely scapegoat for the American loss, and Congressman Thomas Burke of North Carolina was bound not only to place the blame for the loss on Sullivan, but also to have him discharged from the American army. Burke had been present at Brandywine during the fighting and was convinced the blame should fall on Sullivan's shoulders. On October 12, 1777,

179

Burke, from the temporary home of the Continental Congress in York, Pennsylvania, wrote a scathing letter to Sullivan listing his reasons for discontent with Sullivan. Some of the reasons listed by Burke, as Sullivan and his defenders pointed out, were incorrect.

Burke wrote:

> I was present at the action of Brandywine and saw and heard enough to convince me that the fortune of the day was injured by miscarriages where you commanded.
>
> I understand you were several days posted with the command on the right wing, that you were cautioned by the Commander in Chief early in the day to be particularly attentive to the enemys' motions who he supposed would attempt to cross higher up the creek and attack your flank, that you were furnished with proper troops for reconnoitering, and yet you were so ill informed of the enemy's motions that they came up at a time and by a rout(e) which you did not expect. That you conveyed intelligence to the Commander in Chief which occasioned his countermanding the dispositions he had made for encountering them on the rout(e) by which it afterwards appeared they were actually advancing. That when at length the mistake was discovered you brought up your own division by an unnecessary circuit of two miles, and in the greatest disorder, from which they never recovered, but fled from the fire of the enemy without resistance. That the miscarriages on that wing made it necessary to draw off a great part of the strength from the center which exposed General Wayne to the superiority of the enemy.
>
> I heard officers on the field lamenting in the bitterest terms that they were cursed with such a commander and I overheard numbers during the retreat complain of you as an officer whose evil conduct was forever productive of misfortunes to the army.
>
> From these facts I concluded that your duty as a general was not well performed. Otherwise the enemy's motions on the wing where you particularly commanded

would not have been unknown to you during great part of the day of action, nor could they have advanced by an unknown and unexpected rout(e), for you ought to have made yourself well acquainted with the ground. Nor would you have brought up your troops by an unnecessary circuit and in disorder, which exposed them to be surprised and broken.

I also concluded that the troops under your command had no confidence in your conduct, and from the many accounts I had officially received of your miscarriages, I conceived, and am still possessed of an opinion, that you have not sufficient talents for your rank and office, tho I believe you have strong dispositions to discharge your duty well.

I consider it as one essential part of my duty to attend to the appointments of the army, and where I perceive that any person so unqualified as I deem you to be has got into a command where incompetence may be productive of disasters and disgrace, it is my duty to endeavor at removing him....I urged your recall with all the force I could, and thought it, and still do think it, necessary for the public good....Your personal courage I meddled not with. I had no knowledge of it, and I was cautious to say nothing unjust or unnecessary. My objection to you is want of sufficient talents, and I consider it as your misfortune, not fault. It is my duty, as far as I can, to prevent it being the misfortune of the country.[1]

Burke's vicious attack on Sullivan amounted to uncalled interference with the running of Washington's army by a member of Congress. Burke's letter, as Sullivan and Sullivan's defenders pointed out, contained many inaccuracies. Even though Sullivan did not undertake his own investigation of the fords, Sullivan only reached his position the day before the battle, didn't have adequate members of cavalry under his command, and he faithfully relayed to Washington all intelligence he received, contrary to Burke's claims. Burke's charges set off a heated exchange of letters among Congress, Sullivan, and officers in the American army.

Sullivan's ability as an officer was already under scrutiny by Congress because of his conduct during the American loss at Staten Island. Congress resolved on September 14 that "General Sullivan be recalled from the army until the enquiry heretofore ordered into his conduct shall be duly made."[2] Washington, for his part, stood by Sullivan. On September 15 Washington asked Congress to allow Sullivan to continue serving because of the "critical and delicate" situation of the army, and Congress concurred on the next day.

Sullivan's fellow officers also came to his aid. On September 20 General Adam Stephen wrote to Sullivan, "I am astonished at a Report in Camp, whispering, that you are Suspended, by a Resolve of Congress: and That your Intention is to resign. It is alarming to me, and I suppose to ev'ry Officer of Spirit, & Reputation: If the Congress have taken upon themselves to suspend you; they seem to have forgotten from whence the present Evil, partly, Originated; Namely the determination of British Government, to Condemn Americans without being heard."[3] Likewise, Major William Willcocks wrote to Sullivan on September 25, "The place which I have the honor to hold in the army naturally gave me, the best opportunity of observing the behavior of every General officer, in the center of the line, and to my great concern, I saw you and my Lord Stirling with General Conway, from the commencement of the action, until you were deserted almost by every man, ride from right to left encouraging and driving the soldiers to their duty, till the enemy were pouring a severe fire on both flanks and pressing on with charged Bayonets in front. Some time before this I thought you had exceeded the bounds both of Prudence and courage."[4]

Sullivan asked for a "Court of Enquiry" to be immediately called to clear this name. Washington agreed but said the situation of the army prohibited an immediate hearing. On September 27 Sullivan pressed the matter by writing a long letter to John Hancock, president of Congress, about what he considered to be unjust charges leveled against him for his conduct at Staten Island and Brandywine. In his letter Sullivan wrote about Burke, "I was Still more astonished to find that upon the vague Report of a Single person who pretends to know all about the Late Battle of Brandywine (Though I am Confident he Saw but Little of it) Congress Should Suddenly pass a Resolve to Suspend me from the Service which Resolve was afterward Rescinded: If the Reputation of General officers is thus to be Sported with upon Every vague & Idle Report Those who Set Less by their Reputation than myself must Continue in the Service — Nothing can be more mortifying in a man who is conscious of having Done Every thing in his power for the good of his Country has wasted his Strength & often Exposed his Life in the Service of it Than to find the Representatives Thereof Instead of Bestowing on him the Reward of his Services Loading him with Blame Infamy & Reproaches upon the false Representations of a Single Person who Don Quixot Like pranced at a Distance from the fight & felt as Little of the Severity of the Engagement as he knows about the Disposition of our Troops or that of the Enemy."[5]

The letter to Hancock also detailed Sullivan's version of the fighting at Brandywine and related that Sullivan had "never yet pretended that my Disposition in the Late Battle was perfect." He wrote that at 2:30 p.m. he received orders to march with his division and to take command at Birmingham. Sullivan contended he didn't know the position of the British army or that of the other two American divisions on Birmingham Hill. Five minutes after receiving orders from Washington to march, Sullivan began and after going less than a mile he came across Colonel Moses Hazen who reported the principal part of the British army was at his heels. At Birmingham Hill, Sullivan reported finding the other American troops to his right and he began to move his men to form with them. While repositioning his troops, the British attacked and threw Sullivan's men into confusion. Sullivan wrote that he took a post in the center of the line with the artillery and gave orders for the artillery to "play briskly to stop the progress of the enemy." Sullivan and four aides tried to rally his troops but to no avail, according to Sullivan. He wrote that he felt he had to hold the hill and if he failed a total rout would take place. Some of the troops rallied but others "could not by their officers be brought to do any thing but fly."

The British attacked with their main force and the fire was "close and heavy" for a time and five times the British drove the Americans from the hill and five times it was retaken, Sullivan wrote to Hancock. Sullivan also praised the work done by Lord Stirling and General Conway and estimated that the fighting lasted one hour and forty minutes with almost an hour of that fighting disputed "almost muzzle to muzzle." The hill was abandoned, Sullivan wrote, after the British were in the process of turning both flanks. When the hill was abandoned, Sullivan worked to rally his troops to prevent the British from pursuing Washington's army. His work, Sullivan wrote Hancock, allowed the whole American army, artillery, and baggage to escape. Sullivan also took another dig at Burke: "I would now beg Leave to ask this warlike Son of Achilles who has Censured my Conduct whether it is proper for the Best officer in the world to make a perfect Disposition of Three Divisions of Troops to Receive an Enemy vastly Superior in numbers already formed and advancing in order of Battle when he has not time upon the Swiftest Horse to Ride from the Right to the Left of the Line before he is attacked."[6]

The root cause of the American defeat was a lack of solid intelligence concerning the British movement of troops and the stolen flanking march. Sullivan, in a letter to Hancock on October 6 contented he had warned Washington of a possible flanking attack and gave his opinion on numerous occasions. "I wrote him that morning that it was clearly my opinion: I sent him two messages to the same purpose in the forenoon & the very first intelligence I received, that they were actually coming that way, I instantly communicated to him."[7] When conflicting information came from Major Joseph Spear he said he had a duty to send the report to Washington. "That if my opinion or the intelligence I had sent to General had brought him into a plan of attacking the enemy on the advantageous heights, they were posses'd of & a defeat shou'd follow, that I shou'd be justly censur'd for withholding from him part of the intelligence I had receiv'd & thereby brought on the defeat of our army; I therefore sat down & wrote Major Spear's account, from his own mouth & forwarded it to his Exc by a Light Horseman."[8]

Washington did not blame Sullivan for forwarding Spear's report and in fact said it was Sullivan's duty to do so. In a letter to Sullivan dated October 24, Washington wrote, "That, although I ascribed the misfortune which happened to us on the 11th of September, principally to the information of Major Spear, transmitted to me by you; yet I never blamed you for conveying that intelligence. On the contrary, considering from whom, and I what manner it came to you, I should have thought you culpable in concealing it. The Major's rank, reputation and knowledge of the country gave him a full claim to credit and attention. His intelligence was no doubt a most unfortunate circumstance; as it served to derange the disposition that had been determined on, in consequence of prior information of the enemy's attempt to turn and attack our right flank, which ultimately proving true, too little time was left us, after discovering certainly, to form a new plan, and make adequate arrangements to prevent its success. Hence arose that hurry and consequent confusion which afterwards ensued. But it was not your fault that the intelligence was eventually found to be erroneous."[9]

Sullivan's failure to verify conflicting reports showed him "at his worst, dilatory and indisposed to check conflicting reports himself. In any such situation, where one man sights the enemy and another sees nothing, a commander's presumption must heavily favor the man who sees 'something,' not the one who sees nothing, if only because one normally does not see something that is not actually there. In Sullivan it was derelict not to confirm personally the truth of the situation. For him to act as though the British were not there was to expose the American army to destruction."[10]

After receiving Burke's letter of October 12 detailing the charges against him, Sullivan again communicated with Hancock on October 25 and answered the allegations. Sullivan again said he faithfully executed Washington's orders to guard the fords deemed passable and was faithful in passing along all information he received from scouts. He also disputed the contention that his officers did not have any faith in him and pointed out a number of those officers wrote letters to Congress affirming their high regard for Sullivan's ability as an officer. Congress never censured Sullivan for his conduct at Brandywine.

The controversy over Sullivan's conduct at Brandywine wouldn't dissipate. Sullivan wrote to printers in Boston about misinformation distributed there and as late as 1847 Sullivan's grandson was defending his relative's honor. Dr. Alfred L. Elwyn was about to publish an unflattering article about Sullivan when grandson John Sullivan wrote a letter to Elwyn on March 29, 1847. "It is a matter of regret that at this late period, after the lapse of seventy years since the battle, after he and every prominent officer of the army is dead, and many facts relating to it must be forgotten, it was regarded as necessary to publish the personal and acrimonious letter of Burke to Gen. Sullivan, as the foundation of a history of the conduct of an active officer of the Revolution or of any fact connected with the history of the Revolution."[11] Grandson Sullivan went on to point out that the country was hilly, covered by a dense forest with bad roads, inhabited with people of unknown loyalties, and a thick fog enveloped the whole area on the morning of the battle. He wrote that General Sullivan didn't have the responsibility for exploring the fords or keeping an eye on the British since he only had a few light horsemen and shouldn't be blamed for the defeat. The grandson also attacked Burke for being biased against Sullivan even before the battle took place.

* * * * *

Sullivan was not the only American officer to be criticized for his performance at Brandywine. General George

Washington "conducted the Brandywine operation as if he had been in a daze," Washington biographer Douglas S. Freeman wrote. In general, Washington failed to use his cavalry to explore the battleground and to gain information on the British movement, to anticipate Howe's flanking maneuver, and to firmly take charge of the battle by giving more detailed orders. In a book about John Marshall, Jean Smith wrote, "Washington was badly outgeneraled at Brandywine."[12] And Washington himself, in a dispatch dated September 14 from Germantown to Major General William Heath called Brandywine a "disaster."

Not only did Washington receive blame for the handling of the army during the Battle of Brandywine, but he also caused dissension within the ranks for his passing out praise for work done by his troops. General Nathanael Greene felt a particular slight by Washington, who worried about being criticized for praising his fellow Virginia troops too much. Greene wrote a letter from camp at White Plains, New York, to Henry Marchant, a member of Congress from Rhode Island, on July 25, 1778, concerning his feelings. He wrote:

> In the action of Brandywine last campaign, where I think both the general and the public were as much indebted to me for saving the army from ruin as they have ever been to any one officer in the course of the war; but I was never mentioned upon the occasion.
>
> I marched one brigade of my division, being upon the left wing, between three and four miles in forty-five minutes. When I came upon the ground I found the whole of the troops routed and retreating precipitately, and in the most broken and confused manner. I was ordered to cover the retreat, which I effected in such a manner as to save hundreds of our people from falling into the enemy's hands. Almost all of the park of artillery had an opportunity to get off, which must have fallen into their hands; and the left wing posted at Chasdsford, got off by the seasonable check I gave the enemy. We were engaged an hour and a quarter, and lost upwards of an hundred men killed

and wounded. I maintained the ground until dark, and then drew off the troops in good order. We had the whole British force to contend with, that had just before routed our whole right wing. This brigade was commanded by General Weedon, and, unfortunately for their own interests, happened to be all Virginians. They being the general's countrymen, and I thought to be one of his favorites, prevented his ever mentioning a single circumstance of the affair.[13]

For the most part General William Maxwell received praise for his handling of the American light infantry against General Knyphausen's advance during the morning hours of September 11, but he too came in for harsh words from a fellow officer, Lieutenant Colonel William Heth of the Third Virginia Regiment. Heth, who had served in Daniel Morgan's riflemen, was attached to the light infantry under Maxwell at Brandywine. Heth wrote Morgan on September 30 and castigated Sullivan and Maxwell for their work at Brandywine. Sullivan, according to Heth, didn't arrive at Birmingham in time to stop the British and Maxwell proved to be "unfit for such a command." An unfounded charge was made that Maxwell was drunk during battle. In another letter to Morgan, Heth wrote that Maxwell's corps "Twas expected would do great things – we had opportunities – and any body but an old-woman, would have availed themselves of them – He is to be sure – a Damnd bitch of a General."[14]

* * * * *

Despite the overwhelming victory gained by the British army at Brandywine, General William Howe also couldn't escape criticism. Howe's greatest sin was not following up on his success and destroying Washington's army. "The poor organization of the American army was of course well known to the British commanders, and they took advantage of the fact. Had they been dealing with an organization as efficient as their own, their course would have been foolhardy. On the other hand, when we consider the relative strength of the two armies, it is clear that the bold move of Cornwallis ought not simply to have won the field of battle. It ought to have annihilated the American army, had not its worst consequences been averted by Washington's promptness, aided by Sullivan's obstinate bravery and Greene's masterly conduct of the retreat upon Dilworth."[15]

A majority of Howe's army had either been marching or fighting since before sunrise and he decided to break off the engagement and allow Washington and his men to slip off toward Chester, to gather, rest, and fight another day. "Though far from decisive, Brandywine was a skilful action, very creditable to Howe considering that he had little or no superiority of numbers. There has always been a conspiracy to belittle Howe, but, whatever his failings, he could fight a battle and handle his troops on occasion with uncommon ability."[16]

Captain Friedrich von Muenchhausen also had words of praise for Howe. He wrote in his diary about the day of the battle:

> We all admire the strong and unexpected march of General Howe, and the special bravery, which the English showed in the battle, and I am convinced that everyone in Europe would admire General Howe if they were as familiar with all of the obstacles he faces, as we are.

> As usual, the General exposed himself fearlessly on this occasion. He quickly rushed to each spot where he heard the strongest fire. Cannon balls and bullets passed close to him in numbers today. We all fear that, since he is so daring on any and all occasions, we are going to lose our best friend, and that England will lose America.[17]

* * * * *

While Howe defeated Washington's army, the rebels certainly didn't retreat in disorder. John Fiske's 1891 work on the American Revolution states, "The American soldiers came out of the fight in good order. Nothing could be more absurd than the careless statement, so often made, that the Americans were 'routed' at the Brandywine."[18] The rout was averted by "Washington's promptness, aided by Sullivan's obstinate bravery and Greene's masterly conduct of the retreat upon Dilworth," according to Fiske. The author also judged Howe's decision to send Lord Cornwallis on a flanking movement fully justified.

The American army was not annihilated as their losses totaled about 1,300, almost 10 percent of the total forces engaged. Washington never made an exact accounting of casualties, at least one has not been found, but estimates were placed at 300 killed, 600 wounded, and 400 taken prisoner. General Greene also estimated between 1,200 and 1,300 American casualties. As for the British, Howe reported losing 90 killed, 480 wounded, and 6 missing. Those numbers have been disputed as being underreported and one unverified report places his losses at 1,976. That number comes from an alleged report from an unnamed British officer found at Germantown and revealed to the public many years after the Philadelphia campaign concluded. Scrutiny of British regimental records reveals losses were in line with Howe's reporting and not that of the Germantown paper, and noted historians, including Washington biographer Douglas Southall Freeman, have discounted the Germantown report.

The February 28, 1778, edition of *The Providence Gazette* and *County Journal* of Great Britain carries a report on page three of the edition on the Philadelphia campaign. That article is datelined London and makes reference to a report of November 19, 1777, a little over two months after the battle. The article details the British losses at both Brandywine and Germantown. "In the general engagement with the rebel army at Brandywine" the report states the British army lost 3 captains, 5 lieutenants, 5 sergeants, 68 rank and file killed. As for British wounded, the newspaper reports 1 lieutenant colonel, 1 major, 16 captains, 22 lieutenants, 5 ensigns, 35 sergeants, 4 drummers, and 372 rank and file. The Hessians lost 2 sergeants and 6 rank and file killed and 1 captain, 3 lieutenants, 5 sergeants, and 23 rank and file wounded. That totals 89 killed and 488 wounded, almost exactly the number Howe reported. The same article said the British captured eight pieces of cannon and a great quantity of military stores at Brandywine. The newspaper article reported the British losses at Germantown almost matched the casualties at Brandywine with 64 killed and 451 wounded.

* * * * *

In winning Brandywine Howe accomplished one of his main objectives—the route to Philadelphia was clear. Howe failed to crush Washington's army, which should have been his main objective. The rebel army survived Brandywine and the Philadelphia campaign. They would fight the British all the way to Yorktown and win independence for the young nation.

Lafayette's Headquarters

General Lafayette used the home of Quaker Gideon Gilpin as his headquarters during the Battle of Brandywine. Lafayette revisited the home in 1824 during his tour of America.

Chester County Historical Society, West Chester, Pennsylvania

Twelve

Philadelphia Falls

After his military victory on the fields of Brandywine, General William Howe took time to regroup his army. Howe spent four days upon the ground before beginning his final march to capture his valued prize, Philadelphia, the center of the rebel government. While the main British force was anchored at Dilworth, Howe's army, as described in Captain John Montresor's journal, secured the immediate area, searched for supplies, tended to the wounded and dead and searched for rebel soldiers.

Montresor, chief engineer of the British army, recorded the following: On September 12, "At 2 o'clock this afternoon Major-Genel. Grant with the 1st and 2nd Brigade marched from Chad's Ford towards Concord. The patrols from each Corps in scouring the woods near them picked up Waggons, Horses, Ammunition, Provisions and cattle and several Rebels that had secreted themselves. (On September 13) The peasants about (are) employed in burying the dead Rebels...who have now become very offensive. This day the 71st Regt. Took possession of Wilmington, the rebels having left 7 pieces of Cannon unspiked and also 2 Brass field pieces taken from the Hessians at Trenton. (On September 14) A detachment at 6 this morning escorted our wounded men to Wilmington. (On September 15) Prisoners taken, found in the woods, that could not escape. The rebel wounded sent off to the Turks Head Tavern, 5 miles from Dilworth."[1]

Burial parties, including local residents drafted for the duty, spent days gathering the dead on the battlefield. Many were placed in unmarked graves, including a long trench dug on the property of the Birmingham Meeting House, where Washington's troops bravely contested the British advance. Residents "found it necessary to call in the assistance of their neighbors, to re-bury many of the dead who lay exposed to the open air, having been washed bard (heavy rains) and some of them had never been interred."[2]

Washington's army, as recorded in the orderly book of General George Weedon, had its own work schedule. Weedon wrote on September 12 from the camp headquarters at Chester that his brigade was "immediately to draw two Days Provisions and cook it, they will also draw a gill of rum per man....The Commanding Officer of each Brigade is immediately to send off as many officers as he shall think necessary on the roads leading to the places of action yesterday and on any other roads where stragglers may be found and particularly to Wilmington where it is said many have retired to pick up all the stragglers from the army and bring them on. In doing this they will proceed as near to the enemy as shall be consistent with their own safety and examine every house....Sick and wounded to be sent to Philadelphia."[3] The American wounded were sent to a number of hospitals, including Trenton, Easton, Allentown, Ephrata, and Bethlehem.

On September 13, 1777, from his camp at Germantown, Weedon passed along to his men compliments from Washington for work done at Brandywine. "The General takes the earliest opportunity to return his warmest thanks to the Officers and soldiers of Gen. Weedons Brigade engaged in the late action for their spirited and soldierly behavior, a conduct so worthy under so many disadvantages cannot fail of establishing to themselves the highest military reputation....The General has the pleasure to inform the troops that notwithstanding we gave the enemy the ground, the purchase has been at much blood, this being by far the greatest loss they ever met with since the commencement of the War....Although the Event of that day from some unfortunate circumstances were not so favourable as could be wished, the General has the Satisfaction of Assuring the troops, that from every Account, he has been able to obtain, the enemy's loss greatly exceeded ours and he has full confidence that in another appeal to Heaven (with the blessing of Providence which it becomes every officer and soldier humbly to supplicate) we shall prove successful."[4]

* * * * *

Successes would be minimal for Washington and his army for the remainder of the Philadelphia campaign of 1777 despite the commander in chief's optimism, as Howe captured and occupied Philadelphia. On September 14 Washington wrote to Major General William Heath from Germantown, "On the 11th instant, we had a pretty general engagement with the enemy; which from some unlucky incidents terminated against us, so far as to our being obliged, to quit the field, after an obstinate action; with the loss of some men and artillery. But from every account, we have reason to believe, the enemy suffered much more than we did in the number of killed and wounded. Our troops have not lost their spirits, and I am in hopes we shall soon have it in our power to compensate for the disaster we have sustained."[5]

Another American defeat was in the making on September 16 as British forces forced units of Washington's army to withdraw east of Turk's Head and through the Goshens. Washington's troops were in a disadvantageous position when a rainstorm developed into a deluge and fighting stopped as ammunition on both sides became ruined. The Battle of the Clouds was a frustrating encounter for both sides.

Washington slowly retreated attempting to protect not only Philadelphia, but also supply depots in the area of Reading. Howe's army was also searching for the American supplies in an attempt to destroy them, especially the ones near Valley Forge. While the two armies were maneuvering in the western environs of Philadelphia, the Continental Congress decided to evacuate Philadelphia on September 19, eight days after the defeat at Brandywine. The Liberty Bell was sent to Allentown as the Americans were afraid that the British would melt it down and use the material for ammunition. As Congress fled to first Lancaster and then York, General Anthony Wayne with 1,500 troops at Paoli planned to attack the British. Wayne was camped close to his boyhood home and he was preparing for his assault when British Major General Charles Grey with 5,000 men under his command launched a surprise attack in the early morning hours of September 21. Grey, after placing troops to the east to guard against an American retreat in that direction, ordered his men to use bayonets during the assault and to take the flints from their rifles so they couldn't fire and ruin the surprise attack. He was then known as "no flint Grey." The British attack by the 42nd and 44th Foot led to 53 American deaths and more than 100 wounded and another 71 captured. The British lost four dead and seven wounded. Wayne faced a court-martial for the affair at Paoli but was cleared of any wrongdoing.

After suffering the defeat at Paoli Washington watched as Howe's army marched into Philadelphia on September 26, 1777, with Cornwallis in the lead. Howe kept 9,000 troops at Germantown. Washington had decided to protect the military stores scattered around the countryside rather than defend the abandoned capital. After seeing Howe take Philadelphia, Washington decided to strike the British at Germantown. On October 2, 1777, the Americans attacked and achieved some success in the early fighting. The British rallied, and put up a stubborn defense at the Cliveden mansion. In the end Washington again retreated, suffering another 1,000 in losses. The British casualties numbered less than 600. As at Brandywine, American soldiers felt Germantown was a unfortunate defeat and not the fault of their abilities as soldiers. As Howe and the British secured the port of Philadelphia and captured Fort Mifflin, Washington began to prepare for the long winter. Before Christmas, 1777, troops began to arrive at Valley Forge, about 20 miles from Howe's army in Philadelphia. Valley Forge would be Washington's base until June of the next year.

* * * * *

As the two armies left Brandywine behind and marched and skirmished toward Valley Forge, both Washington and Howe had many concerns about their armies and the civilian population of the area. On October 1, 1777, Howe issued a proclamation offering pardons to those in the Philadelphia area who wanted to return to the British fold to take an Oath of Allegiance to His Majesty by October 25. Those failing to do so "will be considered as persons out of his Majesty's Peace, and treated accordingly."[6]

Two days after the proclamation Howe wrote to Washington concerning Washington's alleged treatment of the general population. "Sir, Your parties having destroyed several mills in the adjacent country, which can only distress the peaceable inhabitants residing in their Houses, I am constrained from a regard to their sufferings and a Sense of the Duty I owe to the public, to forewarn you of the calamities which may ensure and to express my abhorrence of such a proceeding. At the same time I am inclined to believe, that the outrage already committed have not been in consequence of your orders, and that this early notice will engage you to put an effectual stop to them. If not, I do in the most direct terms disclaim any (blame) in creating the general scene of distraught among the inhabitants, which such destruction must inevitably come."[7]

Washington didn't allow Howe's assertions to stand unchallenged. He replied on October 6:

> I cannot forbear assuring you that I am somewhat at a loss to understand the design of your letter of the 3rd Instant. I can hardly believe you to be serious in remonstrating against a procedure fully authorized by the customary practice of armies. Countenanced by the conduct of your troops at Trenton, and obviously calculated to answer a purpose very different from that of distressing the inhabitants, and increasing the common calamities

incident to a state of War. If this is the consequence of it, it is an unavoidable one, and had no part in producing the measure. I flatter myself this public is sufficiently sensitive, that it is not my wish nor aim to destroy but to protect the inhabitants, and know how to interpret anything with to individuals may seem to deviate from this end. Nor will they be easily persuaded, to consider it as any injustice or cruelty to them, that my parties should have rendered useless for a time, a few mills in the neighborhood of your army which were so situated, as to be capable of affording them no inconsiderable advantages.

I am happy to find you express so much sensibility to the sufferings of the inhabitants, as it gives room to hope that those wanton and unnecessary deprivations, which have heretofore, in too many instances marked the conduct of your army will be discontinued for the future. The instances alluded to need not be enumerated; your own memory will suggest them to your imagination— from the Destruction of Charles Town down to the more recent burnings of mills, barns and houses at the Head of Elk and in the vicinity of Schuylkill. I am Sir, With due respect, Your most Obedt Servant, Signed G. Washington.[8]

Howe also had to deal with deserters from his own army. On October 8 from Germantown he issued another proclamation that those soldiers "bearing arms at this time in support of an unnatural rebellion against their King and Country" voluntarily surrendering before December 1 would receive a full pardon.[9] The dwindling number of troops concerned Howe as he wrote to Lord Germain on October 22 requesting additional soldiers. In the same letter, Howe, citing a lack of support in London, asked to be relieved of his command.

Howe was also fielding complaints from the captured American soldiers and officers. Those complaints led to an exchange of letters with Washington in which the two generals accused each other of mistreating prisoners. Colonel Persifor Frazer, taken after Brandywine on September 16, had contacted

Washington about conditions in Philadelphia and the hope that a prisoner exchange could take place:

> I have been favored with your letter of the 9th ultimo. And was sorry to find that the situation of our officers was so disagreeable. You are well acquainted with the treatment of the prisoners in our hands, and therefore can determine without difficulty how just the grounds for your confinement are.
>
> In respect to a general exchange of prisoners, it has ever been my wish that it should take place on just and equal terms; my letter to Genl. Howe on the subject I trust this (intention) to have been the case. I have written to him again. I shall be happy if we can effect so desirable an object on proper principles. If this cannot be done, I have proposed that it should be no impediment to the exchange of all the officers as far as circumstances of ranks and number will apply—and if any should then remain, that they may be released on parole. The first mode mentions for the liberation of the officers, I expect will be most agreeable to both parties. You may imagine your letter upon this subject might have received an earlier answer, I assure you the delay has not proceeded from inattention to the distress of our prisoners or want of inclination to afford them every possible relief.[10]

The exchange of letters, but not soldiers, continued between Howe and Washington. Howe, in a November 6 letter says he would like to exchange prisoners but Washington has not complied with his proposed terms. Howe also complains that his own prisoners are not being properly treated and are "most injuriously and unjustifiably loaded with Irons."[11] Washington's next letter denies allegation that British prisoners are put in irons but Americans are "treated in a manner shocking to humanity and that many of them must have perished through hunger had it not been for the charitable contributions of the inhabitants....The friends of these unhappy men call upon me for their relief and the people at large insist on retaliating on those in our possession."[12] The American officers wrote a letter to Howe on November 17 detailing those complaints, including not being allowed exercise, being falsely accused of acting as spies, not receiving enough food, not receiving proper medical care, money being taken from them, and especially bad treatment of officers taken from the Delaware frigate, and a watch being taken from the home of Colonel Hannum after Brandywine.[13]

* * * * *

Washington's army needed time to regroup and reorganize after the Philadelphia campaign, and especially after Brandywine.

For the Pennsylvania troops defending their homeland, the battle was costly. "The Pennsylvania Line's bloodiest battle was Brandywine with 74 reported casualties."[14] The First Pennsylvania reported 14 casualties as it fought with Wayne at Chadds Ford along with the Second, Fourth, Seventh and Tenth Pennsylvania. Captain Thomas Robinson was wounded at Brandywine and then promoted to lieutenant colonel. The Third Pennsylvania, under General Thomas Conway, an Irish-born volunteer from the French army, was part of the right flank and received the initial surprise attack by Cornwallis. Captain Thomas Butler rallied fleeing troops and received a personal commendation from Washington. The Fifth Pennsylvania was stationed just above Chadds Ford and sustained a number of casualties. Two members of the Sixth Pennsylvania were wounded. The Ninth Pennsylvania fought at Birmingham Meeting House and had one man killed and another wounded.[15]

The Pennsylvania Line had a number of heroic encounters at Brandywine. At Chadds Ford, Major Stephen Bayard of the Eighth Pennsylvania was wounded when a cannon ball knocked him head over shoulder."[16] The Eleventh Pennsylvania fought with Wayne and lost a number of officers. Captain James Calderwood died of the wounds he suffered two days after the battle. Three second lieutenants were killed, another one wounded and another was captured while a first-lieutenant was wounded and another captured. The regiment also had four privates wounded.[17] Hartley's Regiment lost Major Lewis Bush on September 15 from wounds received at Brandywine, and Captain Robert Hopes was killed at Brandywine. The Independent Pennsylvania Artillery had two men wounded.

The battle, as with all battles, brought out the best of soldiers and human frailties. Captain John Stoner of the 10th Pennsylvania was charged with leaving his regiment in a cowardly manner at Brandywine and was found guilty of leaving his regiment improperly but not in a cowardly manner. Ensign William Russell lost his leg at Brandywine and was rendered incapable of future duty, but "behaved well."[18]

*   *   *   *   *

For more than two centuries the Battle of Brandywine has not received the recognition it deserves. For sure, some of the reason is that the battle was a strategic loss for the Americans, and Washington wrote little concerning the engagement. Even though Brandywine was a clear British victory, the loss of the war diminished the importance of the battle to those in England.

Both the British and the Americans had their disappointments at Brandywine. Howe allowed the American army to escape and fight another day. Howe failed to rally the civilian population to the side of the British and his presence in Pennsylvania meant he couldn't aid Burgoyne's forces in New York. For Washington, he failed to secure credible information concerning the fords of the Brandywine and allowed Howe to flank his army and drive it from the field.

Washington downplayed the loss and blamed the reversal on outside factors. On October 10, he wrote to Thomas McKean, "If the uncommon fogginess of the morning and the smoke had not hindered us from seeing our advantage, I am convinced it would have ended in a complete victory, but we should rejoice that our ranks are as full or rather fuller than they were before."[19]

For the British, Howe accomplished his goal of capturing Philadelphia. A revolutionary new weapon, the Ferguson Rifle, demonstrated its potential on the fields of Brandywine even though Howe took the rifle out of service and disbanded Ferguson's corps of riflemen. The British commanders, Howe, Cornwallis, and Knyphausen, all performed admirably as they successfully executed Howe's risky tactic of splitting the British army and undertaking an exhausting flanking maneuver.

For many reasons Brandywine was important to the American fight for independence. Some of them were:

- Brandywine was the largest land battle of the American Revolution, stretching from Kennett Square where the British began their march, past the Forks of the Brandywine, through Chadds Ford where Washington was headquartered to Dilworth and Concordville. Howe's troops marched 17 miles during the day and Washington's troops retreated from Chadds Ford to Chester that night.
- The first documented firing on the Betsy Ross American flag was at Brandywine.
- LaFayette made his debut with Washington's army at Brandywine and suffered a leg wound.
- Count Pulaski, future cavalry leader of the American army, commanded dragoons at Brandywine.
- Brandywine was the major engagement of the Philadelphia campaign and led to the capture of the capital city and the flight of the Continental Congress.

The most important reason the Battle of Brandywine was crucial to the American cause for freedom was the confidence the American army received from standing up to the British army, one of the most professional in the world. "This battle upset all previous conclusions. It had been claimed that the Americans could not stand before the King's troops in a fight in the open and upon equal conditions."[20] The Americans knew they could hold their own with the British. Their time at Valley Forge gave them time to rest, regroup, and receive valuable training from Baron Friedrich Wilhelm Augustus von Steuben.

Washington and his Americans fought hard and bravely at Brandywine. Even though suffering a clear defeat, the Americans didn't fold and went on to secure independence for America. September 11, 1777, and the Battle of Brandywine deserve an honored place in the history of the United States.

Notes

CHAPTER ONE

1. Samuel S. Smith, *The Battle of Brandywine* (Monmouth Beach, N.J.: Philip Freneau Press, 1976), 12.
2. Ibid.
3. Duane Christman, "Squire Thomas Cheyney: The Paul Revere of the Brandywine," Chester County Historical Society Collection, 2–3.
4. Edward P. Cheyney, *Thomas Cheyney, A Chester County Squire: His Lessons for Genealogists*, an address before the Pennsylvania Historical Society on May 11, 1936, vol. 60, July 1936, *Pennsylvania Magazine of History and Biography*.
5. Christman, 3–4.
6. Robert Leckie, *George Washington's War, The Saga of the American Revolution* (New York: HarperCollins Publishers, 1992), 351.
7. John W. Shy, *George Washington's Generals and Opponents: Their Exploits and Leadership* (New York: Da Capo Press, 1994), 40.
8. Sir John Fortescue, *The War of Independence* (London: Greenhill Books, 2001), 52.
9. Mark M. Boatner III, *Encyclopedia of the American Revolution* (Mechanicsburg, Pa.: Stackpole Books, 1994), 1112.
10. Fortescue, *The War of Independence*, 60.
11. Ibid., 61.

CHAPTER TWO

1. Carl Emil Curt von Donop, *Letters from a Hessian Mercenary*, vol. 62 (The Pennsylvania Magazine of History and Biography).
2. Captain Friedrich von Muenchhausen, *At General Howe's Side 1776–1778: The Diary of Gen. William Howe's Aide de Camp*, trans. Ernst Kipping and annotated by Samuel Smith (Monmouth Beach, N.J.: Philip Freneau Press, 1974), 11.
3. John F. Reed, *Campaign to Valley Forge* (Philadelphia: Pioneer Press, 1980), 22.
4. George Washington, *Writings of George Washington*, vol. 9 (Washington: U.S. Govt. Printing Office, 1931–1934), 99.
5. Reed, *Campaign to Valley Forge*, 57.
6. George F. Scheer and Hugh F. Rankin, *Rebels and Redcoats* (New York: Da Capo Press, 1994), 233.
7. *Diaries of Two Ansbach Jaegers, The Feilitzsch Diary*, trans. Bruce E. Burgoyne (Bowie, Md.: Heritage Books, Inc., 1997), 12.

8. Ibid., 11–16.

9. Reed, *Campaign to Valley Forge,* 69.

10. Public Records Office, Kew, London, document CO 5.95–8690870.

11. Robert Leckie, *George Washington's War* (New York: HarperCollins Publishers, 1992), 349.

CHAPTER THREE

1. Public Records Office, file 30/55/6, document 651.

2. Sir George Otto Trevelyan, *The American Revolution,* vol. 3 (London: Longmans, Green, and Co.), 244.

3. Major Carl Leopold Baurmeister, "Letters of Major Baurmeister during the Philadelphia Campaign, 1777–1778," vol. 59 (*Pennsylvania Magazine of History*), 392.

4. Ambrose Serle, *The American Journal of Ambrose Serle,* ed. Edward H. Tatum, Jr. (New York: The New York Times and Arno Press, 1969), 246.

5. Ibid., 241.

6. Smith, *The Battle of Brandywine,* 5.

7. Trevelyan, *The American Revolution,* 243.

8. Sir William Howe (London: The National Army Museum File of letter book from Howe to Lord George Germain), file 7204–6.

9. Serle, *The American Journal of Ambrose Serle,* 246.

10. Howe, The National Army Museum File number 7204–6.

11. Nathanael Greene, *The Papers of General Nathanael Greene,* vol. 2, January 1777–October 1778.

12. *The Papers of George Washington,* ed. Philander D. Chase and Edward G. Lengel (Charlottesville: University Press of Virginia, 2001), 103.

13. John Montresor, "Journal of Captain John Montresor July 1, 1777 to July 1, 1778, Chief Engineer of the British Army," vol. 5 (*The Pennsylvania Magazine of History and Biography,* 1881), 411.

14. Baurmeister, vol. 59, 399.

15. *The Papers of George Washington,* 141–42.

16. George Washington, *The Papers of George Washington,* 133.

17. Greene, vol. 2, 149.

18. Henry Steele Commager and Richard B. Morris, eds. *The Spirit of 'Seventy-Six'* (Bonanza Books, New York, 1983), 610.

19. James McMichael, "The Diary of Lt. James McMichael, of the Pennsylvania Line 1776–1778," vol. 16, no. 2 (*The Pennsylvania Magazine of History and Biography,* 1892), 129.

20. Harry M. Ward, *General William Maxwell and the New Jersey Continentals* (Westport, Conn.: Greenwood Press, 1997), 67.

21. Montresor, 410.

22. Ibid., 412.

23. Johann Ewald, *Diary of the American War, A Hessian Journal, Captain Johann Ewald, Field Jager Corps* (New Haven and London: Yale University Press, 1979), 77–78.

24. Christopher L. Ward, *The Delaware Continentals, 1776–1783* (Wilmington, Del.: The Historical Society of Delaware, 1941).

25. Montresor, 393.

26. Muenchhausen, 28.

27. Ewald, 78.

28. Montresor, 413–14.

29. *The Diary of a Scottish Grenadier 1776–1782*, ed. Ira D. Gruber (Somerset: Sutton Publishing Company for the Army Records Society, 1997).

CHAPTER FOUR

1. Public Records Office, document A.O. 12 vol. 40, 78.

2. Ibid., A.O. 12 vol. 39, 5.

3. Ibid., A.O. 12 vol. 38, 355.

4. Ibid., A.O. 12 vol. 40, 45.

5. Ibid., A.O. 12 vol. 42, 244.

6. Boatner, *Encyclopedia of the American Revolution*, 408.

7. Reed, *Campaign to Valley Forge*, 114.

8. *George Washington's Generals and Opponents*, ed. George Athan Billias (New York: Da Capo Press, 1994), 109.

9. Ibid., 110

10. Boatner, *Encyclopedia of the American Revolution*, 454.

11. John Fiske, *The American Revolution* (Boston and New York: Houghton, Mifflin & Co., 1891), 197.

12. Text of notes of the Philadelphia Yearly Meeting supplied by Ted Brinton of Chester County. The full text of the directive is:

PHILADELPHIA YEARLY MEETING

1ST OF THE 9TH MONTH OF 1777

Dearly Beloved Friends of Birmingham Meeting,

In this time of deep probation and affliction the Philadelphia Yearly Meeting finds it necessary to give our sense and judgment to the monthly meetings so that our conduct is uniformly consistent with Spirit of our Religious Principles. The fate of our Religious Society in these provinces hath now been very mightily considered and we pray for divine Wisdom in our solemn deliberations on these important subjects.

We have taken under our mighty Consideration the sorrowful account given to the public deviation of many in our Society from our Ancient Testimony Against War. This testimony means that Friends must not join with the Multitude in warlike exercise nor instruct themselves in the Art of War. Friends are advised to avoid all acts, including being spectators at training grounds, which might in any way compromise the Principles upon which this Society was founded.

The Constitutional Convention has adopted an ordinance requiring those who are conscientiously opposed to bearing arms to pay a fine of 20 shillings per month in lieu of military service. It is the united Sense of this Meeting that such a fine cannot be paid by Friends or their children, servants or apprentices, consistent with our Christian Testimony.

The Continental Congress has resolved that anyone not accepting the new currency Should be treated as an enemy to his country. The weighty and important Subject of accepting currency and paying Taxes imposed by those now in power, it is agreed to refer the same to the deep and serious Consideration of a Committee we have formed to make a report to our Yearly Meeting so that we can provide guidance to the monthly meetings.

In the Spirit of our Religious Principles we exhort and advise Friends to withdraw from being active in Civil Government due to its founding in the Spirit of War and Fightings. We find it necessary to give our Sense against being concerned either in electing any Person or being themselves elected to such Stations that cannot be consistent with our Christian Peaceable Testimony.

And as many of our Brethren have of late been brought under Sufferings for the Testimony of Truth, the Continuance and Increase of which there is reason to expect, it is recommended to the Monthly Meetings to keep a regular Record of the persecution and sufferings of Friends and sent to our Meeting for Sufferings in order to be laid before the Yearly Meeting when necessary.

Considering the present difficulties and the prospect of their continuance we have desired each of our Quarterly Meetings to nominate four Friends to join with our Meeting for Sufferings in deliberating and concluding on the weighty concerns of our religious Society.

It is our united Concern and Desire, that faithful Friends in their respective Meetings may speedily and earnestly labour on the Strength of God's love for the reclaiming of those who have thus deviated from our ancient Testimonies. A united effort must be maintained to strengthen each other in the way of truth and righteousness. But where any continue to oppose the Judgment of the Meeting now expressed, monthly meetings should make it manifest that such behavior disregards the foundations upon which our Society was formed and disownment must be considered an outcome of this disregard.

The great effusion of human blood and the loss of the lives of men since the commencement of the present tumults induce us to pray for the restoration of peace to our colonies. Our Meeting now being near closing, we again salute you in a degree of the Love of the Gospel and are

Your affectionate Friends and Brethren.

13. Ibid.
14. Ibid.
15. Ibid.
16. Ibid.
17. Gilbert Cope, "Chester County Quakers during the Revolution," files of the Chester County Historical Society (West Chester: *Daily Local News*, 1902).
18. Ibid.
19. Ibid.
20. Ibid.
21. Ibid.
22. Ibid.
23. Ibid.
24. Ibid.
25. Ibid.
26. Ibid.
27. Ibid.
28. Ibid.
29. Sol Stember, *The Bicentennial Guide to the American Revolution* (New York: E. P. Dutton & Co., Inc., 1974), 94.
30. Reed, *Campaign to Valley Forge*, 254.
31. Ibid., 93.
32. Author's interview with Quaker historian Ted Brinton on October 16, 1998.
33. Reed, *Campaign to Valley Forge*, 209–10.
34. Joseph Lee Boyle, *Writings from the Valley Forge Encampment of the Continental Army* (Bowie, MD.: Heritage Books, Inc., 2001), 83.
35. George Weedon, *Valley Forge Orderly Book of General George Weedon* (New York: Dodd, Mead and Company, 1902), 31.
36. Samuel Hazard, *Pennsylvania Archives 1776–1777*, vol. 5 (Philadelphia: Joseph Severns and Company, 1853), 587.

37. Reed, *Campaign to Valley Forge*, 109.
38. Weedon, 39.
39. Ibid., 42.
40. Billias, *George Washington's Generals and Opponents*, 111.

CHAPTER FIVE

1. Jean Edward Smith, *John Marshall: Definer of a Nation* (New York: Henry Holt and Co., 1996), 58.
2. Muenchhausen, *At General Howe's Side*, 28.
3. Smith, *The Battle of Brandywine*, 6.
4. Trevelyan, *The American Revolution*, 247.
5. *Papers of the Governors*, vol. 3, ed. George E. Reed (Pennsylvania Archives, 1900), 657.
6. McMichael, The Diary of Lt. James McMichael, of the Pennsylvania Line 1776–1778, 129.
7. Smith, *The Battle of Brandywine*, 7.
8. Ibid., 9.
9. Reed, *Campaign to Valley Forge*, 115.
10. *Writings of George Washington*, vol. 9, 203.
11. Pennsylvania Historical Society records, from *Magazine of American History*, April 1885, 281.

CHAPTER SIX

1. *American National Biography*, vol. 14 (New York: Oxford University Press, 1999), 564.
2. *British Army Orders: Gen. Sir William Howe, 1775–1778*, prepared by the New York Historical Society (Boston: Gregg Press, 1972), 491–92.
3. Muenchhausen, *At General Howe's Side*, 31.
4. Ibid.
5. Frederick B. Robins, *The Queen's Rangers* (London: The National Army Museum, 1954), 7–10.
6. *Brandywine Battlefield: The National Historic Landmark Revisited* (Delaware County Planning Department, 1992), 16.
7. Sol Stember, *The Bicentennial Guide to the American Revolution* (New York, E. P. Dutton & Co., Inc., 1974), 91.
8. *Brandywine Battlefield: The National Historic Landmark Revisited*, 18.
9. Ibid., 19.
10. Chester County Historical Society files, 100 Box 39.
11. Baurmeister, 392.
12. *The Papers of George Washington*, 195.
13. Christopher L. Ward, *The Delaware Continentals 1776–1783* (Wilmington: The Historical Society of Delaware, 1941), 198–99.
14. Howard M. Jenkins, "Brandywine, 1777" (London: *Lippincott's Magazine*, September 1877), 334.
15. Donald S. Hoke, "The Scotsman and His Gun—Patrick Ferguson" (Chadds Ford: article for Brandywine Battlefield Park Associates), 8.
16. James Ferguson, *Two Scottish Soldiers: A Soldier of 1688 and Blenheim. A Soldier of the American Revolution* (Aberdeen: D. Wylie & Son, 1888), 63–64.
17. David Patten, "Ferguson and His Rifle," vol. 28, no. 7 (London: *History Today* Magazine, July 1978), 446–54.
18. Ibid.
19. Laing Manuscripts from University of Edinburgh Library.

20. Ferguson, 66–67.
21. Patten, 446–54.
22. Ferguson, 67.
23. James Murray, *Letters from America 1773 to 1780. Letters of Scots Officer, Sir James Murray*, ed. Eric Robson (Manchester: University Press, 1951).

CHAPTER SEVEN

1. Douglas S. Freeman, *George Washington – Vol. IV Leader of the Revolution* (New York, Charles Scribner's Sons, 1951), 489.
2. *The Papers of George Washington*, 190.
3. Ibid.
4. Ibid.
5. Ibid.
6. Ibid., 197.
7. Ibid., 196.
8. Ibid., 190.
9. Smith, *Battle of Brandywine*, 13.
10. Ward, *The Delaware Continentals 1776–1783*, 201.
11. *The Papers of George Washington*, 191.
12. Washington, *Writings of George Washington*, 477.
13. Ward, *The Delaware Continentals 1776–1783*, 202.
14. Lewis H. Garrard, *Colony and the Revolution* (Philadelphia, J. B. Lippincott and Co., 1856), 49–51.
15. Montresor, 415–16.
16. Muenchhausen, *At General Howe's Side*, 31.
17. *Brandywine Battlefield: The National Historic Landmark Revisited*, 23.
18. Jenkins, *Brandywine 1777*, 335.
19. *Brandywine Battlefield: The National Historic Landmark Revisited*, 22.
20. Smith, *Battle of Brandywine*, 13.
21. Joseph Townsend, memoir (Chester County Historical Society files), 18–20.
22. Ibid.
23. Ibid.
24. Ibid.
25. Ibid., 21–25.
26. Trevelyan, *The American Revolution*, 249.

CHAPTER EIGHT

1. *The Papers of George Washington*, 191.
2. Ibid.
3. Cornwallis quote. John F. Reed, *Campaign to Valley Forge* (Philadelphia: Pioneer Press), 128.
4. Smith, *Battle of Brandywine*, 16.
5. Smith, *John Marshall: Definer of a Nation*, 59.
6. Smith, *Battle of Brandywine*, 16.
7. Montresor, 416–17.
8. Smith, *Battle of Brandywine*, 16.
9. Ibid., 17.
10. *Brandywine Battlefield, the National Historic Landmark*, 25.

11. The Hubbard Collection, Lafayette College.

12. J. Thomas Scharf, *Chronicles of Baltimore* (Baltimore: Valley Forge Park collection, 1874.)

13. Albert Lee, *History of the 33rd Foot* (Norwich: Jarrold and Sons, Ltd., The Empire Press, 1922), 107.

14. Trevelyan, *The American Revolution*, 249.

15. Smith, *Battle of Brandywine*, 19.

16. Ibid., 19.

17. Baurmeister, 397.

18. Townsend, 26.

19. Washington, *Writings of George Washington*, 206.

20. Hugh F. Rankin, *The North Carolina Continentals* (Chapel Hill: The University of North Carolina Press, 1971), 105.

21. Smith, *Battle of Brandywine*, 20.

22. The Hubbard Collection, Lafayette College.

23. Ibid.

24. *Lafayette in the Age of the American Revolution, Selected Letters and Papers, 1776–1790*, vol. 1, ed. Stanley J. Idzerda (Ithaca and London: Cornell University Press, 1977), 114.

25. *Papers of George Washington*, 192.

26. Robert Leckie, *George Washington's War* (New York, HarperPerenial, 1992), 355.

27. *Brandywine Battlefield, the National Historic Landmark*, 27.

28. Ward, *The Delaware Continentals 1776–1783*, 208.

29. Brandywine article, vol. 111, no. 6 (Portland Transcript, Saturday, May 18, 1839).

30. Smith, *Battle of Brandywine*, 21.

31. Montresor, 393.

32. H. G. Purdon, *Memoirs of the Services of the 64th Regiment (Second Saffordshire)* (Strafford, Great Britain: W. H. Allen & Co.), 13.

33. A. J. Baker, *The East Yorkshire Regiment (the 15th Regiment of Foot)* (London: Leo Cooper Ltd., 1971), 50–51.

CHAPTER NINE

1. Allen G. Eastby, "Battle of Brandywine, Setback for the Continental Army" (*Military History Magazine*, December 1998), 63.

2. Trevelyan, *The American Revolution*, 250.

3. *The King's Own: The Story of a Royal Regiment*, ed. Col. L. I. Cowper (Oxford: University Press, 1939), 267.

4. Garrard, 49–51.

5. Baurmeister, 406.

6. *George Washington's Papers*, 193.

7. A.D. L. Cary and Stouppe McCance, *Regimental Records of the Royal Welsh Fusiliers* (London: Royal United Service Institution, Whitehall, 1921), 166.

8. Robins, *The Queen's Rangers*, 9.

9. Benjamin M. Nead, "A Sketch of General Thomas Procter, With Some Account of the First Pennsylvania Artillery in the Revolution," vol. 5 (*The Pennsylvania Magazine of History and Biography*, 1881), 393.

10. Ibid., 460.

11. Fortescue, *The War of Independence*, 68.

12. Smith, *Battle of Brandywine*, 23.

13. John B. B. Trussell, Jr., *The Pennsylvania Line: Regimental Organization and Operations 1776–1783* (Harrisburg, Pa.: The Pennsylvania Historical and Museum Commission, 1977), 195.

14. Ibid., 205.

15. *Brandywine Battlefield National Historic Landmark*, 31.

16. *The Spirit of 'Seventy-Six*, ed. Henry Steele Commager and Richard B. Morris (New York: Bonanza Books, 1983), 613.

17. Montresor, 393.

18. Baurmeister, 407.

19. Robert J. Jones, *A History of the 15th (East Yorkshire) Regiment (The Duke of York's Own)* (London, National Army Museum, 1958), 209.

20. *The Spirit of 'Seventy-Six'*, 614.

21. Freeman, 483.

22. Eastby, *Battle of Brandywine, Setback for the Continental Army*, 64.

23. John H. Hawkins, "From the diary of Sergeant Major John H. Hawkins, of the Congress Own Regiment, commanded by Col. Moses Hazen," vol. 20 (*The Pennsylvania Magazine of History and Biography*), 421.

24. Trussell, 248.

25. Lee, *History of the 33rd Foot*, 107.

26. Jones, *A History of the 15th (East Yorkshire) Regiment (The Duke of York's Own)*, 209.

27. Albert Lee, *The History of the Tenth Foot* (London: Gale and Polden Ltd., 1911), 248.

28. Ward, *The Delaware Continentals 1776–1783*, 211.

29. Scharf, September 23, 1777 letter from Major John Stone to William Paca, Valley Forge Collection.

30. Charles W. Upham, *Life of Timothy Pickering*, vol. 2 (Boston: Little, Brown and Company, 1873), 82.

31. Josiah Quinch, *The Journals of Major Samuel Shaw* (Boston: Wm. Crosby and H. P. Nichols, 1847), 37.

32. Freeman, 483.

33. *The Papers of George Washington*, 201.

34. *Spirit of 76*, 616–17.

CHAPTER TEN

1. Chester County Historical Society files.

2. Sarah Frazer, "A Reminiscence," Chester County Historical Society papers, 1840.

3. Samuel R. Slaymaker II, *Mrs. Frazer's Philadelphia Campaign Journal*, vol. 73, no. 4 (Lancaster County Historical Society), 187–90.

4. Ibid., 194.

5. Ibid.

6. Ibid.

7. Ibid., 187.

8. Portsmouth, N. H., Journal, Chester County Historical Society files (Envelope 8, Item 3).

9. Stephen Kemble, *Journals of Lieut. Col. Stephen Kemble* (Boston: Gregg Press, 1972), 492.

10. Public Records Office File 30/55/6, Document 664.

11. Ibid., Document 665.

12. *The Papers of George Washington*, 215.

13. Carl Binger, *Revolutionary Doctor Benjamin Rush (1746–1813)* (W. W. Norton & Company, Inc., 1966), 131.
14. Ibid., 128.
15. Public Records Office File 30/55/6, Document 673.
16. Ibid., File 30/55/6, Document 674.
17. Ibid., File 35/55/7, Document 749.
18. Thomas Paine, *Common Sense* (Philadelphia: Sept. 12, 1777).
19. *The Papers of Benjamin Franklin*, vol. 25, ed. William B. Wilcox (New Haven and London: Yale University Press, 1986), 244–45.
20. Historical Society of Pennsylvania files.
21. Robert D. Bass, *The Green Dragoon* (New York: Henry Holt and Company, 1957), 34.
22. Kemble, 492.
23. Ibid., 493.
24. *The Papers of George Washington*, 211–12.
25. Ibid., 212.

CHAPTER ELEVEN

1. *The Spirit of Seventy-Six*, 617–18.
2. *Journals of the Continental Congress*, vol. 8, 742.
3. *Letters and Papers of Major-General John Sullivan*, ed. Otis G. Hammond, vol. 1 (New Hampshire Historical Society, 1930), 455.
4. Ibid., 458.
5. Ibid., 461–62.
6. Ibid., 466.
7. Ibid., 475.
8. Ibid., 476.
9. Ibid., 541.
10. Leckie, *George Washington's War*, 350–51.
11. Historical Society of Pennsylvania records, John Sullivan's letter to Dr. Alfred L. Elwyn of March 29, 1847.
12. Smith, *John Marshall: Definer of a Nation*, 59.
13. Greene, 471.
14. Harry M. Ward, *General William Maxwell and the New Jersey Continentals* (Westport, Conn.: Greenwood Press, 1997), 73.
15. Fiske, *The American Revolution*, 325.
16. Fortescue, *The War of Independence*, 69.
17. Muenchhausen, *At General Howe's Side*, 32.
18. Fiske, *The American Revolution*, 326.

CHAPTER TWELVE

1. Montresor, 34–35.
2. Reed, *Campaign to Valley Forge*, 143.
3. Weedon, *Valley Forge Orderly Book of General George Weedon*, 44–45.
4. Ibid., 46–47.
5. *The Papers of George Washington*, 227.
6. Public Records Office, PRO 30/55/7, Document 691.
7. Ibid., PRO 30/55/7, Document 694.

8. *The Papers of George Washington*, 409.

9. Public Records Office, PRO 30/55/7, Document 699.

10. Ibid., Document 734.

11. Ibid., Document 735.

12. Ibid., Document 746.

13. Ibid., Document 749.

14. Trussell, 268.

15. Ibid.

16. Ibid., 107.

17. Ibid., 131.

18. Ibid., 214.

19. Chester County Historical Society records.

20. Ibid.

Bibliography

Adams, John Quincy. "Oration on the Life and Character of Gilbert Mothier De Lafayette." Boston: S. Coleman and Russell, Odiorne & Co., 1835.

Anderson, Troyer Steele. *The Command of the Howe Brothers during the American Revolution*. New York: Octagon Books, 1972.

Atkinson, C. T. *Regimental History: The Royal Hampshire Regiment, Vol. 1 to 1914*. Glasgow: The University Press, 1950.

Baily, J. D. *Commanders at Kings Mountain*. Greenville, S.C.: A Press, Inc., 1980.

Baker, A. J. *The East Yorkshire Regiment (the 15th Regiment of Foot)*. London: Leo Cooper Ltd., 1971.

Bass, Robert D. *The Green Dragoon*. New York: Henry Holt and Company, 1957.

Billias, George Athan, ed. *Journals of Lieut.-Col. Stephen Kemble, 1773–1789; and British Army Orders: Gen. Sir William Howe, 1775–1778; Gen. Sir Henry Clinton, 1778; and Gen. Daniel Jones, 1778*. Boston: Gregg Press, 1972.

———. *George Washington's Generals and Opponents: Their Exploits and Leadership*. New York: Da Capo Press, 1994.

Binger, Carl. *Revolutionary Doctor Benjamin Rush (1746–1813)*. New York, N.Y.: W. W. Norton & Co., Inc., 1966.

Boatner, Mark M., III. *Encyclopedia of the American Revolution.* Mechanicsburg, Pa.: Stackpole Books, 1994.

Boyle, Joseph Lee. *Writings from the Valley Forge Encampment of the Continental Army: December 19, 1777–June 19, 1778, Vol. 2.* Bowie, Md.: Heritage Books, 2001.

Burgoyne, Bruce E. *Ansbach-Bayreuth Diaries from the American Revolution.* Bowie, Md.: Heritage Books, Inc., 1999.

——. *Diaries of Two Ansbach Jaegers, the Feilitzsch Diary.* Bowie, Md.: Heritage Books, Inc., 1997.

Cannon, Richard, ed. *Historical Record of the Fifteenth, or, The Yorkshire East Riding Regiment of Foot.* London: Parker, Furnivall, & Parker, 1958.

Carrington, Henry B. *Battles of the American Revolution 1775–1781.* New York: A. S. Barnes & Company, 1877.

Cary, A. D. L., and Stouppe McCance. *Regimental Records of the Royal Welsh Fusiliers.* London: Royal United Service Institution, 1921.

Chase, Philander D., and Edward G. Lengel, eds. *The Papers of George Washington: Revolutionary War Series, vol. 11.* Charlottesville: University Press of Virginia, 2001.

Cheyney, Edward P. "Thomas Cheyney, A Chester County Squire. His lessons for genealogists." *The Pennsylvania Magazine of History and Biography.* Vol. 60 (July 1936).

Christman, Duane. "Squire Thomas Cheyney (A Short Biography): The Paul Revere of the Brandywine." Chester County Historical Society, n.d.

Commager, Henry Steele, and Richard B. Morris, eds. *The Spirit of 'Seventy-Six: The Story of the American Revolution as Told by Participants.* New York: Bonanza Books, Inc., 1983.

Cope, Gilbert. "Chester County Quakers during the Revolution." Chester County Historical Society Records, from newspaper article of *Daily Local News* of November 20, 1902.

Cowper, Col. L. I., ed. *The King's Own: The Story of a Royal Regiment.* Oxford: University Press, 1939.

Daniell, David Scott. *Cap of Honor: The Story of the Gloucestershire Regiment (The 28th/61st Foot) 1694–1950.* London: George G. Harrap & Co., 1951.

Davis, Burke. *George Washington and the American Revolution.* New York: Random House, 1975.

Eastby, Allen G. "Battle of Brandywine: Setback for the Continental Army." *Military History Magazine.* Vol. 15 (December 1998), Number 5, pp. 58–64.

Ewald, Johann. *Diary of the American War, A Hessian Journal, Captain Johann Ewald, Field Jaeger Corps.* New Haven and London: Yale University Press, 1979.

Ferguson, James. *Two Scottish Soldiers: A Soldier of 1688 and Blenheim. A Soldier of the American Revolution.* Aberdeen: D. Wylie & Son, 1888.

Fiske, John. *The American Revolution.* Boston and New York: Houghton, Mifflin & Company, 1891.

Fortescue, Sir John. *The War of Independence: The British Army in North America, 1775–1783.* London: Greenhill Books, 2001.

Frazer, Persifor. *General Persifor Frazer, A Memoir.* Philadelphia, 1907.

Frazer, Sarah. "A Reminiscence." September 11, 1840, article. Chester County Historical Society Papers.

Freeman, Douglas Southall. *George Washington – Vol. IV Leader of the Revolution.* New York: Charles Scribner's Sons, 1951.

Futhey, J. Smith, and Gilbert Cope. *History of Chester County, Pennsylvania.* Philadelphia: J. B. Lippincott & Co., 1881.

Garrard, Lewis H. *Colony and the Revolution, A Sketch by Lewis H. Garrard.* Philadelphia: J. B. Lippincott and Co., 1856.

Gruber, Ira D, ed. *John Peebles' American War: The Diary of a Scottish Grenadier, 1776–1782.* Mechanicsburg: Stackpole Books, 1998.

Hammond, Otis G., ed. *Letter and Papers of Major-General John Sullivan, Continental Army.* Concord: New Hampshire Historical Society, 1930.

Hoke, Donald S. "The Scotsman and His Gun—Patrick Ferguson." Brandywine Battlefield Park Associates.

Idzerda, Stanley J., ed. *Lafayette in the Age of the American Revolution, Selected Letters and Papers, 1776–1790.* Ithaca and London: Cornell University Press, 1977.

Jenkins, Howard M. "Brandywine, 1777." *Lippincott's Magazine.* Vol. 20 (September, 1877) Number 117, pp. 329–39.

Jones, Robert J. *A History of the 15th (East Yorkshire) Regiment (The Duke of York's Own).* London: National Army Museum, 1958.

Kemble, Stephen. *Journals of Lieut. Col. Stephen Kemble.* Boston: New York Historical Society and Gregg Press, 1972.

Kipplin, Ernst, and Samuel Stelle Smith, trans. *At General Howe's Side 1776–1778: The diary of General William Howe's Aide de Camp, Captain Friedrich von Muenchhausen.* Monmouth Beach: Philip Freneau Press, 1974.

Leckie, Robert. *George Washington's War: The Saga of the American Revolution.* New York: HarperPerenial Publishers, 1992.

Lee, Albert. *History of the Tenth Foot: The Lincolnshire Regiment.* London: Gale & Polden Ltd., 1911.

———. *History of the Thirty-Third Foot: Duke of Wellington's Regiment.* Norwich: Jarrold & Sons, Ltd., The Empire Press, 1922.

McKeel, Arthur J. *The Relation of the Quakers to the American Revolution.* Washington: University Press of America, Inc., 1979.

McMichael, James. "The Diary of Lt. James McMichael, of the Pennsylvania Line 1776–1778." *The Pennsylvania Magazine of History and Biography.* Vol. 16, Number 2 (1892), p. 129.

Montresor, John. "Journal of Captain John Montresor July 1, 1777 to July 1, 1778, Chief Engineer of the British Army." *The Pennsylvania Magazine of History and Biography.* Vol. 5 (1881).

Nields, John P. "Washington's Army in Delaware in the Summer of 1777." Chester County Historical Society Records: Address given September 9, 1927, at Cooch's Bridge, New Castle County, Delaware.

Patten, David. "Ferguson and his Rifle." *History Today* Magazine. Vol. 27, Number 7 (July 1978).

Purdon, H. G. *Memoirs of the Services of the 64th Regiment (Second Saffordshire)*. Strafford, England: W. H. Allen & Co.

Quinch, Josiah. *The Journals of Major Samuel Shaw*. Boston: Wm. Crosby and H. P. Nichols, 1847.

Rankin, Hugh F. *The North Carolina Continentals*. Chapel Hill: The University of North Carolina Press, 1971.

Reed, John F. *Campaign to Valley Forge*. Philadelphia: Pioneer Press, 1980.

Robins, Frederick B. *The Queen's Rangers*. London: The National Army Museum, 1954.

Robson, Eric, ed. *Letters from America 1773 to 1780. Letters of Scots Officer, Sir James Muray*. Manchester: University Press, 1951.

Sargent, Winthrop. Abbatt, William, ed. *Life and Career of Major John Andre, Adjutant-General of the British Army in America*. New York: William Abbatt, 1902.

Scharf, Thomas. Chronicles of Baltimore. Letter of September 23, 1777, in Valley Forge Park collection.

Scheer, George F., and Hugh F. Rankin. *Rebels & Redcoats: The American Revolution through the Eyes of Those Who Fought and Lived It*. New York: Da Capo Press, 1987.

Showman, Richard K., ed. *The Papers of General Nathanael Greene*. Chapel Hill: The University of North Carolina Press, 1980.

Shy, John W. *George Washington's Generals and Opponents: Their Exploits and Leadership*. New York: Da Capo Press, 1994.

Slaymaker, Samuel R., II. *Mrs. Frazer's Philadelphia Campaign Journal*. Volume 73, Number 4. Lancaster County Historical Society.

Smith, Jean Edward. *John Marshall: Definer of a Nation*. New York: Henry Holt and Co., 1996.

Smith, Samuel S. *The Battle of Brandywine*. Monmouth Beach, N.J.: Philip Freneau Press, 1976.

Stember, Sol. *The Bicentennial Guide to the American Revolution*. New York: E. P. Dutton & Co., Inc., 1974.

Stille, Charles J. *Major-General Anthony Wayne and The Pennsylvania Line in the Continental Army*. Port Washington: Kennikat Press, Inc. (undated but Stille wrote in the era of 1860–1880).

Tatum, Edward H., Jr., ed. *The American Journal of Ambrose Serle*. New York: The New York Times and Arno Press, 1969.

Trevelyan, Sir George Otto. *The American Revolution*. London: Longmans, Green and Co., 1907.

Trout, Rev. Joab. "A Sermon, Preached on the Eve of the Battle of Brandywine, Sept. 10, 1777." *Magazine of American History*, Vol. 13 (April 1885), Number 4, p. 281.

Tustin, Joseph P., trans and ed. *Diary of the American War: A Hessian Journal of Captain Johann Ewald, Field Jaeger Corps*. New Haven: Yale University Press, 1979.

Upham, Charles W. *Life of Timothy Pickering*. Boston: Little, Brown and Company, 1873.

Von Donop, Carl. "Letters from a Hessian Mercenary." *The Pennsylvania Magazine of History and Biography*, Vol. 62.

Von Muenchhausen, Captain Friedrich. *At General Howe's Side 1776–1778: The Diary of Gen. William Howe, Aide de Camp*. Monmouth Beach, N.J.: Philip Freneau Press, 1974.

Walker, H. M. *A History of the Northumberland Fusiliers 1674–1902*. London: John Murray, 1919.

Ward, Christopher L. *The Delaware Continentals 1776–1783*. Wilmington: The Historical Society of Delaware, 1941.

Ward, Harry M. *General William Maxwell and the New Jersey Continentals*. Westport: Greenwood Press, 1997.

Washington, George. *Writings of George Washington*. Washington: U.S. Government Printing Office.

Webster, Nancy. "A Commonwealth Treasure: Brandywine Battlefield Park." Pennsylvania Heritage, Vol. 23 (Fall 1997), Number 4, pp. 14–21.

Webster, Nancy, Martha Wolf, and Susan W. Hauser, eds. *Brandywine Battlefield: The National Historic Landmark Revisited.* Media: Delaware County Planning Department, 1992.

Wildes, Harry Emerson. *Anthony Wayne: Trouble Shooter of the American Revolution.* Westport: Grenwood Press, Publishers, 1970.

Willcox, William, ed. *The Papers of Benjamin Franklin, Vol. 25, October 1, 1777, through February 28, 1778.* New Haven: Yale University Press, 1986.

Sources of Material

Brandywine Battlefield Park.

Ted Brinton interview by the author on October 16, 1998.

Chester County Historical Society.

The David Library.

Delaware County Planning Department.

Historical Society of Pennsylvania.

Lafayette College.

The National Army Museum, London.

The Pennsylvania Historical and Museum Commission.

The Pennsylvania Historical Society.

Philadelphia Yearly Meeting records.

Portland Transcript.

The Providence Gazette and County Journal.

Public Records Office, Kew, London.

United States Army Military History Institute.

Valley Forge National Park.

Index

— The Author —

During his 25-year journalism career Bruce E. Mowday has been a reporter, columnist, city editor, and managing editor, winning numerous awards for writing and reporting. Mowday is president of his media relations company, The Mowday Group, Inc., and hosts his own radio show. A member of a number of historical organizations, he served for two years as president of the nonprofit Brandywine Battlefield Park Associates. This is his third book.

— Cover Illustration —

The Nation Makers
Howard Pyle

*Collection of the Brandywine River Museum,
purchased through a grant
from the Mabel Pew Myrin Trust*

— Also by the Author —

THE SELLING OF AN AUTHOR
A Marketing Guide for Writers to Increase Book Sales

To be successful authors, writers need to market their own books. For more than a decade, Bruce E. Mowday has been researching, writing, promoting, and marketing his four previously published books. This guide contains practical tips told through personal experiences to help those published and self-published authors increase book sales.

ISBN 978-1-57249-363-6 • Softcover

— Of Related Interest —

THE AMERICAN PARTISAN
HENRY LEE AND THE STRUGGLE
FOR INDEPENDENCE, 1776-1780

By John W. Hartmann

Documents Henry Lee's remarkable military career and examines the central role he played in both gathering intelligence and foraging for the Continental army. Also delves into the unique personal relationship between Lee and Gen. George Washington.

ISBN 978-1-57249-226-4 • Softcover

WHITE MANE PUBLISHING CO., INC.

To Request a Catalog Please Write to:
WHITE MANE PUBLISHING COMPANY, INC.
P.O. Box 708 • Shippensburg, PA 17257
e-mail: marketing@whitemane.com
Our catalog is also available online
www.whitemane.com

CPSIA information can be obtained
at www.ICGtesting.com
Printed in the USA
BVOW06s0831121116
467571BV00003BA/3/P

9 781572 493421